AUDACIOUS

AGITATION

VINCENT D. WILLIS

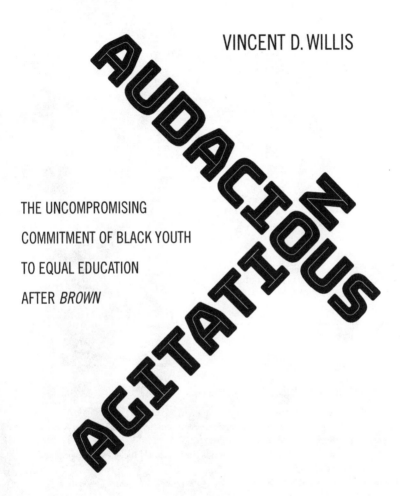

AUDACIOUS
AGITATION

THE UNCOMPROMISING
COMMITMENT OF BLACK YOUTH
TO EQUAL EDUCATION
AFTER *BROWN*

THE UNIVERSITY OF
GEORGIA PRESS
ATHENS

© 2021 by the University of Georgia Press
Athens, Georgia 30602
www.ugapress.org
All rights reserved
Designed by Kaelin Chappell Broaddus
Set in 10/13.5 New Caledonia LT Std Regular
by Kaelin Chappell Broaddus

Most University of Georgia Press titles are
available from popular e-book vendors.

Printed digitally

Library of Congress Cataloging-in-Publication Data

Names: Willis, Vincent D., author.
Title: Audacious agitation : the uncompromising commitment of black youth to equal
    education after Brown / Vincent D. Willis.
Description: Athens : The University of Georgia Press, [2021] | Includes bibliographical
    references and index.
Identifiers: LCCN 2021006512 | ISBN 9780820359694 (hardback) | ISBN 9780820359687
    (paperback) | ISBN 9780820359700 (ebook)
Subjects: LCSH: African American youth—Political activity—Georgia—History—20th
    century. | Student movements—Georgia—History—20th century. | School integration—
    United States—History—20th century. | Discrimination in education—Georgia—
    History. | Georgia—Race relations—History—20th century.
Classification: LCC E185.61 .W7385 2021 | DDC 305.23089/960730758—dc23
LC record available at https://lccn.loc.gov/2021006512

To those born into a world full of
injustices and decided to fight for
a more just world, thank you!

CONTENTS

LIST OF ABBREVIATIONS   ix

PREFACE. The Invisibility of the Activists' Scars   xi

INTRODUCTION. A Unique Divorce between Federal Decisions
and Loyal White Local Southern Officials   1

CHAPTER 1. *Brown* and the Muddled Realities of Public Education   17

CHAPTER 2. The Insatiable Appetite of Jim Crow and
Black Tiftonians' Desire for Full Citizenship   46

CHAPTER 3. A Heavy Tax Levied for Demanding Equality   76

CHAPTER 4. Educational Resources Are Not for White Schools Only   107

CHAPTER 5. When Desegregation Was Not Enough   137

EPILOGUE. The Elusive Nature of Educational Equality   151

NOTES   159

BIBLIOGRAPHY   187

INDEX   203

ABBREVIATIONS

AU	Atlanta University
NAACP	National Association for the Advancement of Colored People
SCLC	Southern Christian Leadership Conference
SNCC	Student Nonviolent Coordinating Committee
TYCSCLC	Tifton Youth Chapter of the Southern Christian Leadership Conference

PREFACE

THE INVISIBILITY OF
THE ACTIVISTS' SCARS

I am invisible, understand,
simply because people refuse to see me.
—Ralph Ellison

How do we see what we are trained to ignore? This question guided a conversation I had with David (Dave) Myles, a physician and my Morehouse brother. I wanted to speak with a medical professional about seeing the emotional and psychological scars of others because the nature of their profession regularly places them in constant proximity to others. Dave revealed that his training at Yale Medical School included a course on how to deal with patients' scars as part of their overall diagnosis. The course was called "Doctor-Patient Encounter." According to Dr. Myles, the class focused on training medical students how to keep the humanity in the practice of medicine by seeing and treating the entire human being.[1] Medical professionals like Dave understand the danger of becoming numb to someone's scars. Equipping professionals with the tools to combat the problem illuminates the importance of using visibility to diagnose an illness.

Hearing Dave describe how his training elevated the importance of using scars in understanding a patient's experience led me to wonder: What of those who have been trained to ignore scars in order to tell neatly packaged narratives that lend to only a part of the story being told? Likewise, how do people who are not medically trained understand the danger of not seeing scars, when the messages of commemorating historical events are plentiful while the atoning for the actions that caused the scars is so scarce?[2] The answer to these questions lies in the undergirding philosophy of the Doctor-Patient Encounter course that Dave describes, which emphasizes a need to become intentional about seeing the totality of one's experiences. Like medical professionals, we must intentionally accept the discomfort that invariably occurs when seeing scars in order to grasp the full humanity of those we commemorate and to benefit from their fight and sacrifices.

History is often referred to as the gateway into restructuring events that influence people to rethink certain events they initially considered as fact. Allan J. Lichtman and Valerie French offer the following definition: "history provides a glimpse of what people have thought and felt in times and places very different from our own. It reveals their successes and their failures, loves and hates."[3] Throughout the data collection and writing of this book, I have become increasingly conscious about not becoming numb to my participants' scars. Although I wanted to know about their audacious stand against inequality, I knew that their story could not be told without them remembering the violence that occurred to them. To achieve this feat, I used reliable historical methodologies that allow for scars caused by activism to be analyzed.

Considering the complexity and the multiple components of the student movements in southwest Georgia, I drew on the theory and methodology of social history. Social history was ideal as a framework for this project because it helped me conceptualize and synthesize human agency and the social process that influence agency or, as Paul Johnson has stated, "it humanizes and historicizes plain people."[4] Participants in this study grew up during a period when their agency was influenced by a number of factors and social history allowed me to account for those societal influences. Elizabeth Todd-Breland asserts that social history "helps contextualize and probe the relationships between historical actors within social networks."[5] Along with social history, this study utilizes a case-study design and oral interviews to construct an interweaving narrative. This case-study design provides an in-depth understanding of the cyclical relationship that existed after *Brown v. Board of Education* (1954). Using southwest Georgia—Tifton, Americus, and Moultrie—as a site of analysis, I investigate the ways the *Brown* decision was implemented (or ignored) and how black and white southwest Georgians responded to the landmark case. These methodologies, individually and collectively, ensured that the totality of my participants' experiences is visible. The following pages use these academic tools to tell the story of black youth advocating for a better educational system in southwest Georgia and the barriers they encountered during their struggle.

Learning how to elevate the scars alongside the activism of those who fought for educational equality after *Brown* developed at the intersection of my personal and educational journey. I grew up in Jacksonville, Arkansas, which is nearly twenty miles from Little Rock, hearing about the heroism of the Little Rock Nine, the laborious work of the NAACP, and the leadership skills of Daisy Bates. I recall being taught at school about the nine black students who desegregated Central High School, but it was not until years later, when my mother, Kathy Landers, was reading *Warriors Don't Cry* by Melba Beals, that I learned about the brutality that accompanied their bravery. My mother noted that she had never entered Central but was able to vividly visualize the institution solely based on Beals's account. Additionally, she recounted how she was able to empathize with the pain articulated in Beals's memoir because the philosophy that undergirded the practice of white opposition in Little Rock existed to a lesser degree in Jacksonville. The inability to contain white opposition encouraged my grandparents, Benjamin and Louise Craft, to get involved with civil rights organizations like the local chapter of the NAACP, which inspired some of their children to get involved in local matters regarding civil rights. These adolescent experiences taught me how to see what was not being shown in the public schools I attended and subsequently shaped my scholarship in ways I can only acknowledge in hindsight.

By the time I embarked on my academic journey, there existed a yearning to see and understand the complexities of the black experience from the lowest depth of their tragedy to the highest peak of their fortune. Like Dave, who was fortunate enough to be trained at an institution that did not shy away from acknowledging human scars, I was fortunate to major in fields of study—African American Studies at Morehouse College, African and African American Studies at Ohio State University, and Educational Studies at Emory University—and work with people—Marcellus Barksdale, Diana Miles, Stephanie Shaw, Walter Rucker, Stephan Hall, Vanessa Siddle Walker, Leroy Davis, Maisha Winn, and Carole Hahn—who shared my philosophy and nurtured me on how to elevate the advocacy of those I wanted to study while not ignoring their pain. The skills and lessons I learned from these scholars were pivotal in my work and I am forever indebted for their encouragement.

Over the last decade, I have read numerous books and articles and have had formal and informal conversations with colleagues, friends, family members, and advocates about the need to reframe how we understand blacks' quest for true democracy in America. The readings and the conversations have provided invaluable insight as to how commemoration is often infused with white comfort at the expense of sharing the advocates' entire experiences and why this narrative must be repeatedly challenged. Colleagues, like Michelle Purdy, Elizabeth Todd-Breland, Malachi Crawford, Celeste Lee, Cynthia Neal Spence, Richard Mizell, Khalilah Ali, Latrise Johnson, Sheryl Croft, Tiffany Pogue, Brandi Hinnant-Crawford, Jillian Ford, Maurice Hobson, Keisha Green, Miyoshi Juergensen, Scot Baker, Kamili Hayes, Kwesi DeGraft-Hanson, Nafees Khan, Natalie Adams, Ellen Spears, James Anderson, Dionne Danns, Philo Hutcheson, and others, encouraged me to portray my participants' pain, along with their ideas and activism, in order to provide more insight into the need to reframe the narrative.

I have experienced a range of emotions throughout the writing of this text. Like my participants, I relied on my family and friends to get me through the days. I was truly inspired by those who believed they could change a system resolved on not seeing them as human beings, and frustrated by the backlash they endured. The questions about the book and the laughter during the writing process from Carla Willis, Benjamin Willis, Isaac Willis, Louise Craft, Darryl Landers, Kathy Landers, Evonne Amerine, Kalisha Willis, Teresa Willis, Anisha Hall, Diana Cox, Lakesa Robinson, Eric White, Damien Miller, Yomund Brown, Greg Hooper, Robert Bennett, Steve King, Joel Williams, Charles Davis, Doug Richardson, my neighbors on Woodruff Way, and others kept me committed to seeing my participants in their totality and making sure the reader does as well. Moreover, the range of emotions that occurred during my conversations with participants whose stories I am sharing—Johnny McBurrows, Mukasa Dada (Willie Ricks), Sam Mahone, Juanita Wilson, Lorena Sabbs, Walter Dykes, Johnny Terrell, Charles Sherrod, Jimmy Holton, Ann Whea Walker, Alton Pertilla, Sandra Mansfield, Dale Williams, Joanne Jordan, Fran Kitchen, Ann Wheeler, and J. W. Green Jr.—solidified my commitment to tell a history that captures the complexities of the period. They deserve a special thanks because challenging people to see what they refuse to see or have been trained to ignore would not have been possible without their willingness to share their ideas, activism, and pain. Additionally, I am grateful to the archivists at the King Center and the Robert W. Woodruff

Library at the Atlanta University Center who had the foresight to preserve what occurred in local communities and within organizations, providing the opportunity to see what is often ignored.

The year 2019 marked the fourth century since people from Africa were kidnapped, sold, and arrived in Virginia to be forced into a life of perpetual servitude. The 1619 Project, docuseries like *Slavery and the Making of America*, and seminal scholarship such as *To Make Our World Anew* illustrate both the dehumanizing treatment that accompanied chattel slavery and that other systemic forms of black subjugation were always met with determined activism.[6] From the heroism that occurred on slave ships to insurrections and nonviolent protest, blacks have spent centuries advocating for equality. The devotion to making "the ideals of American democracy true" has resulted in triumphs but these achievements also came with scars.[7] There is a tendency to elevate the accomplishments achieved by advocates without analyzing their wounds or the opponents who caused the scars, which disregards the pain of activism. An inability to see the activists' scars prevents us from grasping the magnitude of their heroism and why their actions resulted in getting closer to democracy instead of achieving democracy throughout the years. My sincere hope is that within the subsequent pages, the scars of activists become more visible so that a more holistic understanding of their lived sacrifices may be laid bare.

AUDACIOUS
AGITATION

A UNIQUE DIVORCE BETWEEN FEDERAL DECISIONS AND LOYAL WHITE LOCAL SOUTHERN OFFICIALS

Whiteness mitigates the crime.
—Michelle Alexander

The ratification of the Thirteenth, Fourteenth, and Fifteenth Amendments did not prevent states from implementing a racialized public school system. State constitutions and federal judges' misapplication of the Fourteenth Amendment provided protection for an illegal system to be established and maintained. Segregation was the most salient priority of local officials, particularly in the South, and federal judges willingly provided unconstitutional cover from the late nineteenth to the mid-twentieth century. Their laser-like focus on segregation being the foundation of all learning institutions coupled with a federal abetting of systematized educational inequalities. For example, when the Georgia Board of Visitors reported "the presence of white students in the classes of Atlanta University" to Governor John Gordon—Article VIII of the state's constitution prohibited white students at a black institution—he gave this report high priority and wanted to make sure his colleagues in the legislature did the same, so he sent a special message to them. The governor had no intention of providing any exemptions for coeducational spaces to exist within the state of Georgia.[1] In fact, what he sought from the legislature was to reinforce what was already established culturally and authorized legally. The legislature heeded the governor's call and passed the Glenn Bill, which was just as inflexible as the constitution but more punitive. The newly adopted bill used similar declarative language, such as "no school, college, or educational in-

1

stitution in this state now or hereafter," to reaffirm that coeducation was not allowed under any circumstances in Georgia. Furthermore, the bill made "mixing" educational spaces a felony.[2] Demanding public schools be separate as a constitutional matter was not unique to Georgia, but the escalation of offenders potentially being incarcerated as a deterrent to end the anomaly that took place at Atlanta University (AU) illuminates the state's priority.

Two legislators—Anthony Wilson of Camden County and Lectured Crawford of McIntosh County—voted against the Glenn Bill. As the only two black legislators in the Georgia Assembly, their vote against the bill provides a counterreaction to the state's overreaction. Wilson and Crawford made clear during their speeches on the floor that the bill was unnecessary. White students at the historically black AU attended because their parents worked there. The decision was not a challenge to the social order of separate schools. Wilson and Crawford's objection to the bill, however, reflected their constituents' concern with local officials' zealous focus on separation with little attention on equalization. Governor Gordon and the body politic of Georgia used the seven white children attending AU to harden the state's position on segregation. Although Wilson, Crawford, and other black leaders, like the Reverend Cyrus W. Francis, a professor at AU, criticized the Glenn Bill for "making a big fuss out of a small matter," the bill passed and solidified the cultural and legal precedent applying to schools receiving any tax dollars from the state.[3] Through political savviness and what George Lipsitz describes as the possessive investment in whiteness, local officials were able to systemize segregation with no dissent from the highest court in the country.[4]

The unification between local officials and the Supreme Court was fueled by a silent white citizenry who refused to challenge the status quo and hardened segregationists who made it clear they were only willing to accept the status quo. These separate, yet interconnected, facets crystalized a paradigm that confined school resources and educational opportunities within a narrow framework. This framework, by its very nature, was oppositional to the type of education blacks wanted to implement.[5] During the same period when a large constituency of whites pushed for segregation, blacks in Massachusetts, North Carolina, Georgia, Texas, and other places sought to expand the inclusivity of public schools. Their desires, however, were often trumped by a power structure determined to uphold educational barriers that predated the Civil War and extended beyond World War II.

Audacious Agitation: The Uncompromising Commitment of Black Youth to Equal Education after Brown examines the sociopolitical factors that contributed to the perpetuation of a racially stratified educational system in Georgia after the *Brown* decision. Moreover, this book explores the various ways black middle and high school students rejected the educational ethos of the period by pushing for a public school system in which race did not determine access, proximity to schools, intellectual ability, or the distribution of resources. My central argument is that, given the sociopolitical reality of the period, the ideas and activism of black youth, along with the backlash that occurred, shaped public education in the South more than legally outlawing segregation. While *Brown* undoubtedly was a momentous legal victory, the burden of making desegregation a reality and addressing other historical educational injustices was placed largely on the shoulders of black youth. This book elevates what black youth demanded public schools become after *Brown* and what they became by answering four central questions: (1) How did the legal decisions that preceded *Brown* influence the sociopolitical climate of the mid-twentieth century? (2) What were the disputable factors regarding the unconstitutionality of segregation that muddled the definition of educational equality? (3) What barriers to equal education did black youth target after *Brown*, and what solutions did they support? (4) Why did educational equality remain elusive decades after segregation was ruled unconstitutional?

Audacious Agitation is centered on the idea that the struggle for equal education was profoundly shaped by contradictory yet relational variables—opposition and activism—that yielded various outcomes. Black youth sought to bridge the gap between the ideals of democracy and the practice of democracy by addressing educational inequities, whereas proponents of the sociopolitical ethos of the South sought to perpetuate the status quo. These oppositional groups clashed on basic matters of what was considered unequal and more complex matters of solutions that addressed the grievances articulated by black youth. The competing ideas of what was unequal did not vanish with the passage of *Brown*. After segregation was ruled unconstitutional, public schools could no longer *legally* be institutions of inequality, but they remained far from the great equalizing institutions that marginalized communities, particularly black youth, advocated they become. Consequently, public schools eventually reached a degree of desegregation but never became learning institutions void of systematic inequities, primarily because the audacious ideas and actions of black youth were seen as adversarial instead of a communal enterprise with the intention of improving society. In this book, I examine how black youth pushed back against the limited scope of a landmark decision and the regressive understanding of educational justice by whites. I illustrate how these individuals advocated for a robust conceptualization of educational equality with the purpose of constructing public schools into institutions that promoted fairness, regardless of the racial makeup of the student body.

Public Schooling and the Firewall of Whiteness

A basic truth about the creation and maintaining of public schools is that these institutions were never meant to disrupt social norms.[6] Although formerly enslaved blacks were the initial agitators who demanded compulsory education in the South, they were not the primary beneficiaries.[7] Shortly after the establishment of public schools, legal decisions and social norms made it clear that the purpose of these institutions was to reinforce the values of whiteness. For example, curriculum was often taught through the white gaze to keep nonwhites in place.[8] These values predated the formal creation of public schooling but survived the Civil War and Reconstruction. Their survival proved pivotal in wedding southern ideas with federal decisions with regard to matters of education. This legal and sociopolitical relationship between the Supreme Court and local southern officials shaped public schooling in ways that benefited whites. Furthermore, the harmonious relationship between federal decisions and local officials gave nonwhites very few avenues to address legitimate grievances. Consequently, public schooling served as a firewall of whiteness because it blocked nonwhites from having any access to white public institutions while simultaneously providing local white officials unlimited control over nonwhite public schools.[9] This unidirectional approach that gave whites sole authority in matters regarding public education strengthened the relationship between federal decisions and local southern officials. Additionally, this intimate connection was not restricted to a historical period, which meant the social and political ramifications were continuous.

Scholarly inquiry that investigates the ways legal precedent strengthened public institutions as a firewall for whiteness often elevates how the federal decisions aided in shaping racial academic institutions of the period.[10] From *Roberts v. City of Boston* (1850) to *Brown*, race was an essential component of those legal proceedings. Several scholars have illustrated how the justices presiding over those cases were often concerned with how the decisions would affect whites. Therefore, the legal maneuvering African Americans adopted to achieve educational equality was often overlaid with a cost-benefit analysis of equality at the expense of a relationship that elevated whiteness.[11] White officials' ability to use legal precedent as a tool to continue racialized educational customs provided cover for school boards that sought to enforce segregation, which limited blacks' ability to achieve educational equality on their own terms.[12]

Studies by legal scholars of federal decisions that tinkered with the firewall also elevate how legal precedent was used to perpetuate a racial hierarchy in public schools. For example, *State of Missouri ex rel. Gaines v. Canada* (1938) and *McLaurin v. Oklahoma State Regents* (1950) broadened the minimalist framework of educational equality without disrupting the unity between federal decisions and local white officials, which continued the social order of education.[13] Although *Gaines* and *McLaurin* are viewed as victories for blacks, neither decision forced states or local officials to fundamentally shift the way blacks had access to public schooling, which was on a separate and unequal basis.[14] What we see in *Gaines* and *McLaurin* are longstanding legal contradictions that the Supreme Court was too indifferent and too confined by the period to reconcile. For half a century, most of the justices who occupied the highest court accepted that blacks were entitled to equal protection under the law, but they did not interpret that as blacks, and other marginalized groups, receiving resources indistinguishable from those received by white students.[15]

Sweatt v. Painter (1950) was the first legal case on educational equality that examined equality outside the strict confines of *Plessy v. Ferguson* (1896), in which the Supreme Court had upheld the "separate but equal" doctrine. Factoring in the "substantive" component of educational equality moved equality beyond a rudimentary quantifiable equation.[16] Therefore, the *Sweatt* decision is extremely important to the historical legal conceptualization of educational equality, because the justices ruled that the "substantive" quality of a publicly funded institution was based on several components such as faculty appointments, essential materials available to students, and the social and political capital of the students and alumni. Furthermore, this legal decision is relevant because the Supreme Court considered the consequences of marginalized people having to go without and how the state of Texas failed to meet the legal precedent set by *Gaines*.[17] Seminal works by social scientists and humanists illuminate the grave consequences that occurred because states neglected their responsibility to provide equitable education.[18] Historian Carol Anderson notes, "Jim Crow had cost America's black children dearly. . . . The disparity in student-to-teacher ratios . . . was staggering. . . . The overcrowding led to significantly shortened school days, as African American students rotated through on staggered, truncated shifts. . . . The result of such widespread disparities in funding was . . . a sprawling, uneducated population that would bedevil the nation well into the twenty-first century."[19] The justices who decided *Sweatt* did not ignore those consequences, at least in terms of what states failed to provide. The long history of states abandoning their legal obligation to provide basic educational needs to blacks was directly addressed by the Supreme Court, which expanded the legal meaning of educational equality.

In hindsight, it appears that *Sweatt* was a precursor to *Brown*, but at the time it was hard to determine whether *Sweatt* was another paradoxical decision by the Court to evade the fundamental issue of segregation or a gateway for the National Association for the Advancement of Colored People (NAACP) Legal Defense Fund to mount a legal attack directly challenging the constitutionality of *Plessy*. Optimists like Thurgood Marshall saw *Sweatt* as a win and an opportunity to eliminate legal segregation in all public schools. In fact, emboldened by the victory, Marshall called a meeting three weeks after *Sweatt* to plan a direct attack on the validity of *Plessy*. According to Mark Tushnet, "Marshall convened a conference of lawyers to 'map . . . the legal machinery' for an 'all-out attack' on segregation. At its conclusion, Marshall announced, 'we are going to insist on nonsegregation in American public education from top to bottom—from law school to kindergarten.'"[20] The ingenious decision to attack the constitutionality of *Plessy* was not reached overnight or even after a seminal court victory. In fact, Charles Hamilton Houston, Marshall's mentor and adviser, and the lawyers on the NAACP Legal Defense Fund team had known the day would eventually come when legal segregation in education would have to be challenged directly.[21]

A direct attack on the firewall that existed since the creation of public schooling was viewed to be a necessity that would have to occur for a just educational system to exist. It was anyone's guess what public education was going to become once the Supreme Court divorced itself from the stranglehold of uncompromising segregationists that caused a narrow view of educational equality, but the NAACP Legal Defense Fund team believed the context that marginalized students had to operate within needed to be eliminated. The quasi victories that occurred from advocating for equality within the confinements of legal segregation yielded what they could. Therefore, the decision to challenge white opposition through the legal means of testing the legality of segregation itself was based on a calculated strategy that white resistance would fade when federal protection ceased. This might have been the case if righting the wrongs of *Plessy* was top priority, instead of appeasing a segment of the population who had no interests in aligning with the constitution. Local white southern officials and their white constituents immediately went from loyal followers to obstructionists. This reality meant that opposition continued to contextualize public education after segregation was ruled unconstitutional.

Brown challenged the harmonious relationship that existed between the Supreme Court and loyal local white southern officials. Unlike *Sweatt*, *Brown* confronted segregation directly. In fact, the seminal legal decision of the twentieth century decided segregation was unconstitutional. *Brown I* and *Brown II* were admissions by the highest level of the judicial branch that *Plessy* systemically created advantages for whites and grave disadvantages for nonwhites.[22] The justices acknowledged the systemic unleveling of educational opportunity produced by separate but equal, and how those practices impacted the social, economic, and political mobility of marginalized groups. Furthermore, they accepted that legalized segregation was a basic violation of the Fourteenth Amendment. Because *Brown* ruled segregation unconstitutional, that meant the educational customs that were prevalent in the South were unconstitutional as well.[23]

The justices' recognition of the consequences of segregation was significant in that it was a complete reversal from their predecessors. Their turnabout from enabling segregation to prohibiting it should not be overlooked. Although the execution of correcting the wrongs of *Plessy* would prove challenging because of their refusal to penalize white obstructionists, the outlawing of segregation was a necessary phase in expanding the legal definition of educational equality. The racial hierarchy of public schools legitimized by *Plessy* was no longer legitimate under *Brown*. Legal scholars, social scientists, and humanists who analyze educational history during the mid-twentieth century have elevated the immediate backlash *Brown* received. White southern officials, along with most of their white constituents, immediately criticized the decision as a gross misuse of power by the federal government.[24] The same individuals who were fervent supporters of *Plessy* chose not to remain loyal to the highest court in the land when it declared their way of life unconstitutional. Immediately, southern white officials went from being loyal bedfellows to staunch adversaries, dissolving a union that existed for nearly six decades.[25]

The divorce between federal decisions and white southern officials after *Brown* was unusual because there was never a complete severance. In fact, several scholars have articulated how the boldness of the landmark decision was quickly diluted in order to appease white southern officials and their constituents.[26] A prime illustration of the unique divorce that occurred after the Supreme Court's first *Brown* decision was the vague language used in what became known as *Brown II* (1955).[27] While the Supreme Court unequivocally told the South that its public schools were unconstitutional, the enforcement remained nearly absent for more than a decade. The use of vague language such as "with all deliberate speed" fostered a climate that allowed local southern officials to continue to operate in their illegality. The inability of federal decisions to eliminate the prevalent educational injustices taking place in Georgia and in other parts of the country had little to do with power and more to do with misplaced will. The justices were willing to delay educational justice for millions of nonwhite students to appease their former white bedfellows. The boldness of *Brown* and the dilution of *Brown II* simultaneously split and mended the relationship between federal decisions and local southern officials. Several scholars have analyzed this conundrum and concluded that *Brown* was a failure because the seminal case was diluted a year later.[28] The decision in *Brown* directly challenged the firewall of whiteness because segregationists could no longer legally rely on public schools to serve as a barrier. Several legal scholars, social scientists, and humanists have also illuminated how public schooling remained a reliable institution that promoted racialized norms after segregation was ruled unconstitutional.[29] Although this scholarship is often categorized within the framework of focusing on *Brown*'s failures, this book is more interested in their portrayal of how public schools functioned after *Brown*. Furthermore, their conclusions provide a deeper explanation as to why social norms survived the seminal case. Given the fact that public schooling and the firewall of whiteness were more fluid during desegregation, there is a need for an exhaustive interrogation as to why black students who attended public schools after *Brown* had similar experiences to those who went to school under *Plessy*. Moreover, the scholarship that elevates issues unaddressed by *Brown* is critical because those experiences were based on the uncanny persistence of the relationship between federal decisions and local white southern officials in the face of increasing odds.[30]

A Theoretical Framework for
a Contradictory Period

The entrance of black youth—the Little Rock Nine, Ruby Bridges, and others—into previously segregated white schools—Central High, William Frantz Elementary School, and others—and their experiences are manifestations of competing variables that starkly shaped the formula and conclusion of educational equality. Likewise, black youth who fought for educational equality outside the framework of desegregation in places like Georgia, Alabama, North Carolina, and Mississippi found themselves susceptible to similar retributions as their classmates who sought to move *Brown* beyond a legal exercise.[31] This mixture of contradictory variables—access, hostility, advancement, and opposition—did not lend itself to binary results—progress or regress. There was no form of agitation in which black youth participated after the outlawing of segregation that was not interconnected with various forms of white opposition. This means that the conclusions of the defiant acts by the activists were accompanied by the conclusions of the hostile acts by the obstructionists. The activists did not get pure progression, but the obstructionists did not get an unfragmented status quo. The results from this contradictory relationship between activism and opposition are just as opposing as the formula. Grappling with this disorderliness is the only way we can fully understand the multifaceted complexities of the fight for educational equality after the landmark *Brown* decision.[32]

The collective lot of contradictory ideas and actions that shaped and influenced public education is referred to as an educational farrago.[33] Educational farrago operationalizes as a contentious mixture of ideas and events occupying the same space at the same time and yielding varying results based on the power dynamics at play. *Audacious Agitation* employs educational farrago as a theoretical framework to illuminate the interconnectivity of activism and opposition. Black youth who advocated for educational equality after the *Brown* decision were addressing contemporary and historical inequities. Therefore, educational farrago is uniquely applicable to this study because it explains how the competing variables shaped pub-

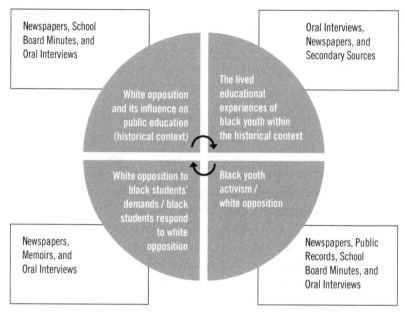

Educational Farrago Conceptual Framework

lic schools and the educational experiences of black students after *Brown* while providing historical context that places the actions of the judicial branch, the opposition of local white southern officials, and the activism of black youth on a continuum. This framework explains the moment as well as the context of the moment, which is critical in any analysis of educational equality.

Black youth, along with black adults, experienced repeated hostile acts that often went unpunished before and after *Brown* because of a power structure that was largely skewed to the side of those who used education to perpetuate hierarchy. The tradition of appeasing white southern local officials and their constituents, perpetuated by the highest court in the land and powerful politicians, helped foster the educational context of the mid-twentieth century. Traditions that subjected black students to second-class resources are directly linked to a history that unapologetically accepted black subjugation.[34] The denominator that solidified the amiable relationship between federal decisions and local southern officials was black subjugation, especially when it came to matters of public education.[35] Federal and local politicians alike justified the treatment of blacks through a deficit lens. For example, President Theodore Roosevelt made several politically charged statements that illustrated how he prioritized his relationship with the South over equality. After he left office, Roosevelt went as far as telling the audience at a National Negro Business League event that blacks "should not whine about privileges they did not enjoy." At that same event, he went on to say that "the best friends the Negroes can have . . . are their white neighbors of the South."[36] Imbedded in his statements are the belief that blacks should not demand to be equal to whites and those who promoted black subjugation were also their friends. White politicians with presidential aspirations, or those who became president, like Roosevelt, had no quarrels with appeasing whites from the South at the expense of black progress.

Like Roosevelt, his presidential successor, William Howard Taft, made conciliatory speeches regarding the preservation of southern traditions at the expense of blacks. At a dinner and talk with four hundred southerners, Taft's address toed the line between dogmatic idealism and pragmatism. He was careful not to offend those who believed in the racial traditions of the South but wanted to be clear that returning to the days of the nineteenth century was not realistic. During this address, he noted that slavery was wrong and the nine million "negroes" who resided in the United States at the turn of the twentieth century deserved to be made "worthy of their responsibilities."[37] He went on to say that bringing in laborers from different parts of Europe made little sense when there were able-bodied blacks to serve in that capacity. Taft continued by stating that industrial education should be available for the masses of negroes with a very select few being provided "higher education for the leaders of the negro race."[38] His philosophy did not deviate from the path of southern politicians. For example, in Hoke Smith's inaugural address as governor of Georgia he noted, like Taft, that he was in favor of politically disenfranchising the "Negro." However, Smith and Taft sold education for blacks to their constituents as a pragmatic endeavor in regard to their role as workers.[39] Federal and local politicians agreed that the primary purpose of public education for blacks was to train them to be laborers and nothing more.

Despite the deficit language used by federal and local politicians and the context it shaped, blacks showed substantive progress, evidenced by an increase in literacy levels, enrollment levels of black students attending school full-time, and amenities at black schools before segregation was ruled unconstitutional.[40] The context in which black progress existed, however, remained oppositional because they were still treated like second-class citizens. Politicians with aspirations of becoming president, such as Herbert Hoover, Franklin D. Roosevelt, and Harry S. Truman, dealt with the nation's de facto and de jure segregation differently. Hoover, some have argued, was more antagonistic to the hostility blacks faced whereas Roosevelt and Truman were more sympathetic.[41] Roosevelt and Truman's penchant to entertain the plight of blacks caused dissension within the Democratic Party that reached a fervor when Truman ended segregation within the armed forces.[42] This decision by Truman disrupted the alignment between federal and local ideals of segregation that had been solidified under *Plessy*. This disruption did not sever the ties, because segregation remained the law of the land. Loyal segregationists like Herman Talmadge, who was governor-elect of Georgia when Truman was elected president in 1948, were so comfortable with him that they supported Truman over Strom Thurmond, the Dixiecrat candidate. Truman's ability to secure southern support, as with his predecessors, was based on southern politicians' and their constituents' belief that their way of life would not be fundamentally disrupted, which held true until the mid-1950s.

While federal and local policies created an adversarial climate for black education to function within, blacks continued to advocate for better education. The consistent challenges that accompanied racialized educational policies also molded the educational farrago. The outlawing of segregation acknowledged what African Americans knew since the inception of public schooling. Several seminal works illuminate how blacks consistently challenged public schools to promote fairness and equality instead of whiteness as the standard.[43] I accept the argument put forth by various scholars who maintain that blacks never accepted the second-class educational opportunities afforded to them under *Plessy* or those that continued after *Brown*.[44] These articulations of the educational agency displayed by people who were legally and socially marginalized have greatly influenced my understanding about the sociopolitical climate that existed when segregation was ruled constitutional and during the time it was outlawed. Moreover, the existing scholarship has helped me develop a holistic framework to capture a contradictory period that was often revealing multiple things and affecting various people in different ways at the same time. Studies that portray the various ways disenfranchised people responded to the social norms and accomplished extraordinary feats despite segregation provide the foundation for the theoretical and methodological framework used in this book.[45]

The constant debate regarding the functionality of education for blacks had political and educational consequences. Because of personal memoirs, reports, and scholarly texts, we know that those outcomes were not all positive or all negative, yet the history of American education is often articulated using a linearity approach.[46] This approach is incomplete because it fails to capture the circular nature of educational history due to the persistent disagreement that surrounded the purpose of public education for whites versus blacks. Influenced by national politicians and federal decisions, local white officials promoted ideas of education that left blacks subjected to second-class citizenship. Meanwhile, an overwhelming majority of blacks desired education that reflected how they saw themselves, which was as first-class citizens deserving of the same type of education as their white counterparts. This contentious mixture of ideas and actions lay at the foundation of public schooling and remained influential after *Brown*.

The sociopolitical climate that birthed *Brown* did not disappear once segregation was outlawed. The educational experiences of nonwhite students continued to be muddled after *Brown* because the landmark case accepted that white schools, white administrators, white teachers, and white students were inherently better than their nonwhite counterparts, a grossly inaccurate conclusion that would prove costly to black schools. The banning of the "separate but equal" ideology reinforced the thesis that the intellectual capabilities of marginalized students were thwarted by the lack of resources at nonwhite schools, so the justices of the Supreme Court sought to address this reality by providing all students access to well-resourced public schools. This linear approach adopted by the justices failed to incorporate best practices that existed outside of white institutions. By doing so, it affected many black principals and black teachers, who lost jobs and positions at an alarming rate, which negatively affected black students. The overreliance on desegregation and the neglect of other critical components of equal education, along with local southern white officials and their constituents' refusal to accept desegregation as redress, continued contradictory tensions that already existed.[47]

The Conundrum of Unsettling Contradictions

Incorporating a different framework—educational farrago—elevates the thorny and auspicious actions that resulted from the strange relationship between blacks' self-determination and whites' refusal to reconceptualize educational equality. These disproportionalities—be it double taxation, desegregation, or lack of equitable resources—do more than provide context for the historical educational experiences of blacks; they help shape those experiences, which means they are partners in this enterprise. In this book, activism and opposition are placed on the same stage to investigate the various contradictory results that occurred in the years following *Brown*. Elevating the ideas and advocacy of black youth along with the opposition they faced illustrates how these individuals profoundly shaped public education in ways that went beyond *Brown*. Archival data and oral histories reveal a poignant story about what occurred when desire for equality came in direct contact with adversarial power.

In chapter 1, I examine the barriers that persisted after the landmark decisions of 1954 and 1955 by portraying how the different responses to *Brown* continued a culture of progress, regress, hopes, and doubts that greatly influenced public education nationally and locally. Organizations like the NAACP and leaders like A. Phillip Randolph and Bayard Rustin played a pivotal role in addressing the barriers by organizing youth after the *Brown* decision. The NAACP was successful in getting *Brown* to extend the legal definition of educational equality, but, I argue, the decision continued using a limited scope that confined equality to access. An interrogation into how youth activism evolved in ideas and actions that included direct action on equal resources, voting, better housing, better-paying jobs, and access to public facilities reveals a much more robust conceptualization of educational equality. This evolution drastically changed the tone of the period and anticipated what youth activism became in the subsequent decades after segregation was outlawed. The chapter ends with my examination of how the evolution of youth activism took root in southwest Georgia, particularly in the cities of Tifton, Americus, and Moultrie.[48]

In chapter 2, I explore the ways in which the small, genteel town of Tifton became one of the first small communities in Georgia to realize that the civil rights movement was not confined to southern metropolitan cities like Atlanta or Birmingham, nor were civil rights just a federal issue. Tifton had been able to function under the ethos of segregation since its founding, but this would all change in the 1960s. In 1962, black youth in Tifton, led by students Walter Dykes and Major Wright, began to challenge the customs of Jim Crow, particularly the educational inequities produced by the segregated system. Inspired by events they attended where Dr. Martin Luther King Jr. discussed what it means to fight for justice, they returned to Tifton determined to organize and fight for equality. In this chapter, I investigate the origin of the Tifton youth movement and those key actors who made the movement possible. I examine the issues black youth believed were salient to them, the ways in which they fought to have those issues addressed, and the opposition they received as they fought to improve their educational experiences. I argue that their desire to acquire political and educational equality reveals an interconnected approach to equality that extended beyond the legal scope of *Brown*. Finally, I contend that the backlash to the youth movement greatly undermined Tiftonians' ability to implement a form of educational equality that could move beyond desegregation.

In chapter 3, I argue that the Americus Movement became a movement about educational equality because the humanity of so many young people was being violated for challenging the disenfranchisement of blacks. I interrogate how essential these black youths' participation was to the Americus Movement. Because Americus is so close to Albany, Georgia, the Albany Movement greatly influenced the events that took place in the rural town. Americus did not have a higher-education institution like Albany State University from which to recruit participants, so the efforts of youth attending primary and secondary school were pivotal. I also examine how the Americus Movement came into existence by focusing on a couple of events that had national implications. I also investigate what motivated several black students to join the movement and the issues they rallied behind. The Americus Movement illuminates why the struggle for equality included the need to be treated as a human being.

In chapter 4, I illuminate how dilapidated facilities and the revocation of many black high schools' accreditation spurred black youth to protest, specifically in Moultrie, Georgia. The customs of Moultrie were like those of Tifton and Americus, which meant that black youth faced several injustices. The focus of this chapter, however, is primarily on the ways they conceptualized educational improvements and subsequently organized and protested to see those improvements fulfilled. I argue that these young boys and girls envisioned an educational system beyond the boundaries imposed by Jim Crow, and they fought tirelessly to see their vision accomplished.

In chapter 5, I contend that desegregation was insufficient in meeting the demands proposed by black youth in Tifton, Americus, and Moultrie. I discuss how pivotal the activism of black youth and the organizing by organizations like the Student Nonviolent Coordinating Committee (SNCC) were to public education after the *Brown* decision. Although a federal decision provided a necessity, I affirm that it was black youth, along with social organizations, who fundamentally pushed public schools to become more equitable from the mid-1950s to the early 1970s.

In the epilogue, I claim that, historically, educational equality for blacks has been difficult to obtain because their ideas and activism have been constantly ignored. Black youth have been intimately involved in the fight for educational equality since the nineteenth century. Unfortunately, only a few policies have been enacted based on their demands. I analyze the real consequences of disregarding the ideas and actions of a group that has been uncompromising in its commitment to educational equality. Black youth asserted that educational equality involved much more than access, even as educational equality largely remained elusive. I argue that public schools failed to achieve a level of equality satisfactory to those they helped marginalize due to the conundrum of unsettling contradictions. Those who are marginalized by public schools hold the answers to creating a more equitable system, but that system has failed repeatedly to recognize their value. Local white southern officials ignored the answers produced by those they were convinced did not even have the capability of having answers. We must understand how the inability to recognize the humanity of the marginalized has continued a cycle of inequality within public schools that is not inevitable but one of choice.

This book provides a comprehensive history of several student movements that took place in southwest Georgia and the barriers that prevented full participation, equal treatment, and equal resources from being implemented. The contestation surrounding the purpose of public schools did not end with the outlawing of segregation. In fact, the arguments were heightened after desegregation for various reasons. For local white southern officials and their constituents, the reasons primarily centered around what they considered to be an infringement on their way of life.[49] For African American youth and adults, *Brown* validated what they already knew, so their fight was a continuation to dismantle public schools from being vendors for whiteness.[50] These contested arguments occupied the same space but did not possess the same power. In this context, *Audacious Agitation* explains how contrasting ideas fundamentally shaped the conceptual framework of educational equality in ways that neither left public schools unchanged nor allowed them to become the institutions black youth desired.

CHAPTER 1

BROWN AND THE
MUDDLED REALITIES OF
PUBLIC EDUCATION

I wish I could say that racism and prejudice
were only distant memories. We must dissent
from the indifference. We must dissent from
the apathy. We must dissent from the fear, the
hatred, and the mistrust. . . . We must dissent
because America can do better, because
America has no choice but to do better.
—**Thurgood Marshall**

Technically, Ann Wheeler was part of the last generation of black children who attended public schools under legal segregation. Growing up in Worth County and Colquitt County, Georgia, during the late 1930s and early 1940s, Wheeler experienced the all-encompassing nature of white opposition. As the daughter of a tenant farmer, she witnessed firsthand how her educational opportunities were intrinsically connected to the economic and sociopolitical norms of southwest Georgia. Wheeler, along with her siblings, experienced shortened school years and interrupted school days due to high labor demands from local white employers. Although her father, Sam McBurrows, like so many other black tenant farmers, saw education as the only vehicle to move beyond the cyclical and limited mobility of tenant farming, pragmatism often outweighed idealism. Wheeler recalled, "In the eighth grade we were out of school so much because in the spring you are going to hit that field. You are going to sit out there, chop cotton, you got to do some of that, so I didn't pass to the ninth."[1]

She internalized this situation as a personal academic failure rather than a result of entrenched social norms that were established and sanctioned at the highest level of government long before she reached school age. Limiting educational barriers linked to inadequate economic opportunities were not confined to Wheeler or her contemporaries. Other black people throughout the South experienced similar barriers due to the enduring practice, after chattel slavery ended, of systemically funneling people into domestic occupations.[2] Additionally, there were restrictions in place that made accessing other professions extremely difficult. Wheeler being forced to repeat the eighth grade was directly linked to the well-established context that predated *Plessy*.[3]

The educational experiences of black youth reveal that no aspect of their journey existed outside of an educational farrago. Being able to attend school, the type of resources available at the school, and the plight of getting to school all yielded contradictory results. The hope of Sam McBurrows and many others that education would be different for black youth from metropolis and/or rural areas in the mid-twentieth century was obstructed by local school boards. Their willful neglect of black students' needs placed financial strains on black schools. That neglect exposed black students to injustices that began on their journey to school. This walk exposed them to hostile spaces that were very different from those of the schoolhouse and their communities. Whites often occupied those spaces to terrorize black students. Ann Wheeler vividly remembers the daily terror she and her classmates faced on the way to and from school: "Walking from school, we see a car coming, we know that they were white people in the car and you gon' hit the ditch. . . . You gon' get down in there and hide until they pass on by. So you were fearful."[4] The exposure to white hostility on the way to and from the schoolhouse sent a similar message of unworthiness as did keeping them home from school to perform domestic duties or grossly underfunding their schools. Legal segregation provided the cover for local officials to send this message boldly and repeatedly. This covering made it nearly impossible for any black student to escape the multifaceted and continuous trauma of segregation.

After the high court banned segregation on May 17, 1954, a logical conclusion for anyone to make was that the educational opportunities and experiences for black youth would improve exponentially. Theoretically, the terroristic customs that were able to thrive and survive under *Plessy* should have limited academic and political ramifications under *Brown*. Under

Plessy, segregation and the educational experiences of black youth were intertwined. There was no reason to believe that this relationship could legally remain nor was there any reason to think the powers that upheld segregation could not uphold desegregation. Thus, several lawyers and many others who were instrumental in quashing segregation were excited about the ruling. The ecstatic response that surrounded *Brown* was undeniable. Journalist Juan Williams recalls the night after the historic decision came down from the Supreme Court: "Marshall and several of the NAACP staff went to his favorite restaurant, the Blue Ribbon, for food and drinks. . . . People at the party began saying the NAACP's work was done and it was just a matter of time before all the nation's schools were integrated."[5] The celebratory aura that characterized the Blue Ribbon reveals the elation that existed among several lawyers because of the potential effect they saw in the legal decision. The lawyers who viewed the decision through an elation lens saw in *Brown* a transformation in the sociopolitical climate responsible for educating black students, which theoretically meant they would encounter less hostility and eventually deem these interactions as aberrations.

While there was consensus among the NAACP Legal Defense Fund team that the *Brown* decision had the power to transform public schools, there was disagreement regarding the order in which the transformation should occur.[6] For some, desegregation was the integral piece missing from the transformative possibility of public education. For Thurgood Marshall, lead council on the team, the seminal decision laid the foundation for public schools to begin to be transformative. According to Williams, Marshall did not join his colleagues as they prophesied about the moment. In fact, Marshall responded to his colleagues by stating "I don't want any of you to fool yourselves, it's just begun, the fight has just begun."[7] Marshall's warning to his peers added somberness to a jovial event. The cautionary statement to his staff who witnessed firsthand the interworking of legal decisions appears to be flippant.[8] This case went beyond equal pay for black and white teachers and providing a law school for black students. The *Brown* decision essentially agreed with what they had spent decades fighting for and here was the lead attorney saying this was only the beginning of the fight. Marshall's refusal to accept desegregation as the end should not be disregarded or treated as cautious optimism. His choice to respond to the seminal decision with trepidation foreshadowed the sociopolitical realities of the period after segregation was ruled unconstitutional. The juxtaposition in the reactions at the Blue Ribbon were not confined to the staff of the NAACP Legal Defense Fund team. In fact, the elation and trepidation that occurred after *Brown* provide a framework for how various reactions continued a culture of progress, regress, hopes, and doubts, which I refer to as an educational farrago that continued to influence public education after 1954.

Muddled Realities

Legal precedent and the educational opportunities and experiences of black youth did not remain as fixed once segregation was ruled unconstitutional, but the politicization of black education proved analogous to what went on in previous generations. Marshall's foreshadowing that the "fight has just begun" speaks to this confusion. He understood whites would not accept blacks as full citizens overnight because for decades the law reinforced what they had been taught culturally. Most blacks, like the McBurrows, resided in places where treating blacks as second-class citizens was an ingrained practice. It was also no secret that a large segment of the white population in these areas opposed any form of integration. So, when the Supreme Court banned segregation in public schools, it created a new policy; it challenged these deeply held views.

As discussed in the introduction, long-held racialized views by whites made it nearly impossible for them to accept the court's decision. Just as damaging was their inability to accept black youth demands for equal education and full citizenship, an inability that was just as instrumental in shaping what public schools became during the mid-twentieth century.[9] Both the events that occurred after May 17, 1954, and the preceding history make it difficult to categorize the struggle for educational equality through a linear lens: segregation to desegregation. The variety of responses inevitably contributed to the degree to which the case was or was not implemented, which invariably determined what public schools looked like after the ruling. Although the responses varied by locale, all of them contributed to the climate of public schools because they aided in the continuation of the educational farrago that became more complicated after *Brown*. Public schools were contradictory bastions when Ann Wheeler was in school and they continued to be after *Brown* because of the combination of a very powerful constituency opposing the new direction of public schools and a frustrated group of young people, who were energetic and organized, attempting to go beyond the court's decision.[10] This does not mean public schools were the same before and after desegregation; it is quite the contrary. What it means is, *Brown* added another variable to an already messy situation that lent itself to contradictory results. At its core, *Brown* assisted in continuing an educational farrago while simultaneously providing an opportunity to change the hostile context by creating new possibilities that had a profound impact nationally and locally.

Those who believed that progress was made after the case turned to recent events to solidify their claims. They used Clinton, Tennessee, and to an extent Little Rock, Arkansas, as evidence. In contrast, others who believed public schooling regressed used the closing of public schools in Prince Edward County, Virginia, and several black students leaving Central High in Little Rock as empirical confirmation.[11] The same bifurcation in interpretation of events is also evident among those who viewed public education through the prism of hope and those who viewed it through doubt. The data, although disproportionately, provide support for each of these competing viewpoints. Whether schools were being desegregated or closed to prevent desegregation, and whether monies were being withheld from or funneled to black schools, the collision between white opposition and black student advocacy illuminates the disputable factors that explain why this was the case.

This chapter portrays how differences in the rhetoric and reality were based on more than the successes and failures of a legal proceeding. National events, such as the Youth March for Integrated Schools in Washington, D.C., and local students' responses, such as the Appeal for Human Rights in Atlanta, Georgia, illustrate the muddled realities of the period. While scholars have done a laudable job articulating what the watershed case did and did not do, an understanding of how the dids and the did nots resulted in a mix of confused responses that shaped public schools in the aftermath of legal segregation being outlawed is required.[12]

The Spaces between What Was and What Is

An image etched in the historical memory of *Brown* is one of Nettie Hunt sitting on the steps of the Supreme Court building with her daughter, Nickie, with one arm wrapped around the young girl and her other hand holding a newspaper that reads, "High Court Bans Segregation in Public Schools." As Nickie looks up at her mother, unsure about the world that lies ahead, and as Hunt looks down at her daughter, perhaps thinking of the daunting journey of the past, the picture suggests that the goal in the relentless struggle for educational equality has finally been achieved, and captures a sense of jubilation for those who thought the ruling signaled an end to the inequalities characteristic of the public school system.[13]

Linda Brown recalled how ecstatic her mother was when the Supreme Court outlawed segregation. She also remembered her father being overwhelmed with joy by the news that segregation was no longer law.[14] James Patterson notes in his work that Harlem's well-known black newspaper, the *Amsterdam News*, called the decision "the greatest victory for the Negro people since the Emancipation Proclamation" and believed it would "alleviate troubles in many other fields."[15] However, this elation in the immediate aftermath of the court's decision was not displayed by the majority; the anecdotes from Linda Brown and others who lived in the period provide insight into the hope that some had in *Brown*. Their hope served as the energy America needed to move *Brown* from a legal proceeding to acts of implementation. While certain lawyers and black newspapers may have overstated the transformative potential of *Brown* and the widespread elation that existed within and outside of the courtroom, hope existed within the possibility of what could be because of something that was no longer. This explains why various laypeople, with limited knowledge as to how a federal decision would be implemented locally, participated in marches and other efforts to implement desegregation.

By ruling segregation unconstitutional, *Brown* put an indelible mark on the ethos of public schooling. The impact of the mark should be neither underestimated nor exaggerated. There was not a complete severance between the past and the future. While a federal ruling told local officials that their primary way of life was unconstitutional, it simultaneously gave states the flexibility to comply with *Brown* on their own terms.[16] Therefore, the elation that accompanied *Brown* was conjoined with trepidation because the legal proceedings did not annihilate *Plessy*. Loyalists of segregation and those silent on the issue were told their way of life was unconstitutional, but no immediate enforcement could make them change. Outlawing segregation was susceptible to a pragmatic component that largely depended on a partnership with local officials and the citizenry.[17] William E. Cox, cofounder of the journal *Black Issues in Higher Education* (now *Diverse: Issues in Higher Education*), stated, "While *Brown v. Board of Education* was a precedent-setting decision and is viewed as a turning point in U.S. social history, it was not a thunderous explosion that rocked the foundation of discrimination. Rather, it was a 'law of the land' lever that civil rights advocates could use."[18] Cox, like Marshall, understood that full implementation of *Brown* largely required the cooperation of those who were staunchly against the decision. Thus, while the watershed case caused jubilation for what it had done, trepidation and hesitancy were also warranted responses because of what the case had not done. As educational historian Vanessa Siddle Walker notes, "By the time the *Brown II* decision on implementation of *Brown I* was read by the chief justice on 31 May 1955, there was enough ambiguity in the court's decision to support a legal confrontation between those who would use legislation to maintain the status quo and those who sought immediate desegregation."[19] The ambiguity created various spaces that often confirmed and contradicted the landmark decision concurrently.

Marshall and certain staff members were not alone in the way they felt about the decision. Several national and local black leaders knew that *Brown* would not cure the racial ills that plagued the United States, particularly in the South. A. Philip Randolph summed up his feelings: "The problem we seek to resolve is largely emotional, with roots deep in a morass of fears, frustrations, desperation, and a guilt complex born of a long history of conflict, contradiction, and confusion. . . . The Supreme Court decisions of 1954 [and] 1955 . . . precipitated a raging controversy. The country has been virtually split wide open into two camps[:] one camp stands for, and the other against, the public-school policy of desegregation and integration."[20] Randolph's words reiterate the idea that the mid-twentieth century did not see a decrease in the struggle for educational equality due to *Brown*, which was anticipated by several of Marshall's colleagues. In fact, the need for civil rights organizations and ordinary citizens frustrated with inequities to become more involved in the struggle increased after *Brown* because white opposition was so widespread.

Legal historian Michael J. Klarman states, "To be sure, *Brown*, which invalidated state-mandated racial segregation in public schools, was an enormous victory for racial equality," and "the ruling in *Brown* reflected the antifascist ideology of World War II." However, he also points out that "residential segregation grew worse, not better. *Brown* was almost completely nullified in the South."[21] Historian Jason Sokol supports Klarman's conclusion when he says, "While the Citizens' Councils proclaimed the day of *Brown v. Board of Education* 'Black Monday,' few white southerners embraced such Manichean portraits. . . . The *Brown* decision did not even register on the radar of many whites."[22] The various ideas and actions, to

Sokol's point, were not inconsequential nor were they neutral. The staunch hostility and/or the complete ignoring of the *Brown* decision adopted by various white communities had tangible political ramifications; so too, did the belief in the possibility of desegregation. Adding to the contradictory chorus was a large segment of people from the black community who looked beyond Marshall's reluctance and saw educational equality being about more than proximity. The various influences and responses to *Brown* portray the unique amalgamation of legal demands with states' rights and individual choices. Merged with the demands of full citizenship and equality was a climate where ideology and actions fervently shaped public education during the 1950s and beyond.

A Reason to Hope and Doubt

The range of ideas and responses to the landmark decision muddled the realities of black youth's educational experiences. Although this disorderliness has often been attributed to public schools, black students enrolled in private and independent schools were not exempt. Educational historian Michelle Purdy investigated the experiences of black students who desegregated a wealthy private school in Atlanta, Georgia, and found her participants' experiences included similar circularities as black youth who desegregated public schools.[23] Purdy and others' portrayal of the complexities of the degrees of access and denials provide evidence as to why several people had hope in *Brown* and why numerous people doubted the decision would transform public schools.[24] An article was published in the *Atlanta Daily World* citing a "quarter million children attending mixed classes in seven Jim Crow states and in Washington, D.C.," with the main purpose of illuminating that desegregation was working, particularly in the South. The article goes on to say, "In the twelve months since that day [May 17, 1954], information compiled by the National Association for the Advancement of Colored People indicates that school desegregation has been initiated in the District of Columbia, and the City of Baltimore, in two towns in Arkansas, 29 counties in West Virginia, 30 communities in Missouri, [and] five towns in Delaware."[25] Based on data from several southern states and a couple of border states, the article contended that the "tiny minority" of black students attending previously all-white schools demonstrated that desegregation was working.

The *Atlanta Daily World* argued that *Brown* was moving education forward and criticized other media outlets for not covering the success of the ruling. The article noted "there have been several unheralded instances of Negro children being welcomed by their new white classmates. The extent to which successful integration has been ignored is something of a journalistic scandal." Furthermore, the newspaper continued, "the inspired strikes, the demonstrations of resistance . . . have been widely publicized." The *Atlanta Daily World* provided some examples to support their claim that black students being welcomed into white schools was "the rule: the hate demonstrations, the exception."[26] The *World's* focus underscores the hope that rested in desegregation and the standard they used to determine the success of *Brown*. Their publication implied that if black students were able to attend a white school previously denied to them with limited incident, then that was reason enough to be hopeful that the landmark decision was working and would continue to work.

Unfortunately, those who hung on to hope faced a chorus of responses that portrayed hostility, in various forms, as the norm. Therefore, the hopes that lay in the hands of the Supreme Court and "unheralded negro children" were accompanied by antagonists who deliberately slowed the speed of states banning segregation, particularly in the South, which made successful integration an anomaly.[27] Given the social and political climate in which *Brown* was passed, the hope in *Brown* was often accompanied by bitterness. For example, on October 2, 1954—nearly five months after the *Brown* ruling—the *New York Times* published a story entitled "Baltimore Crowd Attacks 4 Pupils" that demonstrated the hostility black children faced. The article stated, "An angry crowd of 800 white adults and students attacked four Negro pupils. . . . One Negro boy was punched in the face and an attempt was made to overturn a police car in which the pupils finally were taken away. . . . The trouble at Southern High School, which is in the heart of a residential area largely inhabited by white and Negro industrial workers, began early in the day when picketing students appeared with signs reading, 'Negroes Not Allowed,' 'On Strike' and 'Keep the Germs Spreading.'" The article goes on to depict how, later that evening, "near Cherry Hill, a Negro neighborhood in the southern section of the city, a bus carrying Negroes was stoned and a Negro boy was struck in the face."[28] The aforementioned acts of violence extended beyond Baltimore. The strategy of violence to impose fear was akin to what occurred when blacks attempted to exercise the right to vote. Hostile acts employed as a strategy to prevent black students from exercising their rights were a quintessential expression of white opposition during the period.

In addition to the violent resistance experienced by black youth, whites demonstrated their opposition to integration through nonviolent protest. In Washington, D.C., according to the *New York Times*, a number of white students, representing seven junior high and senior high schools, protested integration by staging walkouts. Their primary grievance was that they felt integration occurred too quickly. The students had been assured that "a few Negroes would come in September and a few in February." Therefore, when "400 [negroes] in a school of 1,000" began the school year, white students found this unacceptable.[29] The *Atlanta Daily World* also covered this story and outlined another grievance elevated in the white students' petition, that "they do not want to take showers with Negroes."[30] Although a committee of students—four whites and four blacks—was created to deal with the grievances caused by integration, these reports reveal the various forms of opposition black students faced. Even when white resistance was nonviolent, authorities felt that violence could ignite at any given moment. The *New York Times* stated that Negro students at Anacostia [a Baltimore school where there were also protests] had motorcycle escorts part of the way home, which aligns with Ann Wheeler's concern about the possible danger of encountering whites on the walk between her home and the schoolhouse.[31]

Unfortunately, black youth were the primary figureheads for *Brown*. They bore the brunt of spreading the message of desegregation to Virginia, Arkansas, Tennessee, Washington, D.C., and other places. Where the law could only go in theory, black youth went physically. The Little Rock Nine and Ruby Bridges are often used as quintessential examples for school integration that illustrated progress. However, when they recall their experiences, they are overwhelmingly characterized by white opposition within and outside of school. All these students had to be escorted to school by the National Guard because of white vitriol. Minnijean Brown, one of the Little Rock Nine, stated in an interview with southern historian Elizabeth Jacoway that her experiences at Central were not so pleasant, because whites at Central assumed that "[we were] one dimensional [*sic*]," that "we had no intellectual life, that we had no creative life, that we had no capability for any of that." Later in the interview, Brown discussed how Central never tried to cultivate black students as human beings: "They didn't ask me at Central what I wanted to be, who I was, how are you, do you have a mind, what have you read. The assumption was I'd read nothing, that I really should be scrubbing the floors with a toothbrush."[32] Another black student who desegregated Central with Brown, Melba Pattillo Beals, noted in her recent memoir how the trauma she experienced at Central affected her decades later.[33] The emotional tax that accompanied being the burden-bearers of implementing *Brown* was heavy and long-term.

Incidents that received national attention, such as Little Rock, and lesser-known events, such as in Norfolk, Virginia, illustrate how hope for integration and opposition to desegregation varied, but one rarely voided the other. The nine black students who entered Central High School in Little Rock in 1957 and those seventeen who attempted to desegregate three previously all-white schools in Norfolk in 1959 all had hope in the transformative possibilities of integration. Unlike the hostility experienced by the nine black students in Little Rock, students in Norfolk, according to the *Daily Defender*, expected "the orderly reopening [to be] completed as smoothly and as quickly as possible so that [they could] proceed with [their] immediate objective to obtain an education." The article went on to state, "the Negro students were expected to come to the schools individually and without escorts," which is drastically different from the Little Rock Nine, who had the National Guard escort them to Central.[34] The article does not provide great detail regarding Norfolk's desegregation plan, but it does portray that black Norfolkians experienced parallel circumstances despite their optimistic expectations.

Before Norfolk administrators attempted to desegregate, they took precautionary measures. The *Daily Defender* reported that "fifty policemen were assigned to the school area. Floodlights, set a week ago, have illuminated the school grounds every night to guard against arson or bombing attempts." The newspaper goes on to report that "Arlington segregationist Jack Rathbone said the Defenders of State Sovereignty and Individual Liberties . . . would picket at the school" to show their opposition to desegregation.[35] While the black students who attempted to enter previously white schools in Norfolk were not punched like those in Baltimore or treated with such venom as the Little Rock Nine, they did experience opposition. The fact that black students in Norfolk asked for an "orderly reopening" implies that they experienced school closure, just like many black students in the South did when whites refused to obey the law. Notwithstanding the attempts to accomplish desegregation and suppress white hostility, archival data show that white hostility was constant, and that hostility gravely affected the educational experiences of black students.[36]

Examining what occurred in Norfolk along with incidents in Baltimore, Washington, Clinton, and Little Rock, we see that black students who integrated white schools faced opposition from white adults and students. The trepidation of Thurgood Marshall and others within the black community stemmed from the constant opposition displayed by local white politicians, business leaders, and laypersons. Despite the staunch objection and the doubts that anticipated effects of *Brown* would not fully materialize, hope remained. This optimism came from an internal belief that institutions could be transformed with the right organizational strategies employed by people who were willing to implement and endure. A pamphlet entitled, *A Call* articulates this hope: "Throughout our history, dramatic action by deeply concerned people has served to awaken the whole nation to its sense of duty. . . . Sincere, earnest, disciplined, and dedicated people will influence those who have not yet taken a clear stand. Such a demonstration presses forward the cause of democracy and social progress in the courts, legislature, and all areas of American life."[37] Black youth who attempted to integrate public schools accepted this audacious call by interacting with hostility in a dignified manner with the hope of transforming these hostile spaces that were accustomed to relegating the self-worth of black students as "less than." As in Thurgood Marshall's philosophy, black youth saw desegregation as a component of larger principles in the long struggle for equality, principles that embraced the idea that black bodies were entitled to occupy the same spaces as their white counterparts. Accompanying the desire for access was the attitude held by black students who attended previously all-white schools that they should be treated with dignity. It was a hostile act within itself for them to be made primarily responsible for correcting a social issue they did not create.

Regardless of the enormous burden placed on black students, they remained committed to using desegregation to bring about real change. For nearly two decades, black youth gave reasons for encouragement to those who believed desegregation would serve as a component to achieving educational equality, even while the hostility they encountered provided evidence to the contrary. Black students continued to enter hostile spaces to seek the education they knew was possible. This display of undeterred hope for a better public school system and their willingness to enter white public primary and secondary schools and public colleges and universities brought disruption to a country that was comfortable with ignoring the educational inequities black youth had experienced since public schools were established.

The NAACP, the most prominent civil rights organization of the 1950s, did not ignore their suffering nor did they allow the sacrifices of black students to go unrecognized. The organization's celebration of black youth's sacrifices spoke to their actions and endurance. According to the *Atlanta Daily World* and the *New York Amsterdam News*, a rally sponsored by the NAACP was held to honor the youth who had participated in the fight for civil rights. The event was held in New York with nearly two thousand youth in attendance. The NAACP called the youth "freedom fighters" and honored them for their bravery and their drive to see "all move forward together toward our supreme democratic goal of assuring equal rights, evenhanded justice, and equal opportunities for all our people."[38] This recognition of the bravery of the youth elevates the sociopolitical climate they encountered while trying to transform a social institution. Their willingness to desegregate warranted enough praise in itself, but their bravery in the face of constant hostility showed a deeper level of courage and conviction. The NAACP celebrated black youth because they, like the organization, believed that segregation was the antithesis of democracy and decided to fight against it.[39]

The purity of the motivation and goals of black youth sought was also highlighted at this event. Legal scholar Ellen Levine posits that black students were celebrated during this period because their fight for equality was not driven by self-gratification: "Uncluttered by concerns of power or fame, they had the simplest and clearest of political urges, the impulse for freedom."[40] Bobby Cain, Jolee Fritz, Fred Moore, Earnest McEwen, and Gloria Lockerman were honored at the event because their actions made public schools less segregated. Bobby Cain, who was one of the black students who integrated Clinton High School in East Tennessee, stated that "only through personal sacrifices on the part of young people will desegregation become a reality."[41] The purity and the belief of black youth encapsulated by this night of celebration reveal the hope in the possibility of *Brown*.

Unfortunately, the celebration also illuminated various reasons to doubt that desegregation would move public schools forward. First, it overstated the transformative effect of the presence of a few black students. Second, it showed that access did not alleviate white hostility. The former is prob-

lematic because the personal sacrifices Cain mentioned in his speech reveal
the toll he and the other honorees paid for a component of equality while
their white counterparts were exempt. The latter elevates the gap that continued to exist between their "impulse for freedom" and their educational
realities.[42] Although the NAACP saw the heroism of Cain, Fritz, Moore,
McEwen, and Lockerman worthy of celebrating, many of their white counterparts saw them as invaders. This juxtaposition is another example of the
challenges those intent on creating racial harmony in educational spaces
faced during the period.

Celebrating those who adopted the legal action of desegregation as a
means of achieving educational equality indirectly overlooks the other ways
black youth were striving toward the same end. The NAACP's celebration
of certain black youth advocates shows how the organization prioritized desegregation as the primary vehicle to transforming public schools, despite
the fact that federal and local officials were just as slow to implement desegregation as they were to address a host of issues that would improve
the education of black youth. Other forms of advocacy by black youth illuminate that they were not as committed to desegregation as the primary
means to achieving educational equality. For example, nearly three thousand black students in Snow Hill, North Carolina, decided to protest their
inadequate facilities. Their primary concern was that their school was without a gymnasium and that the auditorium was too small. According to the
Chicago Defender, "Black students' main grievance[s] were overcrowded-
ness and inferior equipment."[43] What made matters worse for the students
was that a white school in the same county was getting a newly built school
costing $450,000. Because whites saw blacks as second-class citizens, what
black youth experienced in Snow Hill was not an anomaly. The lumbering
pace with which any form of improvements occurred reiterated the racial
beliefs that permeated the country, and black youth could not escape the
educational consequences of these attitudes, regardless of the rhetoric of
Brown.

Despite the overwhelming evidence that the 1950s would present similar challenges as earlier decades, black students continued to illustrate their
hope in equality, using desegregation as one of many vehicles. Their support of integration was not based exclusively on entering white schools. Archival data, such as organizational correspondence and meeting minutes,
portray how these young people participated in several events that reinforced their support for *Brown*, one being the four-year anniversary cele-

bration of the historic case. A memorandum from the leader of the NAACP Youth Program, Herbert L. Wright, states that "NAACP youth and college units throughout the country are making plans to sponsor programs on May 17th in the celebration of the anniversary of the Supreme Court's decision."[44] The memo went on to disclose the groups involved and the dates of programs, which implies that this was a nationwide event that took place on university and college campuses, like Shaw University and the University of California, Los Angeles, as well as at high schools in Greensboro, North Carolina, and Paterson, New Jersey. Another illustration of the hope that existed after *Brown* and youth support of desegregation was the national event, Youth March for Integrated Schools.[45] Very few scholars have elevated this event to a level of historical significance, but the NAACP Youth File papers, Bayard Rustin Papers, and A. Philip Randolph Papers illustrate how relevant the event was to the struggle for educational equality.[46]

Before hundreds of thousands marched to the nation's capital in support of civil rights in 1963, tens of thousands marched in support of integration in 1958 and 1959. Primarily organized by A. Philip Randolph and Bayard Rustin, the purpose of the events was to show that solidarity existed between young and old, black and white, and different civil rights organizations. In addition to showing solidarity, the march was to demonstrate that people of different races could come together and learn from each other. The memorandum sent by A. Philip Randolph articulated why he believed the event was necessary. "It is my belief that young people are anxious for a way to affirm their wish to live, study and play together without regard to racial distinctions. . . . I conclude by expressing my firm conviction that in this crisis in our national affairs, no cause demands more and requires the thought and the clear leadership of our great national youth organization than that of integration of our schools."[47]

Like Randolph, Rustin also believed that public schools were in a crisis due to segregation. Jervis Anderson, Rustin's biographer, quotes Rustin: "segregation is a basic injustice. Since I believe it to be so, I must attempt to remove it. There are three ways in which one can deal with an injustice. (a) One can accept it without protest. (b) One can seek to avoid it. (c) One can resist the injustice nonviolently. . . . To resist by intelligent means, and with an attitude of mutual responsibility and respect, is much the better choice."[48] Rustin's choice about how to deal with segregation permeated the Youth March for Integrated Schools event. As a career organizer, Rustin believed that youth had a pivotal role to play in the struggle for educa-

tional equality. In a speech reflecting on the event, he wrote, "in many re-
spects an expression from them [youth] is more meaningful than from the
generations, like myself, decades removed from the schools."[49] A delegation from the Youth March for Integrated Schools was also organized to
meet with President Eisenhower at the inaugural event.[50] Out of the eleven
delegates, six were black youth—Minnijean Brown, Paula Martin, Norman
Brailey, Leon Thompson, Offie Wortham, and Fred Moore—which is not a
surprise, considering Rustin was co-coordinator of the event.

While Rustin took responsibility for handling the logistical components
of the march, it was A. Philip Randolph who took charge of controlling
the message. A letter sent from Randolph stated, "an organized, interracial, march . . . will be centered primarily around youth of high school and
college age. In planning our program, we have had the support and active
participation of religious groups of every faith, labor unions, and civic organizations."[51] Randolph promoting the march as interfaith and multiracial
was probably a rebuttal to those who attempted to tarnish the purpose of
the event by claiming that it was being organized by communists. Although
sensitive to such critiques, he continued to focus on the purpose and the
mission. He stated, "The Organizing Committee has assured that on the
day of our demonstration the outpouring of citizens will be such as to make
a deep and effective impression upon President Eisenhower and other government officials. We believe that this is one event that can contribute to
the mobilization of public opinion in enforcing the school desegregation
decisions."[52]

On the 25th of October, 1958, the Youth March for Integrated Schools
took place in Washington, D.C. Based on newspaper accounts, the march
was considered a success, drawing nearly ten thousand people. Letters
from the NAACP, Rustin, and Randolph files suggest that they were satisfied with the turnout but even more enthusiastic about the responses from
those in attendance, as well as the demand to have another march the following year. Randolph received letters from students and parents stating
how they enjoyed the march and the usefulness of the event. A group of
students from Brooklyn College who were surveyed about the event stated,

> This is the first time in over a decade that college students have been able to
> raise themselves above the stifling atmosphere of conformity and the tragic in-
> difference to vital issues so prevalent in the academic world and to demonstrate
> for so great a moral cause. . . . Your leadership has been a source of real inspira-

tion to us. . . . We pledge to come back to Washington again and again. . . . We must be firm and resolute in bringing to the attention of our national leaders the conviction of American young people that immediate steps must be taken to assure safe and speedy integration of our school system.[53]

A similar letter by a parent was sent to Randolph expressing how pleased she was with the march. Olivia Frost wrote, "My daughter and I were greatly inspired by the entire program. It was thrilling to see the youth from so many different parts of the country. It should have proven to all that the youth are sincere and deserve to have their views received and considered by the White House Administration."[54] Although letters received were an affirmation of the event, it was the achievements and the resolutions that made the second march possible. An interim report that covered the march in 1958 elevated four achievements. First, it dramatized the nationwide support among young people for the students in the South who were bearing the brunt of the fight for integrated schools. Second, students and young people in general were awakened and mobilized to active participation in the movement for racial equality. Third, individuals and organizations worked together in harmony to make the march the tremendous success it was. Finally, a solid foundation was laid for the petition campaign and youth march on a vastly expanded basis in the spring of 1959.[55]

Nearly ten thousand youth left Washington, D.C., pledging to fight for "full equality in our schools, equal opportunities in our chosen careers, and equal treatment in society at large. We shall come back to Washington again and again to consult the leaders of our nation, to petition Congress, to press for the laws which will guide and sanction our advancement to a fuller, more interracial democracy."[56] With the enthusiasm and commitment displayed by youth at the initial march, Randolph and Rustin wanted the next event to be bigger and better. They began organizing the next event aware of the logistical errors that occurred in the first march and were determined not to have those mishaps happen again.

Most of the youth who participated in the Youth March for Integrated Schools in 1958 lived in the northeastern region of the country, particularly New York. Two primary factors could explain the regionalism: the time organizers had to distribute information, and the fact that Dr. King was stabbed weeks before the event. Although Randolph and Rustin felt the march in 1958 was a success, they knew that some changes needed to be made in the organizational strategies. According to historian Paula Pfef-

fer, the primary adjustment made was to start organizing for the event earlier. Not even a month after the first march, "Randolph called a meeting
of one hundred leaders at his office to plan a 'continuing civil rights youth
program.' After formal dissolution of the *ad hoc* committee that sponsored
the first youth march, a new committee was formed to conduct the Youth
March and Petition Campaign in 1959."[57] In addition to starting the planning for the march earlier, Randolph solicited support from the NAACP,
which offered more than their sponsorship for this event. For the second
march, the NAACP offered "their experience, organizational and financial
support."[58] The shift in organizational strategies and the assistance from
more organizations benefited the second march tremendously.

On April 18, 1959, over twenty-six thousand youth from all over the
country participated in the second Youth March for Integrated Schools,
which was an even bigger success than the organizers had hoped. After
some jubilant opening remarks to start off the event, A. Philip Randolph
stated,

> We have come again to Washington because the job of achieving integrated
> schools and civil rights legislation is not yet finished, although some progress
> has been made. . . . Youth and their allies have come back to Washington be-
> cause, in this fleeting moment of history, the problem of integrated schools has
> become the conscience of the nation. We have returned to our Nation's Capi-
> tal today with a democratic participation in a great mass demonstration by youth
> and adults to indicate the uncompromising commitment . . . to secure an educa-
> tion in the public schools free from the insult of discrimination or segregation.[59]

Randolph's opening comments suggest that several states were still out of
compliance with the Supreme Court's decision and a range of emotions following the case was still prevalent. Although the organizers of the march
were excited about the upsurge in youth participation, the large numbers
say much about the lack of progress occurring throughout the country, particularly in the South. Randolph's remarks at the event gave credence to the
idea that there was limited educational progress occurring, and bore witness to the regress and doubts surrounding *Brown*.

On the other hand, Dr. King's and Roy Wilkins's comments reflected the
hope that remained in the possibilities of integration. At the second Youth
March for Integrated Schools, Dr. King declared that the generation going to school after the *Brown* ruling would benefit greatly from integration. As he looked out into the crowd of black and white marchers, he said,

"I see only one face—the face of the future." He continued, "I cannot help thinking—that a hundred years from now the historians will be calling this not the 'beat' generation, but the generation of integration."[60] Although Dr. King's speech had a hopeful tone, he did indict America for disenfranchising black people from the ballot box. Given that political empowerment would become a primary focus for many black leaders in the early sixties, it is not hard to understand why Dr. King gave a political speech to a crowd of youth who were not eligible to vote. Being a forward-thinking leader, he may have really believed that equal education was drawing near, and the focus should shift to political empowerment. Regardless of the political undertone in Dr. King's speech, the belief that the generation he was speaking to would have a different educational experience permeated the crowd.

The *Los Angeles Tribune* reported how Wilkins and Dr. King thought the march would bring about real educational change.[61] Wilkins stated that knowledge of each other would come from integration and that "respect and dedication to the ideal of liberty and equality" would come as well. According to Wilkins, integration was more than people of different races occupying the same space. It was also about upholding the traditions of freedom by learning about and respecting each other. Dr. King agreed with Wilkins, but he saw integration doing much more than providing knowledge and respect. He believed that the principles of democracy could only be fulfilled through integration.

Both marches encouraged leaders like Randolph, Rustin, Dr. King, Wilkins, and others because it showed that people of different backgrounds and races could coexist in one space. If thousands of people came to the nation's capital to march for integrated schools, then it was reasonable to think that school integration was the next step. Black leaders concluded that this event was significant because it illustrated the possibility and the benefits of integration. This conclusion was reached by several youth who attended the event as well. Youth organizers, according to the *New York Amsterdam News*, viewed the event as a success. A youth quoted in the paper stated, "I believe that this day will be remembered as one of the most glorious in Negro history." Another young person stated that "this youth march for integrated schools is significant because it shows how willing we are to fight for what is rightfully ours."[62] Both of these quotes give insight into how black youth believed that integration would change their educational experiences. Even though they criticized President Eisenhower for not attending either march, the young attendees were able to get a statement from his administration committing to "eradicating racial discrimination from [any sector]" in America.[63]

While the data do not suggest students demanded another march or made another youth pledge, the events may still be interpreted as successful because some victories did occur. For example, the petition campaign garnered two hundred fifty thousand signatures, which were presented to the White House "urging an executive and legislative program to speed integration."[64] Second, despite the fact that the participants in the event were not able to meet with the president directly, delegates from the Youth March for Integrated Schools were able to have a meeting with President Eisenhower's aide, Gerald D. Morgan, to discuss their grievances. Finally, after the meeting with Morgan, Eisenhower issued a statement admitting that the pace at which public schools were being integrated was unacceptable. Such an admission from the highest office in the land was tremendous, since it indicated the president agreed with the primary goal of the event.

A statement from the president acknowledging their concerns was very different than a policy being created to address those concerns. Similarly, getting politicians to admit that the implementation of *Brown* was not going as smoothly as initially intended was something totally different than federal politicians having the fortitude to force local leaders to implement the decision with "all deliberate speed."[65] The fact that they had to march for two years just to get the president to admit that the pace at which integration was occurring was unacceptable proved that officials—federal and local—had little intention of implementing the court's decision on their own. Lacking federal and local politicians courageous enough to ensure the implementation of *Brown*, students marched for integration on the national level and fought for better conditions locally.

Essentially, black youth wanted officials to act with the same vigor on integration as they had done to uphold the separation principle of *Plessy*, but securing that action proved to be an arduous task. Regardless of where such events occurred, whether in a national march or local protest, students realized that most officials were not willing to implement any policies that could be construed as an attack on the status quo. This position created a very difficult terrain to navigate, because if officials refused to integrate or fund black schools equally, then the fundamental changes black youth sought were in doubt. Consequently, they had to maneuver through a quadripartite system—characterized by failure to admit guilt, lack of urgency to implement Brown, lack of courage to disrupt the status quo, and the refusal to fund black school—that yielded varying results but rarely led to full citizenship and educational equality, despite great sacrifice and perseverance on their behalf.

Parallel Citizenship or Something Else

Regardless of the fierce opposition to *Brown*, the fact was that public schools were less segregated in the decade following the decision than the decades that preceded it. In a sense, the *Atlanta Daily World*, a black-owned newspaper that was often criticized for being too conservative, was right about the landmark case working, because black students, although a select few, had access to white schools, and funding for black schools had increased, with such schools in some cases receiving more funding than white schools. If the educational experiences of black youth were quantified from the perspective of "the select few" during the late 1950s and early 1960s, these facts might support the conclusion that public education was becoming more equal. Those who believed that some measure of success had taken place could point to examples provided by legal scholars, such as Donohue, Heckman, and Todd, that "white and black school systems in Georgia had become virtually identical according to quantifiable measures."[66] The problem with trying to quantify educational improvements using selected metrics is the tendency to overstate the percentages of black students who experienced the improvements, while ignoring the status quo and/or decline that occurred during the same period. Although it is true that after *Brown* more black youth were attending schools where resources improved, a large majority of them remained at black schools that were overcrowded and continued receiving secondhand materials white schools no longer found useful.[67] Also, the increases in monetary support and in black teachers' salaries were not a result of local officials trying to right the wrongs of *Plessy* but were used as a means to circumvent *Brown*, which yielded some measured progress but represented regress as well.

Blacks experienced the paradoxes of progress and regress for so long that the contradictory message of increased funding for black schools was not foreign. Blacks throughout the South realized that more money was being funneled to black schools not as an affirmation of citizenship but as a reinforcement of something else. Local whites did not want black students having access to white schools, and they were willing to pay a hefty price to keep them away. Thus, avoidance was a significant factor in the increased funding of black schools during the mid-twentieth century. Those that were not state of the art received some structural improvements such as auditoriums, gymnasiums, and science labs. As a result, some black youth were able to obtain an education with some first-rate resources without ever having to attend a previously segregated white school. Nonetheless, the limited resources and will maintained a gulf in funding between black and white pupils well into the 1960s. Even with the passage of *Brown* and the increased funding for black schools, historian Marcia Synnott concluded over two decades later that "structural racism in politics, economics, and social relations persists," which had profound consequences for black education.[68] Throughout the South, local leaders remained rigid in their belief that blacks were not full citizens, so they did not have to provide them the same opportunities afforded to whites. Because of these long-standing ideologies and city leaders' capacity to reinforce them through policies, several black students continued to attend schools where conditions were hazardous and resources scarce. The consequences of local officials' dogmatic refusal to make substantive improvements to education for most black youth meant that their educational experiences often mirrored what the historic case was supposed to fix.

The attitudes of many local southern white officials and their constituents remained constant throughout the 1960s, but the tone of black youth changed considerably. Once youth activism became more localized and occurred more frequently, it significantly shaped the educational agenda of the civil rights movement.[69] Prior to the 1960s, youth activism was largely influenced by national organizations like the NAACP, which meant its primary goals reflected such organizations' agendas. As movements became more localized, however, the goals became less those pushed by such organizations and instead focused on the issues important to the local community. Local priorities varied state to state, so a pragmatic approach proved pivotal to improving local conditions. In addition to focusing on local issues, black youth displayed their frustration in a different manner. Their tactics were more confrontational and their language more direct. In addition to constant white opposition, the shift in tone by black youth provides another example as to why Marshall's hesitance to accept *Brown* as the end to the struggle was correct.

Black youth knew the educational injustices they experienced were based on local practices that consistently treated them as second-class citizens. As with *Brown*, there are images of what social and political historian Carol Anderson denotes as "white rage" etched in our collective memory of how whites responded to desegregation: Elizabeth Eckford being harassed by a crowd of whites, Virginia closing its public schools, and Governor George Wallace standing in the schoolhouse door at Foster Auditorium at the University of Alabama.[70] These images illustrate actions that were impediments to desegregation. They are useful because they portray tenets of southern white opposition—vitriolic, lasting, and powerful—that were practiced throughout the South. Georgia was just as committed to preventing desegregation as Arkansas, Virginia, and Alabama. In fact, no other southern state proved its commitment to implementing barriers for nonwhite students than Georgia. From the ratification of the 1877 constitution to the Glenn Bill in 1887 and the Sibley Commission in 1955, Georgia was constant and stubborn about preserving segregation, even after it was ruled unconstitutional.

Opposition by white officials in Georgia and their white constituents to both the decision and black student activism provides salient examples of how and why public education continued to be muddled during the implementation and lack of implementation of *Brown*.[71] Georgia did not differ from other southern states when it came to the choice between keeping a violation active or not being a hindrance to those who were actively trying to eliminate the violation.[72] Like South Carolina, North Carolina, and Mississippi, Georgia decided to simultaneously fight to uphold what should have never been legally allowed—segregation—and fight against those who wanted to align states' educational practices with the constitution. The allocation of resources was a tool often used by local officials to demonstrate where they stood on issues around educational equality.

A report by the Atlanta Committee for Cooperative Action published in 1960 stated that "students [in Georgia] attending Negro Schools have been known to attend classes for weeks without being able to secure the textbooks required for the courses; meanwhile, the practice continues of supplying Negro students with used or outdated texts disordered by white students." The report went on to note that white institutions received $31,632,057.18 of the educational and general expenditure of Georgia whereas black institutions received $2,001,127.06.[73] Gross underfunding points to local officials' hands-on approach to ensuring black students were not treated the same as whites. Furthermore, the expenditure gap in Georgia included government spending on employment, housing, and health. These interconnecting sectors made it increasingly difficult for black students to experience full citizenship as those in power continued policies that denied them their rights as full citizens. Although black Georgians contributed to the state's educational and general fund, local officials did not have an issue with allocating their tax dollars to facilities that restricted black bodies: white schools, recreation centers, pools, and parks.

In Georgia, there was a cavalier attitude toward implementing desegregation and the ramifications of the resource gap. Local officials were oppositional on all fronts. An article published by the *Pittsburgh Courier* entitled "Southern School Desegregation Bogged Down in 'Tokenism'" portrayed the age-old custom. The article stated, "The plain fact is: What the Supreme Court ruled in 1954 and what Negroes have strived through the courts to get since 1938 just ain't happening." In answering the question of why desegregation was taking so long to be implemented, the article simply stated that "local school boards have been able to adopt 'desegregation' plans which cut numerical integration to the barest minimum the courts will accept."[74] This position was definitely problematic, but the failure of public officials to embrace and implement *Brown* was not the primary concern among young black Georgians in the 1960s. The source of their frustration stemmed from white Georgians' unwillingness to distribute resources evenly. Black youth believed that they could navigate whites' refusal to accept desegregation because desegregation was not a top priority for most of them. Nevertheless, the resource disparities caused great concern because that meant black students were going without while their white counterparts had an abundance of resources. Public officials refusing the landmark decision was one thing, but perpetuating a system that made it impossible for black students to compete academically in a racially and economically progressive state was something different and unacceptable. The frustration this caused among black youth can be seen in a number of youth-led events that surfaced during this period.

One of the first examples showing the frustration felt by young black Georgians during this time was a manifesto entitled "An Appeal for Human Rights." The manifesto was written by students from the Atlanta University Center and published in the *Atlanta Daily World* on March 10, 1960. The manifesto stated, "Among the inequalities and injustices in Atlanta and in Georgia against which we protest, the following are outstanding examples," and went on to list and address the areas of education; jobs; housing;

voting; hospitals; movies, concerts, restaurants; and law enforcement. The manifesto was authored by six students—Willie Mays, James Felder, Marion D. Bennett, Don Clarke, Mary Ann Smith, and Roslyn Pope—and it spoke to the frustration black students who were in primary and secondary schools were feeling because the majority of black students, whether in college or primary and secondary schools, were exposed to educational disparities. According to the *Daily World* article, the manifesto received so much statewide and local attention because it "served as an awakening and a challenge to Atlanta and the South as to the mammoth torment of minority youth over inequities and denials which confront them in everyday life. In publicizing deficiencies Negro youth faced in education, jobs, housing, voting . . . [the manifesto] served to enlighten a large majority of our population as to the inadequacies of opportunity and provided a platform for remedial action."[75] Even though student-led events took place prior to the manifesto, it was the appeal that captured the frustration of black students in Georgia and their need to respond. Interdisciplinary historian Winston Grady-Willis has argued that the manifesto and the subsequent rise of student activism "signaled to the world that a fundamental concern of the Black freedom struggle was in securing human rights, and that principal among them was the right of self-determination."[76]

There are poignant examples that not only show the gap between the promise of *Brown* and the educational realities black youth experienced in Georgia, but also how black youth attempted to align those promises with their realities and the white opposition they experienced. For example, in Leesburg, Georgia, Charles Wingfield "was suspended for demanding his school have new and better equipment." The *Cleveland Call and Post* was more specific than the *Atlanta Daily World* in that it disclosed Wingfield's demand: "he asked for better school, library, and gymnasium [equipment]."[77] According to the *Daily Defender*, "the student pointed out to NAACP officials that their building houses approximately 1,200 students from grades 1 through 12."[78] The poor conditions black students faced nearly a decade after *Brown* spurred responses throughout Georgia. Another example that illuminates the frustration young black Georgians felt took place in Atlanta. Students at Washington High School disliked their "inadequate school conditions and decided to march to city hall," according to the *Atlanta Daily World*.[79] The *Chicago Daily Defender* reported that a "high school student declared, 'we're sick of the situation at this raggedy old school. . . . Our library is good, but the textbooks are mostly second hand. The building itself is horrible.'"[80] This concern with poor school conditions offers an important portrait of the extent to which black students understood the injustices that many of them were exposed to on a regular basis. In Leesburg and in Atlanta, the penalties for demanding better conditions were suspension and arrest. The response of white officials and local white citizens went against *Brown* and the First Amendment. The rights of black youth were repeatedly trampled on as a strategy to quell their desire to have a public school experience like their white counterparts.

One of the many things black schools did exceptionally well before and after *Brown* was training black teachers, who did not view black students through a deficit lens. The Historical African American Pedagogical Network shared educational and professional best practices geared to reinforce the full citizenship of black students.[81] Black teacher organizations existed throughout the South and this network served as the catalyst for this model, which was adopted by a multitude of black teachers from 1860 to 1968. Scholarly work on black teachers from the Civil War through *Brown* portrays black students as beneficiaries because such teachers reinforced their humanity in a society that taught them they were second-class.[82] Black teachers pushing black youth beyond societal limitations never sat well with local white officials who controlled the purse and made the hiring decisions.

Unfortunately, the uneven power structure of public education meant that the desires of blacks regarding their schools were often encroached upon by what whites wanted black schools to be. For example, in 1961, Al Cheatham, the principal of Sol C. Johnson High School in Savannah, Georgia, was fired by the Chatham County board of education, for being too progressive. The *Atlanta Daily World* covered this story for several days and all of the articles discussed how Cheatham was well educated—he held a master's degree from Harvard and a bachelor's from Howard—and the students of Sol C. Johnson really liked him. It also reported that the principal was fired because he was "active in a Savannah group called the Crusade for Voters which encourages Negroes to register and vote and supported candidates it felt help Negroes the most." Additionally, Cheatham wanted Sol C. Johnson to implement an ROTC program.[83] Firing qualified and progressive black principals was another standard oppositional strategy employed by school board members who felt that blacks should be satisfied with any form of education. Progressive black educators were disruptors of the cultural ethos by influencing the ideals of black youth and how they operationalized educational equality. Local white officials found this unacceptable and this led to the firing of Cheatham. The protest that ensued in Savannah illuminates the seeds black educators had planted of black students being worthy of a first-class education, which blossomed after *Brown*.

Black youth dealt with a range of issues that called for multiple responses because white opposition ran the gamut from resistance to desegregation to refusal to allow black school improvement. The Appeal for Human Rights was one response. The protests in Leesburg, Atlanta, and Savannah were another. This book focuses on the enduring responses of black youth and white opposition that occurred in southwest Georgia during the 1960s. Southwest Georgia is uniquely situated within the historiography of the civil rights movement because of Albany, Georgia, a small town about three hours from Atlanta. More notably, the activism and opposition that occurred in the early 1960s served as the groundswell for the Albany Movement.

The Albany Movement was extremely important to the period because it extended the movement beyond Atlanta. Historian Stephen Tuck argues that besides Atlanta, "the Albany Movement received most of the national headlines, largely because of the involvement of Martin Luther King Jr. and the huge scale of protestors."[84] The movement's extension beyond Atlanta was important because it showed that blacks faced injustices throughout Georgia and the number of young people who were willing to respond. Furthermore, the location of Albany was vital because of the number of blacks that resided in southwest Georgia. One of the original organizers of the Albany Movement was Charles Sherrod. In an interview he recalled "the movement being a protest and an affirmation. We protest[ed] and took direct action against conditions of discrimination. We affirm[ed] equality and brotherhood of all men." He also noted that a large component of the movement was to "organize and recruit youth" because they believed youth were vital to its creation and survival. The demands for "equal service at lunch counters, in the libraries, bus terminals, and swimming pools" came from the youth.[85]

The Albany Movement became pivotal in the region for the boldness in the way its demands were made. The youth in Albany, like their peers in Atlanta, promoted ideas that directly challenged the social ethos of southwest Georgia. Being the targets of violent acts was often the reward black youth received for their boldness. Sherrod noted, "We had to go through some suffering, [besides] going to jail, people were getting shot at, some people [*sic*] houses were burned, churches too."[86] In the midst of all of the violence, the Albany Movement survived and influenced places like Tifton, Americus, and Moultrie.

A valuable lesson learned from the Albany Movement, according to a letter written by a SNCC member who participated, was voicing one's frustration despite the backlash. The letter stated, "What is most impressive is black youth suddenly felt able to express their frustrations in action which forced the white power structure to listen to them."[87] Because of the activity in Albany, suffering injustice in silence was no longer a practical option in the 1960s. This was not only true for those who lived within the city limits of Albany; it permeated the region and emboldened black students throughout southwest Georgia to voice their frustrations and demand equality. While the Albany Movement is often criticized for not yielding fundamental changes, the inspiration it provided for the youth activism that sprang up during and after the Albany Movement cannot be diminished. When black youth revolted against the ethos of Jim Crow in Albany, it gave other youth in the region a script they could adopt to tackle the issues they faced in their own communities. The case of the Albany Movement is not an anomaly in youth activism during this period in Georgia. Tifton, Americus, and Moultrie also had protests linked to the activity taking place in Albany. Youth in these three locales grew weary of political disenfranchisement, the economic immobilization their parents often endured, and educational disparities. Inspired by the activism in Albany, they formulated a plan of action that directly attacked the status quo.

The Fourteenth Amendment granted blacks equal protection under the law. Nearly a century later, *Brown* decided that equal protection could not occur under the umbrella of legal segregation. The political ethos, however, of the creation and continuation of public school under a practice later ruled unconstitutional was so engrained that the educational experiences of black youth after *Brown* often mirrored the experiences of those who went to school under legal segregation. Therefore, elevating the ideas and actions of black youth after *Brown* without examining the hostility and opposition that preceded and accompanied their advocacy yields an incomplete narrative, because both variables aided in shaping public schools of the day. For example, Ann Wheeler's younger siblings attended school after *Brown*, but their experiences were connected by white hostility. Johnny McBurrows, Wheeler's younger brother, remembered his educational experiences this way: "Living in a farm community, most of the parents were farmers and most of the kids didn't get a chance to go to school very often. . . . So we were handicapped. We went to school after school had started and then prior to school finishing each term, we were in the field harvesting our tobacco."[88] The disregard of black minds and the exploitation of black bodies that the McBurrows experienced were long-held practices that predated both the Fourteenth Amendment and *Brown*, but influenced the educational experiences of black youth after each of them. These influences, accompanied by the desire of black youth wanting better learning conditions, continued a reality that often saw hope, doubt, progress, and regress occupy the same space. White opposition contributed to the doubt and regress that existed within the educational farrago because of local whites' refusal to accept *Brown* the way they accepted *Plessy*. Black students, on the other hand, mirrored the hope and progress because of their willingness to attend hostile white schools and fight for the improvement of black schools. Local white and black communities viewed *Brown* from two fundamentally different perspectives. Each disagreement muddled the realities of securing educational equality by way of desegregating public schools.

CHAPTER 2

THE INSATIABLE APPETITE
OF JIM CROW AND BLACK
TIFTONIANS' DESIRE FOR
FULL CITIZENSHIP

Education and justice are
democracy's only life insurance.
—Nannie Helen Burroughs

Mott-Litman Gymnasium is located at 2425 Emerson O. Bynes Avenue in Tifton, Georgia. Visitors and residents unfamiliar with the history of the building may conclude that it is just one of many recreational facilities in Tift County. No signs exist outside or inside the gym indicating that this locale was part of a black youth movement that swept through southwest Georgia in the 1960s. Likewise, no historical markers exist anywhere on the property to inform Tiftonians and visitors that the gym was erected out of opposition by local white officials and their constituents to black bodies encroaching on public facilities that were designated as white spaces. But this hybrid white-brick-and-metal building with a green-and-white roof offers a valuable history lesson that reveals what occurred when black students started demanding improvements to their educational facilities and when their access to public facilities conflicted with the ethos of Jim Crow. Only through examining the nuances around the creation of the Mott-Litman Gymnasium can we uncover the loud silence of the educational farrago that continued decades after the *Brown* decision. The opportunity to choose what was just or familiar was presented to Tifton after *Brown*, as in other parts of the county.[1] Unfortunately, a significant number of people who were proponents of the status quo vehemently rejected justice.

Before the creation of Mott-Litman, black Tiftonians did not have access to a recreational center. Jim Crow practices framed a sociopolitical climate that racialized every facet of life in Tifton, including recreation. Blacks did not have access to a gymnasium because their segregated schools, Tift County Industrial Elementary and High School and Wilson Elementary and High School, did not have one. During segregation, local white officials built black schools without amenities, like gymnasiums, auditoriums, and outdoor facilities, necessary for basic out-of-classroom activities. Showing their loyalty to the "separate" aspect of *Plessy* and their willful disregard of the "equal" component, Tifton officials created policies that provided their white constituents with better resources while leaving blacks with castoff materials. While *Plessy* did not place a hierarchy between separate and equal, *Cumming*, which essentially said that as long as black students had access to a form of public schooling, there was no violation of their rights, provided legal cover for states like Georgia and towns like Tifton to prioritize separate over equal.[2] Local officials in Georgia used this protection to create unequal educational practices that had grave ramifications that went beyond *Brown*. What whites saw as their way of life, blacks knew was an infringement of their constitutional rights. Therefore, not having access to a gymnasium was one aspect of a larger issue that existed in Tifton, which was whites' insatiable appetite to perpetuate segregation to the detriment of black youth desiring a fairer system.

Brown did not end the dispute on the constitutionality or unconstitutionality of segregation in the minds, hearts, and eyes of local officials and their white constituents. They believed the highest court in the land could not legislate how they democratically chose to live their lives. Historian Jason Sokol captured the prevailing thought of the period by stating that "Jim Crow had defined the minds and lives of southerners" in ways with which they were comfortable.[3] Therefore, the dismantling of segregation hinged on what local whites were comfortable with at the time and not what was legal. Their ability to completely ignore *Brown*, then parse out part of the law that was palatable, illuminates how local white officials and their constituents were able to treat a landmark decision as if it was a suggestion. The power wielded by local whites in Tifton and throughout the South came at an expensive cost to blacks and other groups. The conscious choice to choose comfort over justice meant that black Tiftonians continued to be politically disenfranchised, banned from city pools, and their public schools remained under-resourced and underfunded. At the root of this decision was the belief that *Brown* allowed for some unconstitutionalities to remain.

Tifton and the Desire for a Progressive Image

A definitive history of race relations in Tifton has yet to be written. There are, however, historical, genealogical, and archival data that foreshadow why and how a social justice movement emerged. The town's founding, decades after the Civil War ended and federal troops left southern states, correlated with several southern cities and towns trying to reestablish life prior to "federal invasion."[4] Although "slavery [was] never practiced" in Tifton, the town chose sociopolitical practices that established racial hierarchy, which in turn reveals what type of place it wanted to become.[5] Simultaneously, the focus on becoming an economically thriving location meant a necessity to present a visually friendly environment that would attract outsiders. For decades, Tifton was able to present itself as a less racially hostile place, which benefitted it economically.

A history of the town's founders focuses on its commercial sector. In the early twentieth century, Tifton was a small town where businesses prospered. According to historian John Fair, "Tifton's founder [Captain Henry Harding Tift] had the foresight to diversify the agriculture and agribusiness operations and to endow both with the scientific expertise of an experiment station and an agricultural college. As late as 1945, 91% of county lands were used for farming. By the mid-1960s, income from agriculture exceeded $15 million yearly."[6] Tifton, which dubbed itself the "Friendly City," was a thriving community that had amenities such as an opera house, silent-movie theater, several saloons, and churches. One of the town's most publicized treasures was the Myon Hotel, which was rumored to be one of the grandest hotels southwest of Atlanta. Tifton continued to see economic and population growth while being able to suppress racial issues that would have damaged the town's brand of being an economically viable place with good race relations.

Continuing a way of life that was no longer constitutional, Tifton, like its neighbor to the northeast, Atlanta, the "city too busy to hate," was successful in promoting a narrative that conflicted with reality.[7] Tifton is approximately fifty miles southeast of Albany and sixty miles from the border with Florida. Being close to Albany, one might think most of the town's norms mirrored Albany's, and to an extent they did. The social and political norms of Tifton were like those of Albany; however, the economic model of commerce overriding racial injustice reflected the ethos of Atlanta. To a degree, this distinguished Tifton from the largest metropolis in southwest Georgia. Being a port city, it made sense for the town to adopt a business model like Atlanta's because commercial exchanges were in high demand. While Tifton's economic foundation was solid, the portrayal of business peace over racial conflict worked best only until social upheaval began. For decades, Tifton was able to escape the social disturbances frequently caused by the inequities of Jim Crow, which allowed the town to perpetuate its image as a racially progressive place. But by the 1960s the rhetoric of progressiveness was challenged by black youth through multiple forms of protest. The reality of what blacks had endured for decades directly contradicted the rhetoric, and Tifton, like Atlanta and Albany, had to deal with a frustrated populace.

The history of Tifton provides an example of how a small town suppressed racial tensions to attract business while practicing customs that were devoid of equality and full citizenship for a segment of its constituents. While Tifton did not have the violent backlash to blacks attempting to change the customs of Jim Crow that Albany experienced, white Tiftonians were just as loyal to segregation as their neighbors in Albany, which meant that opposition looked different, but the purpose was the same. The image that white Tiftonians attempted to portray provides some context for the type of backlash that occurred. Local officials were willing to make concessions to some extent, in order to attract business, but when it came to creating political, economic, and educational systems that were equal, they followed the typical model of other southern towns and cities. The existence of a different approach to maintaining Jim Crow should not lead one to believe that life for blacks was better or less oppressive. The essential components of segregation—from disenfranchising the black vote to maintaining an economic system that tied black labor to land, to limiting educational opportunities for black youth—existed in Tifton. The forms of opposition established and continued a context of opposition that only became more fervent when black Tiftonians advocated to be included in the process.

Tifton's image as a friendly city has been contested throughout its history but these contestations have been all but ignored within the narrative. Although Fair admits that "the omnipresent issue of race . . . looms large in Tifton," he concludes that "the black population . . . never threatened white hegemony that tempered activism during the Civil Rights era."[8]

This conclusion dilutes what it means to challenge white hegemony and ignores the activism of black Tiftonians like Ella "Dee" Melton and her husband, Daughtry "Doc" Melton Sr., who were pioneers in the black community because they challenged white hegemony in the city. Additionally, Fair ignores how the town's hegemony was consistently challenged by black youth and civil rights organizations during the mid-twentieth century. Just because Martin Luther King Jr. did not lead a direct-action movement in Tifton and federal troops were not called to protect the lives of young people does not mean white hegemony was not challenged. Quite the contrary: black Tiftonians challenged white oppression through political action and educational maneuvering.

Dee and Doc Melton were early activists in Tifton. They were prominent black business owners whose various businesses serviced the black community, so segregation was not their issue.[9] Their issue was the inherent message segregation sent, which was that blacks were less than full citizens. This message had profound consequences because it often resulted in black Tiftonians receiving less. The Meltons created the Tift County Improvement Club and organized an NAACP chapter to improve the lives of black Tiftonians, but not necessarily to integrate with whites. In the words of his daughter, Doc Melton "took a stand for justice during the time when there was no representation in Tifton for the black community[,] with his wife by his side."[10] By elevating the voices and experiences of blacks in Tifton, we see that racial violence was not the only igniter of movements: the simple need to be treated as a citizen was a justifiable cause as well. While other representations of the history of Tifton attempt to paint a picture of a small town that was genteel and friendly, brewing underneath the facade of friendliness and tolerance were systematic inequalities that several blacks in Tifton felt compelled to address.

White Tiftonians were proud of the culture they produced and preserved, in contrast to black Tiftonians, specifically black youth, who were weary of the second-class citizenship they faced and its impact on their lives. Their frustration and the moment contributed to the growth of a youth movement in Tifton. Places that were strongholds for segregation became known sites of advocacy. When young black Tiftonians began to challenge long-held customs that treated them as second-class citizens, their ideas, advocacy, and conclusions mirrored events that took place in Greensboro, North Carolina, Selma, Alabama, and McComb, Mississippi.[11] As Ste

phen Tuck observes, "Grassroots protest was influenced by national organizations and headline-grabbing confrontations. During the early 1960s, the
template of nonviolent direct action campaigns was copied and adapted
by activists in communities throughout Georgia."[12] Although they were influenced by organizations and confrontational events elsewhere, grassroots
protests spoke directly to the concerns of the local community. The fight for
full citizenship and equality was a national movement, but it was its applicability to issues facing individual communities that made it attractive and often successful. Informed by their own experiences and the waves of social
movements close by, black youth in Tifton sought to create a movement in
which equality was the priority.

A Community unto Itself

Economic opportunities for black Tiftonians were not numerous but some
were able to obtain decent factory and other industrial jobs. Others were
able to create businesses for themselves, which helped establish a vibrant
black commercial and social district called the New Front. Johnny Terrell,
born and raised in Tifton, remembered "black and white people getting
along because blacks [were able to] move freely around whites." He also recalled that "blacks and whites worked together and had good relationships
until the movement came."[13] Fran Kitchen, who also grew up in Tifton, remembered her childhood as segregated but recalls "not having many problems" with whites.[14] Terrell and Kitchen attribute the lack of physical violence in Tifton to the civility between blacks and whites in the workplace,
where segregation was fluid. Blacks and whites shared the same proximal
space at a local plant despite Jim Crow customs of the day such as separate water fountains and restrooms. In other economic sectors, like domestic work, the concept of separation was just as fluid because interaction between whites and blacks was constant. The fact that those fluid interactions
were not without hierarchy, however, meant that economic prioritization
remained embedded in an ethos that was not physically oppositional but
enabled an oppositional relationship in other ways. While black Tiftonians
had economic opportunities throughout Tift County during the twentieth
century, those opportunities were primarily industrial, domestic, and entrepreneurial fillers structured by segregation. The economic system in Tifton
provided few opportunities for social mobility, so education became the pri-

mary vehicle the black community in Tifton adopted to improve their lives and the lives of future generations, which Terrell and Kitchen agree was less fluid.

Black Tiftonians adopted education as the best method to improve their circumstances; this almost universally accepted philosophy permeated southwest Georgia. As the forthcoming chapters will illustrate, blacks in Americus and in Moultrie sought to create a democratic system by fighting for a more equitable educational system. Education, however, was one sector in which the customs of segregation were not fluid. Even in a quiet and friendly town like Tifton, black and white children were to remain completely segregated, as the Glenn Bill intended. This lack of fluidity would continue nearly two decades after the *Brown* decision. White Tiftonians' opposition to change, especially after *Brown*, did not differ much from other places in southwest Georgia. In fact, according to testimony before the Sibley Commission, most of the witnesses from Tift County favored closing public schools rather than seeing any form of desegregation.[15] Their thoughts regarding *Brown* reflected the sentiment of a large segment of white Georgians. According to southern historian Alton Hornsby, the Sibley Commission found "that Georgians by a three-to-two margin still opposed the changing of their laws and customs on race."[16] The findings of the Sibley Commission were not a revelation to black Georgians; however, the willingness to close schools is important to note because it illustrates that the overwhelming majority of whites were oppositional to a federal decision and willing to impede implementation.[17] It is also important to note that black Tiftonians were not upset with their counterparts' desire to maintain separate schools, because they were proud of their academic institutions. Black Tiftonians knew the power of their academic institutions, which is similar to what educational historians Vanessa Siddle Walker and David Cecelski found when investigating black communities in North Carolina.[18] The dispute that remained after *Brown* centered around local officials providing more resources to white schools in Tifton to the disadvantage of black schools. Black Tiftonians did not accept that whites inherently deserved better schools. The black community's support for its schools served as the vehicle through which this message was delivered. Thus, while white Tiftonians were trying to figure out how to circumvent *Brown*, black Tiftonians focused on improving their schools and increasing political participation so they could continue to educate black students, a legacy that dated back to the early twentieth century.[19]

By the mid-twentieth century, blacks in Tifton were proud of Industrial and Wilson because both institutions "provided an atmosphere" that cultivated the intellectual, artistic, and physical gifts society so often ignored existed among black students.[20] The ability of black educational institutions to treat black students as first-class citizens was not confined to southwest Georgia. Southern historian Sarah Thuesen and others suggest that this characteristic, along with various forms of white opposition, kept black schools in high demand after the passage of *Brown* throughout the South.[21] Industrial was the oldest of the two schools in Tifton that provided a learning environment in which black students could experience citizenship in the absence of a deficit lens. Alums attributed this to the efforts of former leaders of the school, like principals Johnny Wilson, James Deas, Emerson Bynes, and Richard Mack. Wilson was the first principal of Industrial, but it was under the leadership of Principal Mack that attendance doubled. Mack was able to secure buses and add a playground for his students, which was a great feat during this period. Additionally, alums remembered their resources improving under the guidance of Principal Bynes but noted it was Principal Mack who "emphasized a more comprehensible curriculum and required students to complete twelfth grade before graduating."[22] Graduates of Industrial largely attributed their fond memories to the relationships with their principals, teachers, and peers. Those recollections of first-class relationships, however, did not cancel out the experiences of those second-class facilities they endured at Industrial and the complete absence of many at Wilson. The relationships provided solace within contextual opposition.

The history of Wilson differs from Industrial's because Industrial was a typical black school built before *Brown*, meaning that, by the mid-1950s, it needed several improvements. Wilson was built in 1957, so students did not have to deal with poor conditions related to the building infrastructure itself. Like those at Industrial, Wilson alums remembered with pleasure the education and the activities that took place inside the building. According to *The Tiger*, "many students were awarded scholarships, prizes, grants, and opportunities for higher education." Students at Wilson also excelled in other areas such as chorus, band, drama, and athletics. In addition to excelling academically and through extracurricular activities, there was a community component at Wilson. Principal Mack, who succeeded Bynes at Industrial and was the first principal at Wilson, revived an adult program that offered basic reading courses to help adults improve their literacy level.[23] The existence of this program illustrates a relationship between the school and the community, which provided black students another opportunity to learn how their issues were interconnected with their guardians' issues. This community relationship permeated Wilson and those who attended the school recalled its importance. An alumnus from Wilson stated that "Wilson was a vital and integral part of the community from August 1957 until its closing in June 1970."[24]

The recollections from graduates of Industrial and Wilson disclose little regret about their educational experiences. Former students who shared their experiences for this study recalled that their school years were some of the most enjoyable because of what they received from the institutions. They remember Industrial and Wilson as places that provided a space for them and gave them a sense of self and purpose. In a town that designated them as something less than, students were able to find an unapologetic and therapeutic counter-narrative at school.[25] Their intellect and talents were cultivated and not deemed to be something inferior. Students could be homecoming kings and queens and participate in plays that were outside of societal stereotypes. In addition to being cultivated at the two black schools in Tifton, black youth also had models who represented how not to accept the adverse class status that Tifton's societal norms attempted to place on them.

School pride notwithstanding, black youth recognized the inequalities in their education. Black principals and teachers at Industrial and Wilson did a laudable job teaching their students that they were just as intelligent and as much citizens as their white counterparts. In fact, among those interviewed, black teachers and black principals played a pivotal role in the memory of their educational experiences. Alton Pertilla, who attended both Industrial and Wilson, stated that "during segregation there was an intense and practically laser-like emphasis on getting an education, getting prepared. . . . [Although] we were aware of second-class characteristics and the nature of [our] educational experience[s], the thing we had going for us was the teachers were motivators, they were concerned [about their students]."[26] This resulted in youth having a sense of pride in their institution and their principals and teachers. Walter Dykes, another alum of Industrial and Wilson, remembered Principal Bynes: "Mr. Bynes was highly respected. He would get as much as [he could] for black folks, and my grandmother always told me, Professor Bynes is for us."[27] His recollection of how his respect for Principal Bynes was based on the fact that Bynes did not accept that black schools should have less than white schools provides insight into how some black Tiftonians fought against white hegemony before black youth adopted direct action in the early 1960s. Although Dykes remembered how several black Tiftonians accepted "whatever white folks gave us," observing his principal and some of the teachers inspired and provided a roadmap for his activism. Realizing what Frederick Douglass theorized nearly a century earlier, that "power concedes nothing without a demand," Dykes decided to focus on those who were directly challenging white opposition.[28]

The educational experiences of students at Industrial and Wilson went beyond a schoolhouse being able to create an environment that validated their personhood and intellect. Albeit supportive, the climate at Industrial and Wilson did not shield black youth from the constant reminders that local officials and their constituents saw them as less than. Black schools were created out of a necessity caused by policies, actions, and silence over Jim Crow, and their ungirding ideologies were persistent. Regardless of how many times Pertilla, Dykes, and their classmates were told by their principals and teachers that they deserved a first-class education, the gulf in resources between white and black schools was stark and evident. Even when this was not obvious, receiving their white counterparts' secondhand materials or being told that public spaces were for whites only served as a hostile reminder of how society viewed them. Just as much as they remember loving principals and teachers, when asked about their educational experiences they recalled how those experiences simultaneously included inherent inequalities.

White Comfort and Secondhand Education after *Brown*

Tifton had in common with other places in southwest Georgia and throughout the South a public school system that was segregated and inherently unequal. Black youth noticed these inequities, and several felt obligated to demand a change. It did not take long for young black Tiftonians to learn that the friendliness of their locale was largely based on white comfort. White Tiftonians had no problem with the conditions at Industrial and Wilson. Neither were they invested in making sure black Tiftonians were registered to vote nor concerned about county amenities being accessible to all citizens of Tift County. Local white officials and their white constituents were more than apathetic regarding how local customs negatively affected their nonwhite neighbors. Many of them found comfort in the way things operated. Recent studies by social scientists and cultural theorists such as Joe Feagin, Michelle Fine, Robin DiAngelo, and others, describe this rationale of thinking in various terms, including white racial frame, white guilt, and white fragility.[29] DiAngelo suggests whites' response can be attributed to "a state in which even a minimum amount of racial stress becomes intolerable, triggering a range of defensive moves."[30] These contemporary theories have historical applicability because they provide insight as to why white opposition was the default in Tifton when black youth sought to address the educational norms that existed. Challenging those norms directly questioned what had been in place for decades and, regardless of the legitimacy of black youth complaints, whites internalized that as a threat. The illegality of white opposition went beyond refusing to accept desegregation.[31] The ongoing ethos of segregation negatively influenced the educational experiences of black youth who were not trying to enroll in white schools.

The city's decision to choose white comfort over black equality continued to influence black education during the mid-twentieth century.[32] *Brown* had little immediate impact on the educational experiences of black youth in Tifton. Dykes, Pertilla, Terrell, and Kitchen were natives of Tifton and attended segregated schools after the passage of *Brown*. Most of the students who became activists do not remember *Brown* being discussed. Dykes said, "I don't remember anything about [Brown]. All I remember, we saw it on the news, we saw the demonstration[s], they had sit-ins, they were saying separate but equal, but me personally, I don't remember that much about it."[33] Pertilla, who is a little older than Dykes, remembered his family talking about the landmark case because they discussed national events. In addition to *Brown*, his family had conversations about the Little Rock Nine and the Montgomery Bus Boycott. Pertilla does note, however, that "it may not have been, let's sit down and talk about Brown versus the Board of Ed, but I was aware of the struggle for integration."[34] Terrell and Kitchen did not remember the case being "discussed."[35] The various memories by black Tiftonians on the limited influence of *Brown* provide further evidence to support why whites accepted comfort as a valid reason to continue what was no longer constitutional. There were no ongoing talks about ending segregation or any plan in place to desegregate during the 1950s, so it is not surprising that most of these individuals do not remember the case being discussed.[36]

School board minutes confirm the limited discussion that existed about the landmark case. In fact, *Brown* was not mentioned in the minutes for nearly a decade. This silence could be attributed to indifference. Local officials were able to ignore *Brown* because their white constituents placed no pressure on them to address any aspect of the educational injustices that existed. For different reasons, black and white Tiftonians were not pushing for desegregation, so May 17, 1954, and May 31, 1955, held no relevance. It is important to note that just because black Tiftonians were not pushing for the implementation of *Brown*, this does not mean they were not demanding educational equality. Another factor regarding the stagnation of discussion of *Brown* was the black community's prioritization of other issues. Unlike Little Rock, Arkansas, or Prince Edward County, Virginia, there is little evidence of black Tiftonians demanding desegregation or having a willingness to ask black youth to endure white hostility to ensure desegregation. The desegregation history of Tifton public schools occurred after the struggle to improve segregated black schools. Although one could argue that blacks were fearful of white backlash, it is just as plausible that segregation was not their primary concern. They had two academic institutions in Tifton that they were pleased with. Therefore, their primary complaint was not that schools were separate but that black schools always had to go without. Even though blacks had their own institutions in Tifton, they had little to no say as to how resources were allocated. The lack of input created several problems, because white Tiftonians evidently assumed that if blacks had a building, that was sufficient. Amenities and upkeep were afterthoughts.

While the federal decision attempted to solve the problem of resource disparities rampant in schools by putting everyone together in one space, several blacks in Tifton, particularly the youth, believed the town could solve the issue by equally funding black and white schools. Terrell recalled that "black Tiftonians accepted the so-called segregation . . . but wanted equality." From his recollection, the attitude about the educational struggle in Tifton could be summarized as "equal was okay. You've got your schools, we've got our schools." Too often, integration became synonymous with equality after 1954, but for places like Tifton where integration was not the main thing, educational equality took on more of a practical meaning. Terrell elevated this point, saying, "We want the same thing you've got. We pay taxes and we want the same things. We didn't talk about integration. We were okay; we should've had the same size equipment you've got and in all the schools we wanted the equipment like you've got."[37] Things like not having a gymnasium, consistently making do with their white counterparts' used materials, and the inability to access shared spaces funded by tax dollars were the points of contestation. Black Tiftonians who protested as youth constantly reiterated in interviews that it was the disparities that existed between black and white schools that caused them to organize.[38]

Even though black youth's educational experiences in Tifton were in direct contrast with the focus of *Brown*, they did not attribute the contrast to the fact that integration did not occur. They attributed these issues to the fact that black schools remained the depository of white students' hand-me-down materials and whites were determined to hoard city resources for themselves. Black schools in Tifton either needed structural work done, or when black students did get a new building, like they did with Wilson, vital resources were missing. They were constantly aware and reminded that what they had was secondhand and that materials were received from white schools because they were no longer good enough for their white counterparts. This practice, Dykes remembered, occurred even though Wilson was a new school. Pertilla's recollection of the period reveals how awareness of their second-class citizenship was forced upon black youth: "I resented the fact that during my entire public school career, I probably could only remember getting four or five brand new books, because what happened [was] that the white people would give us the books the white students had last year, and we only got new books in those cases where they didn't have enough of the old ones to go around."[39] The custom of blacks being the recipient of whites' outdated materials is often glossed over as a byproduct of Jim Crow. However, these practices had a profound impact on how black youth conceptualized equality, and it influenced them to become active participants in challenging a practice that designated the best resources for whites and the hand-me-downs for blacks.

Reminiscing on his educational experiences, Pertilla said he does not recall being bothered by segregation but fervidly remembered the frustration that accompanied seeing the previous owners' names—Sarah and James—in one of his schoolbooks. While those names were constant reminders of the racial ideologies that justified this practice, he also believes that such experiences "intensified the awareness of my generation of what our struggle had to be about, more so than a set of specific kind of things that happen[ed]."[40] Terrell, a couple of grades behind Pertilla, recalled being bothered not only by the hand-me-down books but by the fact that the used materials were outdated. According to Terrell, black youth became aware that their books were previously owned by whites as early as elementary school, but the discovery of the materials being outdated did not come until he was in high school. He stated, "I had a book in the eighth grade, a science book that was published in 1953, and my mom worked for a doctor and she found [a new edition of the same book] and realized it was published more recently."[41] Once his mother informed him of her discovery, he realized what Pertilla had comprehended a couple of years earlier. For equality to exist, the custom of white students receiving what was new and updated while black students received what was old and outdated had to be eliminated. The legal arena outlawed this custom through litigation but was not as bold in implementation, which allowed Tifton officials to successfully maintain Jim Crow traditions that were noticeable in the educational experiences of black Tiftonians.

Students were also concerned with a lack of resources at Industrial and Wilson. Dykes, for example, vividly remembered how Wilson did not have a football field or a gymnasium, which meant that they had to use the facilities at the white school.

> We didn't have a gym. We didn't have a football team, we didn't have nothing. So, when we had to practice football, we had to practice on the rocks. . . . I told the principal, I said we're practicing on these rocks and they are practicing on the field. They had the stadium. Okay, now when we played our Friday games, our schedule had to center around whatever their schedule was, we had to do our schedule. Because out of their so-called good heart, they let us use the stadium, so when we played at the stadium, at Tift County Stadium, now our grandma's taxes help pay for this stuff. We put our schedule out so we can play at their park if they were not playing. We went to the white people to make the schedule and when they weren't using the stadium, that's when we got to use the stadium.[42]

Nearly fifty years later, Dykes remains frustrated by these experiences. Time has not healed those wounds. In fact, time only reminds him and his peers of what they had to endure to keep his counterparts comfortable. Reflecting on his lived experiences reveals a concept of "equality" that permeated southwest Georgia. Racialized customs assisted in teaching this life lesson. Even though the stadium was owned by the county, whites had priority. Black youth knew this custom, along with so many others, was unjust.[43] Black students in Tifton understood that having to schedule events around their white counterparts was more than a custom of segregation. It was an explicit denial of equality. Having pride in their school, teachers, and principals could not camouflage the ingrained inequalities of being given secondhand materials and not being able to use public facilities in Tifton.[44] These grievances crystallized into an overarching primary grievance, which was the lack of fairness that permeated their town. Determined to leave their own legacy, they sought to change the customs that they felt prevented blacks from enjoying full citizenship. Led by Dykes and Major Wright, they devised a plan that challenged the core of Tifton's genteel image of racial harmony.

Frustrated and Fearless

Unfortunately, the national media did not give a lot of attention to Tifton because it did not have a local politician using armed guards to prevent black citizens from entering public facilities. Nor did Tifton witness any form of terrorism such as the bombing that took place in 1963 at the 16th Street Baptist Church in Birmingham, resulting in the murder of four young black girls—Addie Mae Collins, Cynthia Wesley, Carole Robertson, and Carol Denise McNair.[45] These forms of sanctioned terrorism brought local, national, and international attention. The daily opposition that accompanied segregation was rarely questioned. This presented a problem for places like Tifton, because the incidents occurring there did not go beyond the pale for most ardent supporters of Jim Crow. Even those who merely accepted the practice of segregation as a default could not anticipate how their way of life would fuel the frustration of black youth who sought to directly attack the lifestyle of white Tiftonians.

According to southern historian Hasan Jeffries, by the 1960s, "black political chatter had increased significantly. . . . Conversations about civil rights activities occurred everywhere."[46] The escalation of political chatter was not absent in Tifton, particularly among youth. Black youth in Tifton had grown frustrated with the status quo and they did not believe their parents could solve the issue. Writings by Principal R. L. Mack and a student, Major Wright, illustrate the friction that existed between young and old black Tiftonians. Principal Mack wrote for Wilson's 1962 yearbook that "our boys and girls are acting like a different generation, speaking their own language, and creating their own world. . . . They yearn to be free individuals."[47] In a 1973 article for the *New York Times* published under the name he had since taken, Wright wrote that Mack "was for us, I suppose, something like the proverbial lighthouse, . . . always offering guidance and direction. . . . But the lighthouse of the old guard stood on a lonely island of fear, humility and submission. Its beacon burned atop the rotting carcasses of Booker T. Washington and the pioneers of his Era of Acquiescence."[48] In both texts there is admiration for the other, but tension also existed due to very different philosophies. The fear that consumed adults that Mack spoke about was not warrantless. The students' parents and grandparents lived through and heard stories of the violence that occurred when breaking the customs of Jim Crow. This violence was not just physical but economic and political as well. Their forebears often worked in sectors in which their livelihood was inextricably linked to a cultural ethos that supported segregation. This created unique challenges that are missing in Wright's critique. Likewise, Principal Mack's condescending approach diminished the taxing reality of living in constant frustration. Both camps understood that Jim Crow was unjust, but they had very different ways of going about challenging the system. These intragenerational differences in the approach to securing equality took place in Americus and Moultrie as well. In fact, civil rights organizations like the Southern Christian Leadership Conference (SCLC) and Student Nonviolent Coordinating Committee (SNCC) experienced similar friction when trying to decide the best ways to attack white opposition. Increased participation brought more bodies to the fight for freedom, but that also intensified differing ideas on achieving that goal.[49]

Black youth in Tifton, like several of their peers in the 1960s, felt adults were too comfortable with gradualism and too fearful of whites. Equipped with a newfound frustration and fearlessness, guidance from a civil rights organization, and inspiration from other nearby movements, they sought to blaze a new path forward. For various reasons, several adults shied away from direct-action protest, yet the youth movement was not without allies. They were able to garner public support from a few adults, like Solomon Nixon, who sided with their cause and their tactics. Nixon and his family were known as pillars of the black community in Tifton because they were one of the few self-sustaining black families. Unlike so many black adults in Tifton, Nixon, who was also known as "Pops," did not depend on whites for his livelihood, so he did not have to worry about white backlash.[50] According to Dykes, the aid provided by Nixon was pivotal to the movement. Because of the financial support Dykes, Wright, and Terrell received from Nixon, they were able to attend events that inspired them to act. He helped students from Wilson, including Dykes, attend an SCLC event in Macon,

Georgia, that led them to organize in Tifton. Dykes also recalled how Nixon sponsored their trip to hear Dr. King speak, paying for his and a number of other students' transportation, lodging, and food. He believed this trip was very important because, after hearing Dr. King's speech, they returned to Tifton and initiated the Tifton Youth Chapter of the Southern Christian Leadership Conference (TYCSCLC).[51] Nixon also sponsored another trip for a number of youth to attend an SCLC event in Savannah, Georgia. One of the students who attended the event was Major Wright, who Dykes promoted as the leader of the student movement when he graduated. Terrell said Nixon even let them drive his car on the trip to Savannah.[52] In a place where adult support was limited, black youth found in Nixon a pivotal ally who greatly contributed to the struggle for equality in Tifton.

Besides receiving internal local support from Nixon, black youth received external adult support from known figures of the movement, like Dr. King and his national organization. Although Dr. King never made it to Tifton and the SCLC did not have a substantial presence there until 1963, their support for youth activism was evident in the SCLC's grant of the youth group's charter. In addition to receiving support, the type of activism promoted by Dr. King and the SCLC encouraged the youth of Tifton, which could not be said of the adults in their hometown. For example, Wright felt his principal's approach to dealing with second-class citizenship was antiquated in large part because it lacked the element of confrontation, but King and his organization faced confrontation directly. According to Wright, "Birmingham, Martin Luther King, the Freedom Riders, Autherine Lucy. . . . These were the names and places that had been echoing against the walls of every juke joint, church and bootleg house in Tifton. . . . And these were the names and places that buzzed across the tables of the cafeteria at Wilson—and that led me out of the internal prison of docility."[53] The admiration that Wright and his contemporaries had for Dr. King and certain organizations illuminates that they were influenced by adults who did not allow their fear to prevent them from challenging the status quo. The external support they received increased their resolve, and upon their return from Macon and Savannah, they were more determined than ever to start a movement in Tifton utilizing direct action.[54]

Plotting a Way Forward

In the spring of 1962, the youth movement in Tifton began when Dykes and other members from the TYCSCLC called a meeting at Beulah Hill Baptist Church. The first meeting, according to Dykes, had a low turnout but those in attendance chose a president for the organization and identified the issues they would use to galvanize the youth. Dykes was named the president and voter registration was the first issue they chose to address. After the weak response to the first call for a meeting, Dykes adjusted his strategy. He was not naive. He recognized that everyone did not join social movements because of societal ills. But many wanted to socialize, and Dykes used that component to draw people to the movement. He recalled, "I knew that when the females got into it the brothers were going to follow. . . . The girls controlled everything, so I said I am going to get the girls, so I went back to my class and got with [the] girls." The change in strategy appeared to work because, unlike the first meeting, the second meeting, which took place at Allen Temple A.M.E. Church, did have more attendees.[55] Dykes said the change in strategy was not just about getting people to attend the meeting: he also believed that his female classmates were better organizers, which he knew was a vital component to a successful social movement.[56] Apart from just getting students to attend the meetings, youth leaders—Dykes, Wright, Charlotte D., and others—knew that convincing their classmates to act would be a process.

Black youth from Tifton learned from seasoned activists that the survival of social movements depended on buy-in from the collective. Leaders needed participants to serve as the oxygen of the movement; therefore, a transition from socializing to social activism was necessary. Voter registration began this transition because political disenfranchisement was widespread in Tifton. It was not difficult for black youth to grasp how their mothers, fathers, aunts, uncles, grandparents, and teachers were barred from the day-to-day decision-making process that affected their lives. A voter registration drive resulted in more young people being involved in local issues. Raising the political consciousness of young black Tiftonians was the first feat accomplished by the TYCSCLC. Momentum around disenfranchisement raised awareness, but leaders knew that for a movement to occur on a large scale, they needed a more robust agenda.

The galvanization of the Tifton youth movement occurred when youth leaders were able to illustrate the interconnection of the sociopolitical and educational issues they faced. Leaders of the youth movement associated their guardians' political disenfranchisement and economic restrictions with the educational disparities they faced as teenagers. This interconnection was revealed through posing very simple questions, and all their questions directly related to how the various communities conceptualized equality. Dykes hearkened back to his teenage years to recall, "My whole thing was, [my grandma was] paying taxes, why can't I go to the library? It said county library. It didn't [say] black folk library, it didn't say white county library, it said library, and we pay taxes just like [white folks in Tifton, so] why can't we go?"[57] He and others also began to question why blacks were not allowed to go to the county pool or the county library when black tax dollars were being used to fund these facilities. Asking fundamental questions attacking the logic of segregation often made whites uneasy. Sharing spaces was forbidden under the customs of Jim Crow because if those spaces were desegregated, as proponents of segregation often argued, race mixing would occur, which would contaminate the white race.[58] Consciously or subconsciously, the leaders of the Tifton student movement were attacking the very justification that was successful in passing the Glenn Bill. For black youth, it was much more pragmatic than that. The thought of being around white people was not a priority. Wright and Dykes note that the push to have access to county amenities was about basic rights. Their parents were taxpaying residents of Tift County, which meant they were co-owners of the pool, park, and library. These kinds of amenities did not even exist on their side of town.[59] Posing these simple questions to their peers raised their consciousness and simultaneously brought angst to white Tiftonians. Questioning the status quo was unsettling enough, but the utilization of direct action meshed contextual opposition with physical opposition, which increased the danger level. The escalation of violence did not deter black youth, who had grown frustrated with whites either following 50 percent of the law they liked or refusing to accept 100 percent of law they disagreed with. Despite the fear, whites' comfort level being the essential factor when determining the standard for educational equality had run its course in Tifton.

Oral interviews and archival records show there was a consensus within the leadership on how to go about addressing the educational issues black Tiftonians faced. By the time education became the focus, Dykes had graduated from Wilson and enrolled at Payne College, but prior to leaving, he chose Major Wright as his successor. This unilateral approach did not replicate the bylaws of other civil rights organizations that the Tifton group mirrored, but it was effective in the sense that there was no disruption in philosophy.[60] According to Dykes, Wright was there from the beginning and had demonstrated a commitment to consistently challenging the ethos of Tifton. Furthermore, Wright was one of the few people who did not have to make the transition from socializing to social activism. From the first meeting to the time he became president of the youth movement in Tifton, his commitment was not questioned. Dykes recalled that "Major Wright lived in Brookfield [but] the brother would come to meetings on time. He came [from] ten miles away. So, I [liked the fact that he worked] and was enthusiastic about stuff." In addition to being impressed by Wright's commitment and enthusiasm, he also believed that the "other dudes were clowns" in comparison. Even though Dykes did not elaborate on why he thought the others were not qualified to lead, based on the events that transpired after he left, his decision proved to be an effective choice.[61]

The tactics under Wright's leadership did shift, but the philosophy of the movement was very similar. The youth movement under Dykes ran by a simple yet profound philosophy: if black tax dollars were being used to fund projects in the county, black people should have access to those amenities. During our interview, he reiterated this belief several times, stating, "My thing was this: To be honest, I didn't care about the integration stuff. . . . Wherever my grandmother's taxes are being spent, I should be able to go . . . pure and simple."[62] Wright's vision aligned with the former president's in that both agreed that the movement had to be about equality. The fact that the leaders of the youth movement shared similar philosophies should not be a surprise, because their involvement in the movement was comparable as well. Dykes, Wright, and the others who made up the youth movement in Tifton remembered exactly where they were and who they were with when they decided to become a part of the civil rights movement. While their decisions to become involved in the movement took place at very different locations—Dykes in Macon, Georgia, and Wright in Savannah, Georgia—the person who inspired them was the same. Above all, they remembered who inspired them to believe they could make fundamental changes in their community. That inspirational leader was Dr. King.

Dr. King never made it to Tifton, but the paramount question he posed—"What is the citizen's right of participation in the decisions which so directly affect his community?"—engendered their local movement.[63] Young black Tiftonians went about answering this question from the time they heard King in Macon or in Savannah. King's ideas of agency were echoed in both speeches and, according to Terrell, "When we come back . . . we had gotten our own ideas of what we really wanted to do."[64] Most scholars who examine Dr. King's influence in southwest Georgia tend to focus primarily on Albany and to some extent on Americus, but this limits King's guidance to places he visited. This is problematic not because it devalues King's influence on the area but because it minimizes the importance of rhetoric in creating a cohesive message of a movement. Points raised in Dr. King's speech influenced young black Tiftonians' decision to fight for equality in their community. In addition, rhetoric was also adopted by Dykes and Wright to allow for cohesion and persuade their classmates to become more involved. Dr. King believed, in the words of Stewart Burns, "that his movement, and any that he associated with, should set an example and refuse to be complicit in society's depersonalizing of citizens. Progressive movements had a moral responsibility, he felt, to offer an alternative stance that affirmed people's humanness while standing up to behavior that depersonalized others."[65] These, too, were the beliefs of the leaders of the Tifton youth movement. As the movement in Tifton switched leaders, the philosophy remained intact because the inspirational source behind the movement was the same.

The reason for the sudden shift in strategies, though, is unclear. Dykes suggested that the change was because Wright was much more militant than he had been, but neither archival data nor other participants confirmed the difference in the leaders' intellectual abilities. The data do, however, indicate that Wright believed that the movement in Tifton had to be more confrontational, so direct action was employed under his leadership.[66] Nowhere was direct action more needed than at Wilson and Industrial because the inequalities were so pervasive. Furthermore, the data suggest that Wright appeared to be more of a cerebral leader than his predecessor. He knew the social customs of Tifton as well as their laws. He informed his classmates of city ordinances that were very important to their cause. For example, Tifton had an ordinance, according to Terrell, that no one could protest inside the city limits. He described how they organized the marches: "We couldn't march in the city. The city had orders against marches and parades . . . so we always had to stay outside the city limits. We always had to stay south of 17th Street and we had to walk across the street."[67] Terrell did not recall why this ordinance existed in Tifton or when the ordinance was passed. He did note, however, that white Tiftonians did not cross their picketed area on 17th Street. Regardless of whether the decree was passed to prevent black Tiftonians from publicly voicing their grievances or for economic reasons, the ordinance added another barrier.

Tifton's ordinance created a major issue for citizens determined to bring awareness of social injustices that plagued the area. Due to this systemic obstacle, along with low participation, Wright chose not to begin the movement by pushing for resource equity between black and white schools. He decided to continue to employ tactics similar to those used by his predecessor, which was sporadic protest. Instead of hosting meetings and coming up with a plan, Wright instructed students to meet at the library, the swimming pool, bus station, or any other place that black taxes help fund but black citizens were not able to use. Terrell remembered participating in a number of these protests and how effective they were. "The library was down under the health department downtown, so we went to the library before they could announce we were going to the library. Then [we were supposed] to go to the swimming pool, but we didn't go to the swimming pool. But we did end up at the library and when the lady at the library saw us coming in the door, the director [said] loudly, 'The niggas are here!' That was then and the next time we went to the Greyhound bus station."[68] The response by the director provided insight to the activists on how local whites perceived them as invaders. Like their peers who sat at the Woolworth's lunch counter in Greensboro, North Carolina, or the nine black students who were the first to attend Central High in Little Rock, Arkansas, they were unwelcome. Being uninvited in facilities that you have every legal right to enter displayed the unconstitutional debate that took place after *Brown*, which manifested the farrago that existed in Tifton and throughout the county.

After several sporadic protests, local officials realized that a movement was brewing. Along with being concerned about the small yet frequent youth protests that were occurring in Tifton, they worried about nearby social movements taking place throughout southwest Georgia, especially Albany. Unwilling to sacrifice its reputation as a "Friendly City," Tifton wanted to quell youth activism and avoid the chances of white violence escalating. Political officials attempted to keep both sides happy by making enough small concessions to satisfy black Tiftonians without addressing their core concerns, which would have made white Tiftonians restless. For example, they built Mott-Litman, but the gym was not on school grounds nor was it on a par with what whites had across town. This initial concession still left the black Tiftonians without a swimming pool. The contemporary significance of this gymnasium as a community mainstay does not negate the historical fact that the building was built not as a down payment to addressing future grievances but as the totality of the response to grievances. Local white officials thought that the hastily built Mott-Litman gymnasium for black students would suffice. They could not have been more wrong. Terrell and his peers proved they were willing to defy Jim Crow by entering white spaces and they also knew that "whites didn't want [them] to come over to their white schools to play in the gym so they built one."[69] For this reason, the students did not conclude that obtaining the new gymnasium was a success, although the community welcomed the new amenity.

Tifton officials conceding on certain grievances articulated by black youth in order to avoid addressing their primary concern was not an abnormality. Pertilla and Dykes noted that these concessions were not out of the ordinary. In fact, local officials made similar concessions when Dykes was the leader of the student movement. They recalled, "White people tried to defuse [the movement]. Their tactic was more of concession rather than confrontation and they got rid of one of the so-called hard-core Ku Klux Klan [members in town] because they said we've got good neighbors and we've got good relationships [with the black community]. They didn't want us to come all the way."[70] Concessions that did not force whites to come to terms with their illegality did not impress young black Tiftonians.[71] After Mott-Litman was built, the youth movement gained momentum. The concessions designed to stop the movement emboldened more youth to participate because they saw that the sporadic protests by their peers resulted in a tangible, although problematic, change. They understood that a new gym and a new swimming pool did not end the struggle. As young black Tiftonians continued to enter Industrial and Wilson, they realized that sporadic protest would not change their educational experiences. Therefore, they devised a plan that would directly address the educational inequities they faced.

Attacking Injustice Head-On

Black schools after *Brown* continued to be one of the great paradoxes of segregation. On one hand, they were viable places for black students to learn and be treated with respect. On the other hand, they served as a constant reminder of what black students had to go without and why their schools did not have the resources that nearby white schools possessed. For example, the protest that occurred at Wilson was based primarily on what black youth perceived as unfair. According to Wright/Obatala's article published in the *New York Times Magazine*, "students . . . marched, held rallies, picketed and generally protested the fact that the money needed to build a gymnasium or to buy typewriters for Wilson had somehow ended up on the other side of town, where the whites had just built themselves an ultramodern high school with a warm, spacious gym."[72] Terrell noted that the protesters were concerned about the lack of resources at Wilson but they were just as concerned about the deplorable conditions at Industrial: "The protest included conditions at Wilson and at Industrial."[73] Centralizing the lack of resources illuminates how what continued to take place in the 1960s was not simply a byproduct of Jim Crow. Black youth in Tifton concluded by the early 1960s that their educational conditions served to feed white Tiftonians' insatiable appetite for segregation. The direct message embedded within the confrontational attack on Jim Crow by black youth was that their education along with their guardians' political disenfranchisement and economic limitations would no longer serve as fuel for Tifton's cultural ethos to be maintained.

Black youth in Tifton were angry about having to go without while their white counterparts had an abundance of resources. Besides not having "sewing machines in the homemaking department" and only six typewriters for five hundred students to share, the conditions at Industrial were deteriorating. The conditions were so bad at Industrial, according to an investigation by the NAACP, "the school structure itself was condemned and labeled unsafe" in 1958.[74] Frustrated by decades of inequality and inspired by the events taking place in Albany, Georgia, the youth movement evolved from registering people to vote to walking out of school and demanding full citizenship by means of equal resources. Young black Tiftonians adopted the "three simple words" advocated by Dr. King, "all, now, and here": "We want all of our rights, we want them here, and we want them now."[75] King's words resonated because there was no anecdotal or empirical evidence that suggested black education would improve through gradualism. Young black Tiftonians had spent years in public schools with very little changing. Therefore, those involved adopted an immediacy approach to end all forms of educational inequality. Six months had not passed before the youth movement went from sporadic protest to students filling the streets of Tifton. The urgency of the moment made it clear that black youth had to defy the city's ordinances that forbade protest. A social movement using a direct-action strategy meant they had to directly confront the issue. Black youth sporadically entering public facilities was important because it moved the movement from an embryonic stage. The fight, however, had to include what was going on at Industrial and Wilson because these issues were connected, and that meant they had to fight precisely where the city ordinance prohibited protest from taking place.

As school began in the fall of 1962, the message was clear and concise. Black youth wanted the same types of resources found at nearby white schools. Once they realized that the school board had no intention of allocating tax dollars evenly, the protest was inevitable. Led by Wright, three hundred black students walked out of Wilson High on "a Friday morning in October." Knowing that there was no way to prevent that many students from leaving, Principal Mack "stood in his doorway, arms folded against his chest, eyes focusing on one after another us . . . as nearly half of the students at Wilson thundered out of the front door and into the street."[76] They walked out of school with hopes of bringing attention to the conditions under which they were forced to learn. According to the *Daily Defender*, the youth wanted more resources for their overcrowded school because "their school building houses approximately 1,200."[77] In addition to the school lacking specific resources and being overcrowded, the *Atlanta Daily World* reported that "there [was] no playground equipment for the elementary school children" at Industrial and the students at Wilson remained without a gymnasium. While the NAACP investigated the youth complaints, Mercedes Wright, youth advisor for the NAACP in Georgia, noted that "mass picketing and other demonstrations are being carried out."[78] The methods adopted by young black Tiftonians were similar to other youth protests occurring during this period.[79] Black students at Wilson and Industrial marched and picketed with the intention of bringing attention to the inequities they faced. They stood in front of county buildings and in areas white Tiftonians frequently visited with various symbols to declare the educational cost of white comfort.

Officials from the Tift County School Board faced a dilemma. If they refused to address black youth grievances, the protest would continue. If they addressed the concerns raised by black youth, it would disrupt the racially harmonious narrative that Tifton attempted to project. Black youth learned from surrounding movements that school board members would have to explain why three hundred students were marching in the streets.

In addition to explaining why students were out, they would have to explain why the students did not plan on going back to school. When the protest began, the superintendent of Tift County said it was "a disciplinary matter and should be dealt with by the principal of the school."[80] However, the superintendent could not suppress the fact that this was a protest about resources and he, along with the other white citizens of Tifton, had to come to terms with the fact that the youth in Tifton were not just going to go away.

The school board's initial response was to palliate the issues raised by black youth. Shortly after the students walked out of Wilson High, Tifton's superintendent was quoted as saying that the issue at Wilson should be addressed by Principal Mack, who in turn tried to defuse the situation by asking, "Is there ever any school that could not use more than it has?"[81] The superintendent shifting the onus to Principal Mack placed him in a predicament. Should he side with the valid concerns articulated by his students or with the superintendent who controlled the budget? The maneuvering by the superintendent worked at first, although it was disingenuous for several reasons. He knew that Principal Mack had nothing to do with the lack of resources at Wilson or Industrial. The superintendent's response was also predicated on a belief that the protest would not last long and would not garner much attention, so he initially dismissed the protest. As was the case in the 1950s, white politicians and school officials downplayed the educational realities of black students to portray the actions of black youth as an overreaction. But the superintendent and the white citizens of Tifton quickly realized that dismissing the concerns being raised by their black constituents was not going to work: they were not going away without being addressed.

Black youth did not spend a lot of time trying to decode divergent messages because they knew the reality of the situation. Nor did they spend a great deal of time trying to convince school officials that a boycott was warranted and needed. When Wright reflected on the boycott, he stated, "individual people were never really the issue or the targets of the movement. It was the system, the ante-bellum system of the South, that we were at odds with."[82] In other words, those who attended Wilson and Industrial knew that the superintendent's failure to address their concerns was part of the problem, but it was not the origin of the disparities. The reason black schools were "without a lunchroom and didn't have a proper place to fix the lunch for the children and had to transfer [students] from Industrial to Wilson just to eat" had little to do with the superintendent.[83] Focusing on systemic injustices does not negate the superintendent's role in perpetuating an unjust system, but it illuminates how the walkout moved beyond the realm of attacking individuals who perpetuated the status quo to directly attacking a system that demeaned black students as citizens. Systems are organized and maintained by people, so Wright's comments should not be misconstrued as indicating that students saw their opponent as some abstract matrix. Their daily contact with these customs illustrated the actualization of white opposition, and these constant reminders provided enough evidence that the superintendent's actions were among many factors that contributed to educational inequities.

There is no evidence suggesting that the Tift County School Board had plans to improve the structural conditions at Industrial or provide newer books at Wilson until black youth walked out and the media began covering the event. Terrell remembered being convinced that the walkout was the only way to get white school officials to acknowledge the conditions at black schools. Even though they were not able to get all the students out, enough students walked out to gain coverage by well-circulated black newspapers such as the *Atlanta Daily World* and the *Chicago Daily Defender*, as well as the *New York Times*. The events taking place in Tifton were covered by these media outlets for months. The media coverage, along with the NAACP's investigation, meant that school officials had a very difficult time dismissing the protest as driven by outside agitators. Civil rights organizations could not be faulted for the broken doors and broken windowpanes at Industrial, nor could they be blamed for the lack of new books at Wilson and the fact the students did not have a playing field. The issues articulated by black students stemmed from neglect. The walkout, in combination with the media coverage, forced school officials to switch their strategy from palliating to reluctantly compromising.

The tactics employed by black youth in Tifton succeeded: they were able to improve the conditions at Industrial and Wilson. Terrell remembered that "they started to give us [new] books. They started to put in the panes in the windows. They started fixing the doors, where you could lock them. [They] went back and redid the lunchroom." He also stated that "new pavement was put down."[84] Although black youth did not get all the resources they demanded until years later, the improvements they received were directly linked to the walkout. To a degree, Terrell was correct about the walkout being the only way to get the attention of the school board. Initially, the switch to direct action seemed beneficial to the movement, but participants soon realized there was a price to pay for demanding equality.

Penalizing Activists for Being
Participatory Citizens

The bold vision among young black Tiftonians of what public schools could be was never fully embraced by the larger Tifton community. Black youth envisioned schools as democratic enterprises to hone one's intellectual, emotional, social, and physical skills. Using schools as testing grounds for democratic development had grave consequences that extended beyond the schoolhouse. White Tiftonians' insatiable desire to maintain their way of life served as formidable opposition that prevented schools from becoming what young black activists envisioned. Although the protest proved that local officials could not control a significant segment of the young black community, the opposition was successful enough to prevent a coalition movement. During a time when the movement needed more support, the authorities stifled the movement by penalizing the participants' parents.

The fight for a more just educational experience never extended beyond youth participation because the employment status of the older black community was often threatened. The veiled threat of suppressing participation in a social movement by putting one's livelihood in jeopardy was an oppositional strategy employed by whites throughout the South.[85] Black guardians had to confront an economic reality that black youth did not have to encounter. Threats for supporting the youth movement began shortly after the walkout and parents who allowed their children to participate were subjected to termination from their jobs. A movement that already had little adult support began to see even less support. Terrell noted that at the height of the walkout, only Reverend Rockwell, Deacon Horne, Solomon Nixon, and a few others were willing to support their cause. He stated, "The adults started to move away from us [because we] were drawing too much attention."[86] Essentially, the threat by the opposition limited who chose to participate, then reduced that participation even more by extending threats to include parents whose children were participating. At the same time local officials were making concessions, they were extinguishing the movement by blocking the oxygen needed.

Genteel Tifton, like their neighbors in Albany, Americus, and Moultrie, had various ways of penalizing those who challenged the status quo. Threatening blacks' economic welfare was often accompanied by direct violence. Like those in Albany, black youth from Americus and Moultrie experienced this violence firsthand, which will be described in detail in the following chapters. Young black Tiftonians, on the other hand, were not subjected to the degree of terror experienced by their peers, but this does not mean violence was absent. Participants in the youth movement were correct in their assessment that public officials in Tifton would not stoop to certain hostile actions adopted in Arkansas, Alabama, and Virginia as a response to them demanding a better educational experience.[87] Their parents being threatened was an oppositional approach they did not foresee, but it was the old proven approach of running the people who whites perceived as troublemakers out of town, and it dealt a serious blow to the youth movement in Tifton.

The greatest strength of the movement in Tifton was also its greatest weakness. Wright had been given the reins of leadership because he was one of the few who was qualified to organize and lead an effective movement. Wright took his role seriously and was successful. Within two months, he had organized several spontaneous protests and a walkout that forced school officials to respond to some of the demands that were articulated by black students for over a year. Being the identified leader of a movement, however, also means the opposition knows who to attack when they want a movement suppressed. As the walkouts came to an end and improvements in the schools began to materialize, Wright was expelled from school for "leading a student delegation seeking better conditions."[88] An uproar ensued from the students at Wilson, so the protest that started off being about the conditions of their schools now incorporated the unfair treatment of their young leader. According to the *Atlanta Daily World*, once the students heard of Major Wright's expulsion, half of them walked out.[89] Unfortunately, they were not successful in reversing the expulsion. In fact, the expulsion was just the beginning of the backlash. Wright recalled how the momentum of the movement changed suddenly. "I was proud and happy. . . . The pride lasted, but not the happiness. The school walkout led to a confrontation with Mr. Mack and white school officials, and I was barred from finishing my senior year—barred from all the schools in the state of Georgia for a year, maybe longer." In addition to Wright being expelled from Wilson, white officials were willing to break the custom of gentility to see him forced out of Georgia. Wright stated, "Crosses were burned, there were threats. So one night that November fearing for their lives, I left my grandparents and my home in Brookfield . . . and fled to the safety of Tifton's black community. . . . And a few months later I fled Georgia altogether."[90] The exile of a young activist who led a successful movement illuminates the severe consequences when demands for law and justice collided with the desire to be comfortable and hold on to a way of life that was no longer constitutional.

SNCC activist Sam Mahone and SNCC chairman John Lewis speaking to protestors at a rally at the Sumter County Courthouse, summer of 1965. *All photos courtesy of the Americus-Sumter County Movement Remembered Committee, Inc. (ASCMRC).*

Protest march demanding the release of jailed activists. *Courtesy ASCMRC.*

Protest march from the Americus Movement "Freedom Center" to downtown Americus to initiate boycott of white-owned businesses who refused to hire blacks. *Courtesy ASCMRC.*

Protest at "Freedom Center" marchers assembling to prepare to march downtown. *Courtesy ASCMRC.*

Young student activists assembling at the Sumter County Courthouse, protesting against the arrest of four black women for attempting to vote in the "white women" line. *Courtesy ASCMRC.*

Protest march led by Willie Bolden (SCLC), comedian-activist Dick Gregory, Americus Movement president Rev. J. R. Campbell, and Ben Clark of SCLC. *Courtesy ASCMRC.*

Movement president Rev. J. R. Campbell addressing rally at the county courthouse. *Courtesy ASCMRC.*

Members of the Tifton Youth Chapter of the Southern Christian Leadership Conference (TYCSCLC) meeting at Allen Temple A.M.E. Church in 1962 to discuss the violation of civil rights occurring throughout the region. *Courtesy Walter Dykes's personal collection.*

Young people gathering outside of Allen Temple A.M.E. Church. Allen Temple was one of a few churches in the region that openly allowed its facility to be used as a training site for black youth to learn the philosophy of nonviolence and the tactics of direct-action protest. *Courtesy Walter Dykes's personal collection.*

CHAPTER 3

A HEAVY TAX LEVIED FOR
DEMANDING EQUALITY

Every great dream begins with a dreamer.
Always remember, you have within you the
strength, the patience, and the passion to
reach for the stars to change the world.
—**Harriet Tubman**

According to the *Tifton Gazette*, Americus and Sumter County led the way in refusing federal government mandates. "The Americus and Sumter school systems announced that they would refuse to comply with the new rules issued by the U.S. Office of Education. . . . [Both systems] will face a loss of federal funds unless they file compliance forms by the May 6th deadline." As an explanation to why school systems in Americus and Sumter County refused the federal mandate, Edward N. Bailey, the Sumter County superintendent, stated, "We feel the guidelines go further than the requirements of the law. We have done everything to fulfill the freedom of choice requirements for pupils."[1] Although the educational experiences of black youth reveal that school systems had not done all they could, Bailey's response was typical of a white southerner during the mid-1960s. The entrenchment of local southern officials made it difficult to hope for, let alone see, a changing Americus or public school system. However, by the early 1970s, those same places and institutions that were embodiments of Jim Crow were elevated as examples of true desegregation. When Chicago, New York, and Boston were still trying to figure out how to implement *Brown*, Americus had sorted that aspect out.[2]

On February 12, 1971, *Life* magazine published an article, "Discovering One Another in a Georgia Town," depicting the improvement of race relations in Americus, Georgia, since the upheaval of the 1960s. Centering on desegregation, author Marshall Frady argued that, "for all the continuing scattered incidents of rear-guard viciousness, what is under way in communities like Americus . . . [is] resolution."[3] While major cities like Chicago, New York, and Boston were still trying to find their way through the malaise of desegregation during the early and mid-1970s, Frady suggested that Americus accomplished this feat seamlessly by 1971.[4] As evidence, he noted that blacks and whites now attended football games together, played on the same field, and occupied the same classrooms. Citizens of Americus accepted desegregation and tried to make black youth feel welcome at Americus High by incorporating culturally relevant materials. Frady observed, "In the Americus school system's administrative offices . . . there are displays of black studies programs, including pamphlets of Martin Luther King and Dred Scott and Frederick Douglass, as well as brochures entitled *Racism in America*. . . . In one English classroom . . . there is a poster of James Baldwin, with a quote from his work: 'It is a terrible and inexorable law that one cannot deny the humanity of another without diminishing one's own.'"[5] The inclusion of these cultural artifacts did not mean the absence of racist ideas and practices. In fact, Frady declared that several racial ideologies and practices continued at Americus High. Situating Frady's congratulatory narrative of Americus alongside an acknowledgment of continued racial actions by school officials highlights the unequal distribution that is inherent within the educational farrago. For example, it did not cost Americus or the Sumter County School Board to adopt a more inclusive curriculum. The racialized pedagogy black youth endured at Americus High, on the other hand, had various regressive social and educational consequences.

The persistent belief that black students diminished the academic integrity of the school and were prone to commit behavioral violations did not dissipate with more white educators being in closer proximity to black students. The deficit lens used to assess the academic ability of black students was created in part to justify segregation and disparate treatment. Consequently, black students at Americus High were constantly tracked into lower- and occupational-level classes. Based on Frady's report, "a program of instructional levels . . . tended to pitch more blacks than whites into the slower classes."[6] Another remnant that remained was fear from white adults who believed black males had an uncontrollable desire for white females. As a result, white teachers and parents acted as social and academic buffers. While at school, teachers tried to limit social interactions by hastening students to class when they witnessed black and white students socializing. Outside of school, white parents tried to make sure that social gatherings remained "private," which meant little socialization took place off school grounds. Some white parents removed their children altogether by enrolling them in private schools.[7]

Although Frady noted that Americus still had to deal with racial issues that had plagued the town for decades, his article concluded by quoting the mayor of Americus, Frank Myers: "it's gonna be our children finally who're going to deliver us out of this thing that's been going on down here ever since slavery. They are the ones who'll do it."[8] Mayor Myers may have been unaware that Dr. King and others made a similar declaration at the Youth March for Integrated Schools event a decade earlier. Between the declarations of these individuals lay nearly fifteen years of activism and opposition that illustrate why it was doubtful that the hope of young people who were coming of age after *Brown* would serve as the unicorn to America's race problem. Myers's conclusion about youth delivering Americus from a racist past was disingenuous because, as a mayor, he did little to alleviate the suffering of blacks in Americus when they pushed for the city to become more equitable. Furthermore, the implication that white and black youth were mutual in this deliverance is inaccurate. Black adults, black youth, and civil rights organizations fought throughout the 1960s trying to "deliver" Americus from its racist past, but they were opposed, and their white fellow citizens and classmates were not innocent bystanders.[9]

Americus had changed by the early 1970s, but it was far from the model for Chicago, New York, and Boston to follow, as Frady suggests. White opposition to educational improvements in Americus was continuous and more hostile than it was in Tifton. The backlash blacks in Americus received for challenging the sociopolitical and educational ethos rivaled what occurred in Birmingham, Little Rock, and Grenada, Mississippi.[10] By the time *Life* elevated Americus as a model city in 1971, the activism of blacks was succeeding in shifting staunch white obstruction into reluctant agreement.[11] The federal government was also very influential in forcing whites in Americus to come to terms with a different reality. Americus received

$161,152 from the federal government, whereas Sumter County received $296,699.[12] During this period, the United States Department of Health, Education, and Welfare had the authority to withhold public funds from school districts that refused to comply with the law. Through advocacy and legal means, white youth had to adjust to a different ethos from the one that black youth and others had fought to change for decades. By the 1970s, Americus was a different place because of the sacrifices made by black youth and civil rights organizations like the Student Nonviolent Coordinating Committee (SNCC). The federal government's push for compliance was important, but the scope of federal intervention was too narrow to dissolve the influence of white opposition without local activism.

By the time the civil rights movement arrived in Americus by way of the Albany and Sumter County Movements during the early 1960s, it was clear that a significant number of black youth were ready and excited to join and that desegregation was not their chief concern. Black youth in Americus were motivated by a right just to be. They wanted to be treated fairly; they wanted to be treated like citizens. In other words, they wanted the same things their white counterparts had, which was the ability to enjoy life as children and adolescents. Black youth had to deal with ongoing and persistent educational and social injustices that fundamentally affected crucial periods of their lives. As historian Wilma King notes, "the inhospitable environment that a number of black youth experienced gave rise to mass action."[13] The Americus Movement is about how a number of black youth decided to fight for a society that would value and appreciate their humanity. It also illuminates how several whites were unyielding in their beliefs that blacks were permanent second-class citizens. These irreconcilable differences had real consequences that led to the suffering of many black youth and young adults.

Black youth in the Americus Movement, including Sam Mahone, Sandra Mansfield, Lorena Sabbs, Juanita Wilson, and others, assiduously marched, sang, bled, and nearly died to be treated as first-class citizens in a place that was determined to deny them that right. In a town where race relations were already tenuous, the Americus Movement challenged long-held traditions that predated *Plessy*. The same students who experienced the tragedy of not having their humanity recognized became agents for change in ways that attempted to fundamentally shift the social norms in Americus. That challenge would prove taxing for the advocates involved. This movement depicts how tragedy and triumph shared the same space but yielded unequal concessions due to an imbalance of the social, political, and educational structure that had existed since the founding of Americus.

Being the City We Want to Become

Americus was established in 1832 as a small courthouse town. By the late 1800s, it became known as the "Metropolis of Southwest Georgia." Americus received this name because it had a privately financed railroad system and was known as a key distributor of cotton. In addition to flourishing financially, Americus had numerous attractions, particularly the Victorian-style Windsor Hotel, which lured northeasterners to visit as tourists. According to Sumter County genealogist Alan Anderson, Americus had political and social clout at the close of the nineteenth century and dawn of the twentieth century that brought the likes of Henry Grady, Franklin D. Roosevelt, and Ty Cobb to town.[14] During the 1900s, this metropolis remained politically and socially influential, which had a profound influence on race relations in southwest Georgia.

Unlike Tifton, Americus did not tout itself as a genteel place with a racially progressive ethos; the pretense that existed in Tifton did not occur in Americus. Americus's traditions were born during the antebellum period, so overt practices of white supremacy and black subjugation were publicly displayed. From the Civil War to the passage of *Brown*, white oppression of black residents saturated every facet of the town; the passage of time changed very little. The primary consequence of this fixed ethos was that it prevented blacks in Americus from participating equally in sectors that influenced their lives. Nearly seven decades after the passage of the Fourteenth Amendment, blacks remained excluded from the political process, with very limited economic opportunities that afforded them social mobility. The only sector they were not excluded from was public education and that was on a separate and unequal basis. This levied a heavy tax on blacks in Americus by placing the burden of any progress squarely on those who were the most disenfranchised, economically challenged, and educationally deprived.

According to Anderson, Americus adopted compulsory education in 1879, and all of Americus's children had access to some type of formal education. Formal education for blacks began in church schools, but the students received their own school building, McCay Hill School, in 1884.

Within the educational sphere Americus might have been viewed as progressive after the antebellum period, but by the early 1900s the educational system mirrored other places in Georgia and throughout the South. Although McCay Hill was built in the early 1880s, it remained the only school for black children until 1935. Furthermore, by the twentieth century, the school board of Sumter County had repeatedly addressed the educational concerns (overcrowding, school proximity to home, and older and younger children being grouped together) of white parents, while ignoring those of black parents. For example, when in 1927 a group of prominent black businessmen petitioned the school board regarding the fact that "all 900 black students attended one school; small children [had to attend the same school] with older teenagers after having traversed considerable distances to get there; [and there was] a lack of janitorial services . . . no school auditorium . . . and general overcrowding, sometimes a seventy-four to one pupil-teacher ratio," the majority of them were disregarded by the board.[15] The only concession made by the board was to add another grade, which did little to address the concerns of the black community in Americus. Regardless of whether the public education in Americus could be viewed as being progressive at a point in time in history, the data clearly show that, by the time the NAACP Legal Defense Fund team began to mount an attack on *Plessy*, black schools in Americus mirrored other black schools in southwest Georgia and other parts of the country.[16] In other words, there were few black schools, if any, that existed outside the context of white opposition.

In Americus, the opposition to educational opportunities for black students was especially overt. For example, when A. S. Staley High School was built in 1935, the board refused to contribute financially.[17] Their refusal to allot tax dollars indicates the adversarial relationship that existed between white local officials and their black constituents. Similar to Tifton, black tax dollars in Americus were contributing to shared expenditures, including for the creation and maintenance of white schools, while Staley depended on federal funds and McCay worsened to the point where the conditions "had deteriorated so badly that the Junior Chamber of Commerce, all white, noted . . . primitive outdoor plumbing, stairways with no railings, an inadequate two-room soup kitchen and nonexistent playground equipment."[18] A civic organization stating what blacks already knew was a good first step, but finding people outside of those affected to assist in improving the conditions at McCay proved to be a difficult task.

Throughout the first half of the twentieth century, blacks in Americus had very few, if any, educational allies in the white community. When in 1956 the school board finally built Eastview, a black elementary school, with county tax dollars, it reflected an oppositional shift, not an ideological progression. Towns like Americus wanted to sustain their nineteenth-century ethos, but new sociopolitical realities of the mid-twentieth century required modifications. Modifying the treatment of another group did not necessarily mean race relations progressed in Americus. In fact, despite the addition of Eastview and some improvements to McCay, blacks in Americus continued to interact with a local school system that offered them an education unequal to that of their white counterparts. The school board operated a dual system with the understanding that the city was responsible for educating white students and the county was responsible for educating blacks. Consequently, by the 1950s, the educational customs of Americus were to an extent nonnegotiable. Whites in Americus had grown accustomed to their way of life and any challenge to their way of life met staunch opposition.

Refusing the Ever-Present Alternative

Before the Americus Movement of the 1960s, one of the most noticeable organizations that challenged the racial customs of Americus was Koinonia Farm. Founded in Sumter County in 1942 by two Baptist ministers, Martin England and Clarence Jordan, the organization sought to bring racial harmony to southwest Georgia. Aware of the racial customs, members of Koinonia sought to use Christianity to remove systemic barriers they believed went against the teachings of Jesus Christ. According to public historian Tracy K'Meyer, "Koinonia Farm was an attempt to build the beloved community. . . . They sought to achieve that by bringing whites and blacks together in work, through cooperation and equalized economic conditions."[19] In other words, this organization sought to challenge and reshape the ways local whites thought about themselves religiously, racially, and economically. Purposefully or by accident, the simple creation of the organization opposed the core values of the region and white citizens of Sumter County eventually addressed the organization's philosophy with direct hostility.

The first decade after the organization's inception went by without confrontation. In fact, K'Meyer notes that "in the mid-1950s Koinonia lived a quiet life in an uneasy but peaceful coexistence with the local people."

K'Meyer suggests that this coexistence could be explained by Koinonians' not outwardly demonstrating their opposition to segregation or discrimination: "Koinonians did not believe in making a scene, using the courts, or agitating for legal measures that would advance racial equality."[20] They differentiated themselves from other civil rights organizations because they chose to fight for racial equality and social harmony inwardly. Members of the organization used their farm as a space where their ideals and customs could be discussed and practiced. While Koinonia's subtle yet successful ways of challenging the boundaries of Sumter County avoided violence for over a decade, by the late 1950s it experienced the full magnitude of white opposition.

Koinonia Farm's isolated display of racial harmony eventually met opposition. Historian Stephen Tuck states that following "a Ku Klux Klan terror campaign of bombing and sabotage, starting in the summer of 1956 . . . clergymen from across the country volunteered to patrol Koinonia's grounds. In July, a dynamite attack destroyed Koinonia's roadside market. Six months later, vandals chopped down over three hundred fruit trees."[21] Outside of the physical violence, a letter written to the NAACP suggested that the financial blowback was more severe: "more devastating than either the bombing or the shooting was the announcement last week by the Citizens Bank of Americus [that it] would no longer provide financial assistance to Koinonia Farm. The bank supplied Koinonia with operating capital since the beginning."[22] Even though Koinonia survived the physical destruction and the economic hardship, it is plausible that the destruction of the farm was not the primary objective. The intent behind those events could have been to send a message to the region that southwest Georgia would not tolerate anyone challenging their racial boundaries, even if it was a white, Christian, pacifist organization that did not employ common civil rights tactics (e.g., registering people to vote, boycotts, and sit-ins). Bombings, destruction of property, and eliminating access to capital were tactics whites used to send a clear message that they had no interest in the interruption of the status quo and they were willing to use violence in order to secure their way of life. This unchecked violence, as in other places, attempted to deny an alternative way of life displayed by those living at Koinonia Farm.

Whites in Americus had no interest in treating blacks as equals or sharing spaces with them, irrespective of the *Brown* decision. This was revealed by the overt forms of violence and the ever-present sociopolitical, economic, and educational suppression that continued after segregation was ruled unconstitutional. Although the Ku Klux Klan is often credited for being the executor of fierce opposition, ordinary white citizens of Americus and Sumter County were key contributors as well. Through action and inaction, whites maintained a culture that was oppositional to change, especially when it came to equalizing education or political participation for blacks.

While white opposition was successful in creating obstacles for those who decided to challenge boundaries, it could not prevent the waves of activism in southwest Georgia. The creation and survival of Koinonia Farm was succeeded by different forms of contestation that overtly challenged the status quo.[23] The adoption of direct action by blacks in Americus spoke to a different objective than those desired by members of Koinonia Farm. A template of living without systemic inequities consisted of challenging white opposition. This method was apropos for blacks throughout the region seeking different possibilities. Movements in Tifton, Albany, and Moultrie adopted similar actions with the goal of moving black citizens from the margins of society to the center. Their articulation of full citizenship did not come by way of secrecy or unproven methods. When blacks in Americus decided to contest the context and actions of white opposition, their local movement mirrored what was happening in urban and rural areas throughout America.

The increasing demand for a more equitable society, along with whites' refusal to be amenable, engulfed the South during the 1960s. Blacks' push to move past the restrictions orchestrated by legal segregation illuminate that an alternative was proposed and vehemently refused, for the most part, in southwest Georgia. Local white officials and most of their constituents did not view the rise of civic engagement from their black constituents and neighbors favorably. Blacks gaining greater participation in the functionality of Americus disrupted the life whites had become accustomed to. In real time, the philosophy that undergirded white opposition was constantly being contested by blacks in Americus before the 1960s. Like those in Tifton, black businesses played a pivotal role in Americus because they provided a degree of economic security. Even though blacks were often disenfranchised, they accrued a level of political influence in order to prevent being completely ignored by officials, which aided in their ability to create educational institutions, which had problems but were successful in educating the black populace. This feat was achieved in large part by those who pushed against the confinements of white hostility before those actions collectively formed a social movement. This initial pushback to white opposition provided the foundation needed for a movement to occur.

The Freemans, Campbells, and Barnums were three prominent black families in Americus that were essential in creating various forms of viability that pushed backed against the ideas of black inferiority. Their economic independence provided opportunities to challenge an ethos that blacks who were economically dependent on whites found more difficult to confront. Tuck notes that "the emergence of an indigenous group of black leaders independent from white economic control" meant that they did not have to fear the economic backlash that Koinonia was susceptible to.[24] Self-reliant blacks assisted with preparing Americus for a movement. Consequently, when a full-scale social justice movement reached Americus, there were people like the Freemans, Campbells, and Barnums who were already involved in social justice work. This was extremely important because they provided their homes, places of worship, and businesses as headquarters for the movement. Moreover, those who were already challenging systemic inequities in Americus had information on and experience with how the various forms of opposition shaped the possibilities of moving beyond the status quo.[25]

Blacks growing up in Americus were all too familiar with overt forms of opposition. They became much more familiar with white opposition the more they pushed for alternative ways to live. Sam Mahone, a native of Americus and member of SNCC, recalled the savagery adopted by whites to suppress any movement toward equality. Charging young protesters with sedition was one of the tools local officials used to quell any social movements in Americus. Ironically, this propelled the town into national significance because of the implications the case had for the civil rights movement, and it increased the participation of those involved in the movement.

An October 1963 article in the *Washington Post* reported that four demonstrators arrested in Americus—John Perdew, Zev Aelony, Ralph Allen, and Don Harris—faced insurrection charges, which carried "a maximum death penalty upon conviction." The article began by noting that "a Georgia prosecutor said yesterday that he has changed his mind and will prosecute four civil rights demonstrators . . . on charges of 'inciting an insurrection'" and quoted him as saying that "the basic reason for bringing these charges was to deny the defendants bond."[26] It is important to note that the prosecutor was unaware of the possible severity of the penalty under such charges, but, nevertheless, when he became aware of it, he did not change them. The prosecutor was primarily concerned with how to keep the leaders of the movement in jail, so he reportedly "pored through the law books to find a strong law to keep the young men out of circulation."[27] What began as an arrest for participation in a demonstration in 1962 turned into a death penalty case by 1963.

Although the sedition trial and its ruling proved pivotal to the movement, the events that transpired before the insurrection charges were filed were important as well. According to the *New York Times* and the *Atlanta Daily World*, a demonstration in the summer of 1962 against segregated public facilities, police brutality, and political disenfranchisement led to the arrest of hundreds of people in Americus, including several SNCC workers. The initial reaction by public officials in Americus was to brutalize the leaders of the movement and set their bail at an astronomically high rate that could not be paid. The *Atlanta Daily World* reported that the bail for SNCC workers was set at "forty-three thousand dollars each."[28] One of the strategies adopted by SNCC was to fill local jails, so the high bail was not a major concern initially. This does not, however, negate the intent behind the bail gouge, which was to deter further participation. The fact that brutality and high bail amounts spawned more demonstrations did not sit well with the powers in Americus, so a year later they increased the seriousness of the charges. The escalation in charges exemplified the heavy tax levied on those fighting to improve the conditions in Americus.

Sam Mahone remembered vividly the fear and nervousness caused by this case because of the potential consequences it had on those involved and the movement writ large. He said, "If they had been successful in finding them guilty, it would have literally stopped movements around the country."[29] Had it not been for the panel of three federal judges who agreed to hear the case, it is conceivable that Malone's fears for the movement would have been borne out. However, the judges did intercede and eventually ruled in favor of those falsely accused of insurrection. On October 31, 1963, a federal judicial panel ruled that the jailings and the sedition charges were unconstitutional and ordered the immediate release of Perdew, Aelony, Allen, and Harris.[30] This decision was essential to the continuation of social movements throughout the country because the acts that the defendants were being charged for were strategies taught and used by most civil rights organizations. For this reason, several organizations sent representatives to southwest Georgia because they were concerned that the case could impact local movements everywhere. SNCC had spent three years in the early 1960s in southwest Georgia trying to convince locals why they should not be afraid to participate in nonviolent direct-action protests, and this case gave locals every reason to be afraid. Telling someone that they might be brutalized or jailed was frightening enough, but asking someone to participate in an activity that was punishable by death was even more terrifying.

The trumped-up charges that landed Perdew, Aelony, Allen, and Harris in jail provided clarity on multiple fronts. First, activists pushing for equality were not left completely unprotected by federal officials. The Kennedy administration eventually got involved once it became obvious local officials had no plan to reverse course. Second, local officials and local whites rejected every facet of the plan put forth by local activists and those who came to help. Because many blacks in Americus worked for those who perpetuated the town's racial ethos, this case increased the trepidation that accompanies lack of economic mobility. This context made it difficult for SNCC to recruit adults to participate in voter registration drives or demonstrations, since there were a limited number of adults with economic independence.

Being limited due to economic vulnerabilities also meant that they were restricted in fighting for their own liberation. This issue was addressed in a letter sent to SNCC's headquarters. David Bell and Robert Mants noted that Americus was ripe for a movement, but they were concerned about a lack of qualified leadership. As they put it, "Out of years of oppression comes a feeling of dissatisfaction. From dissatisfaction arises leadership. The proper leadership provides organization. . . . Successful protest leads to the elimination of oppression. . . . The black masses in Americus . . . have been systematically kept in a position of degradation . . . politically ignored, socially segregated, economically exploited. . . . The result of this oppression, as exhibited in the past few months, has been discontent, and open dissatisfaction. [Yet] a responsible and able leadership has not appeared."[31] Coupling the issues articulated by Bell and Mants with the insurrection case reveals the difficult terrain caused by white opposition. The unapologetic rejection of making Americus a more equitable town is why Mahone noted that "Americus probably ranks along with Birmingham and Selma in terms of the historic [conflict] of the movement."[32] The notoriety of Southern towns during this period often came because something tragic had occurred that stained America's standing in the world. Birmingham was left to answer: How can democracy exist if black people cannot worship in a church without being bombed? Selma was left to answer: Where is freedom when people cannot cross a bridge? Americus was left to answer: If citizens cannot peacefully protest, then what good is the constitution?

While questions of protection and the civil right to protest remained fluid after the insurrection case was dismissed, the clearest message was that blacks, particularly the youth, had no intention of relinquishing their right to demand to be treated as equal citizens. Although the case contributed to uncertainty that a different reality could ever exist in Americus, black youth became more determined to live in a world that acknowledged and respected their humanity. The insurrection case served as a paradox because, according to Mahone, the charges galvanized the black citizens of Americus and "it ignited the movement."[33] The ignition occurred because the case failed to terminate the sporadic forms of activism and deter more from joining. Prior to the insurrection case, this small metropolis faced forms of agitation that challenged the town's way of life, but the case inspired a more audacious attack that sought to fundamentally alter political, social, and educational practices. The transition to pushing for something new through more confrontational strategies is demonstrated by the increased participation among black youth during and after the trial. As Stephen Tuck notes, "it was the presence and attitude of local high school students that fueled the movement."[34] Black youth provided the necessary components for the creation and sustainment of the Americus Movement. The ideas they brought with them of what it looked like to be treated as a human being in public spaces and the actions they adopted to challenge dehumanizing spaces provided the necessary oxygen for the movement.

The tinder was provided and the fire was started by white opposition and the escalation to punish those who challenged it at all costs. For this reason, SNCC found it difficult to get many adults to participate in events. Like their peers in Tifton, blacks in Americus were susceptible to economic backlash from their white employers. This setup engendered the need for black youth participation, because they did not have the economic constraints their parents had to consider. It is not a surprise that "most of the [demonstrators] were teenagers" when SNCC organized a protest directed at police brutality. Nor is it a surprise that the "police used clubs and electric prod poles" on the protestors to quell the demonstration and instill fear.[35] This was the most effective method public officials had at their disposal to hinder youth participation. Using local law enforcement to trample on the rights of citizens was not unique to southwest Georgia. Similar tactics were used in Alabama, South Carolina, Mississippi, and North Carolina.[36] The antagonism black youth experienced in Americus did not end with the sedition trial. Use of the tactic of imposing fear on those who dared to offer an alternative increased after the federal judges ruled in favor of the activists. Because black youth were so vital to the movement, they were particular targets. The constant confrontation between law enforcement and black youth reveals the absence of legal protection and the presence of despotic authority. Law enforcement was clearly serving the will of local officials and their white constituents, which meant that, regardless of how logical and constitutional the ideas and actions of blacks were, the goal was to suppress the agitation. Black youth were rarely granted any leniency when it came to them being punished for demanding equality. Although young black students were not charged with insurrection, they could not escape the hostile response of law enforcement. At the same time, members of law enforcement realized that the attempt to use fear as a tactic to sway those involved to quit and others from joining worked in reverse. Instead, the hostility hardened the rebellious spirits of black youth by engendering something greater than fear that encouraged others to become more active. Therefore, fear was not a reliable deterrent given that most young people got involved when it was uncertain whether protesting could be punishable by death, while also certain that they could not rely on law enforcement to protect their rights of assembly and free speech.

The Americus Movement illuminates how those who participated in any form of protest could not allow themselves to be consumed by fear. Besides being fearless, youth contributed to the rise of activism out of pragmatism. For any social movement to be successful, it needed willing and able bodies. Unlike Albany, Americus did not have a state university with eager college students ready to join the movement. However, as Willie Ricks (Mukasa Dada) recalled, the organization did have a number of enthusiastic preadolescents and teenagers ready to participate. He noted, "When the community kids got involved, they took the head, and when the young people took it, it became something else."[37] Black youth like Sam Mahone, Sandra Mansfield, Juanita Freeman (Wilson), Lorena Barnum (Sabbs), and others saw in Americus a town shackled by its racial history and in desperate need of a transformation. In other words, they wanted to supplant the racial ethos they lived under with a more equitable and inclusive one. Growing up in Americus, black youth witnessed and experienced the town's refusal to accept blacks as first-class citizens. Wilson stated, "I would sit and watch the KKK march through the street. I have been on my way home and had spit on my face."[38] In fact, each participant who was raised in Americus remembered how whites would constantly look for ways—socially, politically, economically, or educationally—to remind them of their second-class status. Therefore, black youth, civil rights organizations, and adults who eventually joined the movement understood that they could not focus on improving only one sector of their life in Americus. They had to address political disenfranchisement as well as the educational disparities taking place. They knew that the political, economic, and educational sectors were all interconnected, so improving one without improving the others was futile.

When SNCC arrived in Americus in 1962, they were not shunned by local black adults, but they were not welcomed with open arms either. The fact that SNCC was not embraced by the adult community may explain the difficulties the organization experienced initially. Mahone stated that when SNCC came to Americus, he remembered the first meeting being "held outside the county down in the countryside [because a number] of ministers were too afraid to let us meet at their churches, because there's been a history of church burnings and bombings throughout the entire area. So we met in small churches in the country until we were able to meet in churches inside the city."[39] Eventually, SNCC moved its operation from the countryside to the city of Americus. Their first goal in Americus was registering African Americans to vote. One of the startling facts in Americus was the low number of blacks who were registered. Although there were 6,674 blacks eligible, only 863 were registered.[40] Blacks made up nearly 50 percent of the town's population, but their political influence did not correlate. Given this reality, SNCC and black youth set up a voter registration drive. Believing that political empowerment was essential, an intensive voter registration campaign was employed.[41] They immediately met obstacles because illiteracy ran rampant in Americus and demanded attention.[42] Because the classes and workshops "were taught by local citizens," black youth would prove pivotal in this endeavor. For example, Mahone remembered assisting in the "citizenship schools" as a youth: "I joined SNCC as a high school student. I worked primarily on voter registration, public accommodation, and direct action. I helped to set up freedom schools/literacy classes in Americus."[43] According to Bell and Mants, the campaign would be carried out by "canvassing with the help of local students from six to eight hours per day. Friday and Saturday had been set aside as the days to take potential applicants to city hall."[44]

The agenda set forth by activists provides insight into their pursuit of equality and the opposition that existed. The farrago that continued in Americus during the 1960s was largely fostered by blacks being barred from the political process, which explains why members of SNCC spent so much time pushing for voter registration. Like black students in Tifton, black students in Americus aided in this endeavor. Black youth understood that political disenfranchisement was just one of many ways to deny a person full citizenship. With so many of their parents barred from voting, it was just as important for adults to obtain voting rights as it was for them to be treated like human beings. Unwilling to accept Americus as it was, demands became bolder and the decrease in fear resulted in many forms of activism. As black youth worked with SNCC to acquire voting rights, their demand for human decency within the social and educational sphere grew exponentially louder as well.

The New Same-Old

The educational system in Americus had very similar racial customs in the 1950s and early 1960s as in previous decades. Although some black schools were built to address the overcrowding at McCay, the racial tenets the school board adopted during the early 1900s remained. Whites in Americus remained staunch opponents to any form of educational improvement that brought discomfort to them.[45] Their refusal to budge had a profound impact on the educational experiences of black youth. For example, Ann Whea Walker experienced the dilapidated conditions of McCay. She attended McCay for eight years and throughout her tenure dealt with overcrowding, secondhand materials, and hazardous conditions. She was even afraid to go to the restroom. Walker recalled, "The thing that I remember most about it [was the location of the bathroom]. I don't know if you would call it a basement or what, but that's where the bathrooms were and I remember that I was just so very afraid because when you would go down there all the guts of the structure was under there. . . . The girls would go down on the east section and the boys' was on the west, and it was the most horrible thing for me to go down there and that's what I did for eight years. It terrified me."[46] The fear of going to the restroom was not something isolated to Walker. Sandra Mansfield, who also attended McCay years later, remembered the horrors of the bathroom as well: "It was an old school. It had a basement down there where we had to use the bathroom, it was gross."[47] These conditions at McCay profoundly shaped students' early educational experiences; however, it was not the sum total of their experiences.

When Walker left McCay, she enrolled at Staley, which was a high school at the time. Like other black students who attended segregated schools in the South, she felt black schools became somewhat of a cocoon for her.[48] Walker recalled her time at Staley as heavenly. She summed up her high school experience this way: "It was an honor to go there and more of an honor to graduate and to be there. To be a part of everything. I was academically a very good student. I was always selected by teachers to do things. I never shall forget we organized the student council."[49] Walker thrived at Staley and was the head of her class. Within this cocoon, many black youth flourished and had educational experiences that they believed were second to none, as was the case for Walker.

Mansfield and Wilson had very similar educational experiences as Walker, although they were a few years younger. Wilson's experience differed slightly: she did not have to deal with the horrid conditions at McCay because her school career began at Eastview. When Mansfield was asked about her educational experiences, she did not go into detail but she did say that she remembered the teachers being good and that she was "an A and B student."[50] Wilson, on the other hand, was very detailed about her experiences at Eastview and Staley. She recalled the recitals at Eastview and "how [my teachers] made me learn and that black was beautiful." At Staley, the philosophy of teaching, loving, and rigor was the same. She recounted, "I had a science teacher, Mr. Carter, who gave assignments that were hands-on, you know. You knew that was going to be a part of your grade and everybody dreaded it, but everybody was looking forward to it. All of us knew that there was so much we had to learn. There were expectations from our teachers, our classrooms in elementary, junior high, and high school were the same. The courses were just as rigorous."[51] Still, in examining the educational experiences of Walker, Mansfield, and Wilson, it is evident that *Brown* had very little influence. While each participant fondly remembered the activities, they also remembered being exposed constantly to the same familiar discrimination that inevitably reminded them of their second-class status.

Black youth throughout the South had to get used to the "new same-old" situation. What were new materials for black youth were old materials for white youth. This tradition profoundly shaped the educational experiences of Mahone, Walker, Mansfield, Wilson, Sabbs, and other students in Americus. As each talked about going to school during the 1950s and 1960s, the conversation invariably ended up with them talking about the frustration they felt from receiving white students' old materials. Mahone remembered this practice taking place from elementary school to high school: "The black schools, all the books had somebody else's name in it. So we knew they were passed on to us, so I never had a book without someone else's name in it. So you were getting second-rate materials constantly."[52] Similar to Mahone's experience, Walker stated, "Let me tell you about the books. . . . I can see them now. They would bring books from the white high schools . . . [and] they would have dump trucks enter them at our school. . . . Yeah, in the front yard. . . . They would dump them, and we would pick them up and take them to the classrooms. Yeah, that is how they got them over there. They would dump them, and we would get them, and the most interesting thing I can remember, we would look in the books and see Sally and Jean and Don and Dan, [laughs] all of those names, and those [were] the books we had, you know."[53] Knowing their new books were old white students' books was humiliating enough, but the dumping of the books in the front of the school like they were trash was downright demeaning.

Mansfield's experience at Staley was parallel to Mahone's and Walker's. In addition to having similar experiences as those who attended the same school, her experience was also analogous to those of Johnny Terrell, Walter Dykes, and Alton Pertilla. She remembered the names in her books, and she talked about how the books often were missing pages, which affected her ability to complete homework assignments.[54] Aside from the practical sense in which the custom affected the educational experiences of black youth, there was a psychological aspect that Wilson remembered: "I think part of it was, when we got our books, we got our books with the white folks' name in it. . . . They had the books for five years, then we had to use it for the next five. When they got new books, we got their books. That is second-class. . . . Just think about being [human], and you couldn't see [your humanity recognized]."[55] Similar to the youth struggle in Tifton, black youth in Americus had to find a way, physically and mentally, to maintain their belief that they were citizens and were entitled to the same resources afforded to their white counterparts in a world that reinforced they were anything but deserving.

As in other locations, the *Brown* decision did very little for black youth in Americus in the decade or so after its passage. In fact, Walker is the only participant who remembered *Brown* being discussed in any detail, and that was when she went off to attend Morris Brown College in 1955. The reality of black education in Americus was that it was unequal in every way imaginable. Wilson summed it up this way: "You didn't have a basketball court, you had a concrete slab outside. You didn't have anything."[56] The effect that white opposition had on black education was definitely seen in the ways black schools operated compared with white schools. For example, Sabbs's mother, Thelma Barnum, taught at Sumter and her father, John L. Barnum, had to buy the microscope for her to teach biology whereas white schools were provided microscopes.[57] Likewise, Mahone remembered his graduation being hosted in a church because his school did not have a place to host the ceremonious occasion.

Inherent white opposition created a climate that resulted in black schools being grossly underfunded. Therefore, black youth understood that their educational reality was not going to change unless they responded. Their involvement was not a denouncement of *Brown* but a pronouncement of relevance. Aware of Little Rock, Greensboro, and the movements taking place in Albany, Mahone, Mansfield, Wilson, and Sabbs wanted to address their educational realities and, as the movement came to Americus, they knew they would have to try to fundamentally change those rampant inequities.

A Different Focus but a Similar Struggle

While undoubtedly troubled by the educational customs of Americus, black youth were propelled to act because of how their classmates were treated. Whether it was in the educational, political, or social sector, black youth were frustrated. Their focus on the treatment of black students did not trump the goals of achieving political, social, and educational equality; it unified them. They believed that the failure of whites to recognize and treat them as human beings lay at the center of the inequities in Americus. Members of SNCC agreed that the social, educational, and political issues were interconnected, but an overarching theme would have to be established to make the movement relevant to all blacks, young and old.

A letter sent by Harris of SNCC shows the intersection of social inequities and education issues. It stated that after a local theater was closed, "local Negroes must travel 25 to 40 miles to attend a movie. The staff in Americus feels that a program channeled toward movies, educational as well as recreational, could be valuable in aiding the movement and serving as an activity for young people to become involved during the summer."[58] Parents' political disenfranchisement, students' educational reality, and the lack of social amenities all had to do with some form of mistreatment. For example, Mansfield's account of her involvement in the Americus Movement illustrates how treatment encapsulated her decision to join, when she stated that multiple forms of mistreatment were the reason. In an incident she remembered vividly, she was at the store with her mother and her cousin and there was a "picture of a little black doll painted like a black Sambo. This little white lady said, 'Oh, he [referring to Mansfield's cousin] looks like him [referring to the picture],' and my mama sealed her lips. . . . I thought to myself, my mama would never have to go through nothing like that again."[59] At the age of twelve, Mansfield, like so many young people in Americus, was on the way to making the decision to attack such mistreatment directly.

During the summer of 1963, black youth were reminded that their demanding any change to the status quo would be dealt with violently. As black youth marched downtown they were met by a white mob, which included law enforcement and members of the Ku Klux Klan, and things got violent.[60] A number of students were beaten, arrested, and thrown in jail, where they spent days, and some even months, in a deplorable environment. A notarized letter from Henrietta Fuller described the conditions to which some were subjected: "I am 13 years old and in Leesburg Stockade from August 31 to September 8. There were 32 kids in there with me. There were no beds, no mattress, no blankets, pillows, no sheets. . . . The hamburgers were dry and were not cooked. . . . The smell of waste material was bad."[61] A special report in *Essence* by Donna Owens noted that "everyone had lost weight. . . . Other girls had suffered from a range of ills: ear infections, boils, and high fevers. Some had lice in their hair."[62] The report also noted that parents were unaware that their children were jailed at Leesburg Stockade, which is why those who were unjustly imprisoned are referred to as "the Stolen Girls."

Mansfield, Wilson, Sabbs, and others were also arrested, and they vividly remember this injustice. The deplorable conditions to which several black youth were exposed energized more people to get involved in the movement, especially when a photograph taken by Danny Lyon of SNCC revealing the conditions at the jail was published in SNCC's weekly newspaper, the *Student Voice*, and gained state and regional headlines. Those students who had not been arrested or jailed for long periods knew that only by chance were they not subjected to these dehumanizing forms of treatment. As the summer ended and fall classes began, the school year was disrupted, because several students refused to attend school until their classmates were released from their jail cells.

The inhumane treatment experienced by those who pushed for an alternative was not abstract. It was real and often personal. Black students in Americus decided to join the movement because they had relatives and/ or friends in situations that disregarded their humanity or had experienced second-class treatment themselves. Many of them joined the movement because they were persuaded by a sibling or a peer. Seeing a sibling treated inhumanely was extremely difficult. Such was the case for Sabbs, who followed her siblings into the movement. She remembered how she and others responded to their classmates and siblings being locked up: "We had protested all summer long and of course most of the people who were locked up during that time were students. My own brother had been in jail maybe two months under deplorable circumstances, so when school started to open we campaigned to parents, we did everything, saying, if all of our [classmates] can't go back to school then nobody was going to go back to school."[63] Undoubtedly, the decision to stay out of school was personal. The constant proximity with white opposition left little room for detachment. Black youth knew intimately about their guardians' disenfranchisement and what occurred to those who attempted to change that reality. This personalization drew them to the movement. In Americus, the overlapping of these various forms of personal mistreatment ignited a movement. Mistreatment was the primary reason students petitioned parents to keep their children out of school in the summer of 1963.

The strategy employed by local black youth, along with SNCC, appeared to be ineffective initially because, according to the *Atlanta Daily World*, only thirty-two students did not report to Staley on the first day of class.[64] A tweak, however, in the strategy increased the number of black youth participating, which would eventually change the effectiveness of the movement. Instead of concentrating on the parents, black youth who had been jailed and released became the most effective recruiters of other youth. White officials' tactic of releasing some youth from jail appears to have been aimed at quelling the school boycott; however, freeing those students became the primary reason the boycott increased. Because they were students at Staley, they had access to their fellow classmates. Sabbs remembered recruiting other students in the school. The goal was "to close the school down. And on the first day of school, we were protesting outside in our little perimeter to ask students to turn around and not go in and of course you still had some that went in, but what I personally did along with [other] protestors [was] we went into the school." Sabbs was in the seventh grade and went into the school under the premise that she was going to class. "What we did, though, is go from classroom to classroom asking our friends to please leave." Their recruitment strategy resulted in Wilson being nearly "emptied out."[65]

While Sabbs and the other protestors were able to get several of their classmates to leave Staley, news accounts reveal they suffered the same fate as those they were protesting to support. According to the *Americus Times-Recorder*, "a total of some 45–50 Negro students were arrested outside Staley when they refused to stop singing freedom songs and shouting at pupils inside the school to leave classes and join in a boycott. . . . The arrests came on two different occasions, the first during mid-morning and the second about noon."[66] The response by law enforcement and the school board was typical in that their only priority was to terminate what they deemed as a disruption while ignoring the reasons the students were being disruptive. This "organized brutality in Americus," according to Tuck, was a typical method used and, unfortunately for black youth, they could not escape it. Instead of responding to a simple demand, officials subjected more of them to the inhumane treatment.[67]

The protest at Staley did not fundamentally change school policies or improve race relations in Americus, but the students were eventually released from jail. The school board was satisfied because black youth were back in school instead of outside protesting. Those in power lacked the foresight needed to understand the stages of social movements. When no immediate political, social, or educational concessions were made and students were back in school, these authorities concluded, erroneously, that everything was back to normal. What they did not realize is that their lack of concessions did not mean black youth internalized their concerns or actions as invalid. Those who lived with white oppression daily and the suppression of legitimate demands by force of arrests had no intention of conceding and allowing the status quo to stand. In fact, what was normal prior to the initial protest had changed because the number of blacks being mistreated had increased, which meant they were more vulnerable to dehumanizing conditions. The initial decision to challenge the town's sociopolitical ethos did not require the approval of whites in Americus, so the lack of concessions did not determine the survival or next phase of the movement.

Like their peers were doing in Albany and Tifton, black students in Americus wanted to bring awareness to the nature of the conditions they faced, which they did. In addition to introducing their suffering to the nation, they illuminated their agency. Blacks in Americus and those who were assisting in the fight for equality were not passive victims. From the insurrection trial to the young girls being held hostage in the Leesburg Stockade, the nation saw them as nonviolent participatory actors in the dehumanizing actions taking place in Americus. As black youth experienced various demeaning ordeals, their desire and willingness to be treated as human beings did not diminish. For example, when Carol Barner, one of the Stolen Girls, was asked by a magistrate "if she would promise to stay away from the protests and other 'mess' in the future, [she] retorted angrily, 'Mess, what mess?!'" Barner told the reporter, "We were willing to do what we had to do to gain our freedom."[68] Their perseverance and willingness to sacrifice resulted in more youth becoming aware of their circumstances because of what transpired at Staley. A return to school meant that the tactic of boycotting school to achieve equal treatment had run its course. Irrespective of what members of the school board thought, those involved in the Americus Movement understood they had other tactics available to them and they intended to use all of them. By the time the momentum and participation in the Americus Movement declined in the early 1970s, the political, social, and educational sectors had been challenged.

An Immovable Object Meets an Unstoppable Force

The fight to transform educational and sociopolitical spaces by demanding black people be treated as human beings was never a fair fight. Americus, like other places throughout the South, had developed a level of expertise in treating blacks as second-class citizens by the time segregation was outlawed. The longevity of separate and unequal practices distorted the balance of power toward white citizens to the point that their ideas reigned supreme. Mahone remembered it this way: "Growing up in Americus as a young kid in a segregated society you are taught the lines are clearly drawn.

It's a way of life and from day one there are certain lines you don't cross."[69] Throughout the twentieth century, those norms were thought to be so un-movable, particularly by whites, that political disenfranchisement, educa-tional disparities between black and white youth, and economic exploita-tion were ways of life. Local white officials and their white constituency did not view these practices as systematic injustices. In fact, by the 1960s, Jim Crow and its resulting widespread ideologies were so entrenched that, as Sokol argues, "an abyss separated white racial attitudes from reality."[70] Where blacks in Americus saw inequities caused by segregation, whites saw a system they cherished. Their reverence added to the distortion that ex-isted from the founding of Americus, thereby increasing the unfairness of the fight.

For decades, the immovability of Jim Crow flourished in Americus be-cause whites remained committed to the town's norms and blacks were vul-nerable to white retribution. Against insurmountable odds, enough blacks, particularly the youth, collectively agreed to challenge what was thought to be unchallengeable. The events that began in 1962 and continued into the early 1970s illuminate how those on the margins garnered enough force to alter the status quo. The rise of consciousness and fearlessness created great opportunities for those who were determined to be treated as humans and great challenges for those who wanted Americus to remain the same. In an article entitled, "How It All Started in Americus, Georgia," journal-ist Thelma Hunt Shirley noted that "Americus, a jungle town built on red clay with a population of 13,452, hidden in the backwoods of Georgia . . . fi-nally erupted on the national scene [because] Negroes had gained a rich-ness that was the envy, the fear, and engendered the hatred of their neigh-bors. They became bold enough to believe they had everything to gain, if they spoke up for their rights."[71] The ability to become influential enough to push political and social boundaries can be largely attributed to the pres-ence of organizations like SNCC and local leaders who prepared the town for civil disobedience. SNCC's organizational presence undoubtedly was a significant force, but the steady participation of black youth was just as nec-essary and audacious. Mahone confirms Shirley's report by stating, "I con-sider SNCC the vanguard of the movement in Americus even though you had other organizations like SCLC, but they were much older. The SCLC was more reserved in terms of their approach to direct action. SNCC was confrontational and in the trenches every day . . . and being young, being in the forefront and wanting to rebel, you gravitate towards that sector."[72]

Even though SNCC depended heavily on the youth of Americus, by the mid-1960s adult participation had dramatically improved, which allowed SNCC to protest racial injustices on multiple fronts.

As the Americus Movement gained momentum, members of SNCC continued to listen to the desires of the people to organize the next plan of attack. Leaders of the movement understood movements could diminish if there was not an answer to the question, "What is next?" Sabbs, whose family was very involved in the movement, stated, "People thought that [the activities were] kind of unplanned but it really wasn't. I mean, it was like the next step, you attack public transportation [then] you attack public accommodations. There were battle plans."[73] People finally bought into the idea that a group with shared goals, focus, and a willingness to endure could become an unstoppable force. SNCC was able to mobilize strong leadership, and the buy-in around shared ideas fueled the movement while simultaneously clashing with the immovable object of white opposition.

Shortly after the insurrection charges were dropped and the students were released from prison for protesting, SNCC organized several protests that hit directly at the practices of segregation. Sabbs stated, "The public buses were closed down because we were trying to integrate the public buses. We [boycotted] lunch counters. We did just like [they] did in Greensboro, [North Carolina,] integrating the public lunch counters and whatnot. They closed them, and I'll never forget there was a pharmacy called Red's Pharmacy that I had been going to with my mother for years and years and years, and they had a lunch counter and I had never ever sat at their lunch counter, never had a soda pop or a hamburger or whatever. And when we tried to integrate that lunch counter, they took it out, they went out of business after that. . . . Of course, the school integration was a natural progression."[74] Although directly challenging segregated public spaces became the tactic used to challenge the customs in Americus, it would not be accurate to say that the primary goal of the Americus Movement was to integrate. Leaders of the movement used the approach of pushing for integration because it had been proven effective in other parts of the South and it aligned with their underlining philosophy of having the option to have access because of one's citizenship. If blacks were to be treated as equals in Americus, then that meant they should have access to all public schools and be able to patronize local businesses and public facilities. It was unfathomable to them to envision a world in which they had equal protection under the law, but restricted access. A common belief held by those who participated in the movement for equality in Americus was that one's humanity could not be fully recognized while whites were simultaneously restricting their educational, political, and economic possibilities. Therefore, fighting against mistreatment included fighting for the option to integrate, because of the dehumanizing component of segregation.

Like the young people in Arkansas, Virginia, Louisiana, and Boston, black youth in Americus shouldered the burden of desegregating public schools and paid a similar tax as those who pushed for voter registration and equal treatment.[75] Being the sole burden-bearers did not occur by happenstance. The actions of local officials and their loyal white constituents imply that they felt they had limited or no obligation to make sure desegregation was implemented.[76] More importantly, they were very interested in making sure educational equality did not reach a status in which blacks were afforded the same opportunities as their white counterparts. Whites were not indifferent to desegregation. In fact, they displayed their continued opposition to desegregation even after the federal government threatened to withhold funds from counties that refused to desegregate. The decision by local white officials and a significant number of their white constituents to remain antagonistic toward black students' desire to be treated as equals continued to confine the educational experiences of black youth within a hostile climate. The result of this confinement changed the dynamic of the movement by controlling the number of black students allowed in white spaces. This meant that the demand to be treated as equals came from a small collection of individuals who decided to enroll at Americus High, a historically white school. Demanding to be treated fairly at school was a lonesome ordeal because of the initial enrollment imbalance. Despite being outnumbered, young black students in Americus refused to accept second-class treatment.

Desegregating white schools was the only legal option available to those who remained committed to challenging the immovable customs of Americus. Mahone noted, "It was clear in people's minds that they were not getting as good of an education, so once black students started attending white schools it opened up another world of possibilities."[77] Like the Little Rock Nine, Ruby Bridges, and so many other black youth who spearheaded desegregation efforts to achieve equality, black youth in Americus took up the same fight. In the fall of 1964, Robertina Freeman became one of three Negro girls to integrate Americus High School. Her sister, Juanita Wilson, remembered why this approach was useful during this period: "See, everything with the civil rights movement was to cut the white man's money so he would hurt and give in. The only way they could receive funding for school was [through adopting freedom of choice]."[78] Although the initial desegregation of Americus High convinced other black students to consider enrolling, the major backlash from whites dampened those possibilities. A letter sent by a SNCC representative detailed the status of integration in Americus by stating, "last year, three girls integrated Americus High. This year, during the period for school transfer, some eighty-five students applied to transfer next year."[79] However, by the time the following school year came around, most of the students who had signed up to transfer decided to remain at the all-black Sumter High or Staley. The drastic decrease could be explained by the fact that mistreatment of black students remained a common practice that most tried to avoid.

The initial response of the school board to the original three girls and those who signed up to transfer in 1965 was subtle. According to the SNCC papers, the school board's response, aimed at keeping blacks from attending Americus High, was that supposedly "to relieve overcrowding the city is converting one of the junior highs into a high school. Also . . . teachers are exerting pressure on the kids not to transfer, [telling] them they'll get scholarships if they stay and so on."[80] The letter does not say whether school officials forced teachers to persuade students, but it is clear that integration of any kind was unacceptable to the powers that be. After their initial efforts proved futile, white officials did away with the subtlety and tried to stoke fear in those who chose to transfer. Using Robertina Freeman and Alex Brown as examples, they trumped up charges against the two with the hope of ending the push for integration. An immediate news release by SNCC stated that "Robertina Freeman, 15, and Alex Brown, 15, have been sentenced to incarceration in the Georgia Training School until they are no longer minors. This is the maximum penalty and would mean that Robertina would spend 3 years and Alex Brown 6 years imprisoned on a charge of fornication."[81] A letter in the SNCC files detailed the treatment of Freeman and Brown: "In an attempt to intimidate students who might want to transfer, the cops picked up Freeman and Brown and charged them with fornication. They said they were innocent, and a lie detector test confirmed this. Nevertheless, the judge, James V. Smith, sentenced them to reform school until they reached 18 and 21, respectively. In other cases, he'd just released other kids, but in this case, he used the maximum penalty."[82] The increased hostility designed to prevent desegregation illuminates how black youth experienced treatment that was analogous to the treatment of those held hostage at the Leesburg Stockade. Although these charges greatly affected the educational experiences of Freeman and Brown and infuriated the black community, it was subsequent events that forever changed Americus and the Americus Movement.

While the methods used to prevent black students from attending Americus High angered blacks, the Mary Kate Bell incident elevated their frustration. Bell, a Spelman College graduate, was the first black woman to run for public office in Americus. In a special election to select a justice of the peace, Bell lost under a cloud of suspicion. Most upsetting, however, to the black community and some whites who had sided with the struggle for racial equality, was that Bell and three other women—Lena Turner, Mamie Campbell, and Gloria Wise—were arrested for refusing to stand in the segregated line to cast their ballots. Tuck states that after the women were arrested and refused to post bond, "twenty-five people marched in protest. . . . By the weekend, the marches had swelled to almost eight hundred people."[83] Participants in the movement did not make any new demands; in fact, their demands for political representation had remained constant since the first voter registration drive in 1962. *The New York Times* reported that protesters wanted local officials "to grant longer voting registration hours, to name Negroes to election posts, and to void the segregated justice of the peace election."[84] Similar to how a number of youth used integration as a tactic to challenge Jim Crow, adults like Bell used political participation. Although she was not able to win the special election, her actions, along with those of the other three women arrested, brought attention to the entrenched political disenfranchisement blacks faced. Besides being able to attend the school of their choosing, blacks needed to be able to participate in the political process.

After the fornication charges brought against Freeman and Brown, along with the arrest of Bell, racial tensions increased and so, too, did violent acts.[85] The most violent act in Americus during this period occurred on July 29, 1965, when Andrew Aultman Whatley, a white man from Americus, was killed. Two black males, Eddie Lee Lamar and Charles Lee Hopkins, were accused of his murder, which sharply divided the city. At the same time Whatley was shot, a demonstration to free Bell was taking place. Leaders of the movement realized how the story would unfold. Two black men accused of killing a white man was never good, especially when racial tensions were so high. In fact, the *Los Angeles Times* reported that shortly after the shooting "local residents were unnerved which caused a run on guns and ammunition." Tuck notes that "the *Wall Street Journal* recorded that in the aftermath of the murder, pistols were selling like 'hot cakes.'"[86] In the presence of paranoia and heightened racial tension, black youth provided some sense of hope that the racial tension would subside and the quest to have access to the amenities of being a citizen could be resumed. The *Chicago Tribune* reported that "several hours after the Klan rally, more than 300 integrationists, most of them Negro teenagers, marched to the courthouse, held a rally, and then marched away—through a block of a white residential area. As they marched through the residential area, they sang 'We love the imperial wizard.' Their signs said 'We love the Ku Klux Klan—in our heart' [but] 'We're not pleading for freedom, we're gonna take it.'"[87] The hybrid message of appealing to your antagonists' morality, which Dr. King often utilized, while being willing to "take" what is owed, which mirrors SNCC's methodology of the mid-1960s, was adopted during this march. Neither approach required black youth to mask their demands in order to lessen the racial tension, nor did they send conflicting messages. Loving those who intended to cause you harm was a moral and spiritual value infused in the Americus Movement, but not accepting the harm and advocating against the harm were also essential to the movement.[88]

White opposition was constant, fierce, and taxing to participants involved in the movement. This was especially true for black youth as they continued to try to be the unstoppable force to move an immovable object. By the mid-1960s, this effort became more dangerous because a white person had died and white spaces were being desegregated. Tuck argues that the killing of Andrew Whatley had a catastrophic impact on the movement because it appeared as though SNCC had lost control. He states, "Local SNCC leaders lost control of the demonstrations and despaired of the racial violence. . . . The demonstrations dissipated in the face of retaliatory violence and the uncompromising stance of the city government. Locally, the momentum for mass demonstrations was lost for good." Tuck concludes that this essentially ended the direct-action stage of the Americus Movement.[89] To a degree, Tuck is correct, in that organized resistance to racial inequities in Americus waned after Whatley's death. The tragedy, however, put the movement in a different phase because black youth remained formidable opponents to those who wanted to ignore their humanity. Once the attention faded from Americus, local blacks remained vulnerable to white oppression and schools remained largely segregated. Therefore, the young black students, who had joined the movement to improve voter participation for blacks in Americus and to change how blacks were being treated, continued to challenge the town's customs by entering one of the most sacred bastions of white opposition: public schools. Their willingness to enter hostile learning spaces continued to provide oxygen to a movement in which fighting for improvements proved taxing.

Black youth who grew up in Americus thought they had a great understanding of the opposition they met when they decided to challenge traditions. By the time they pushed against segregated public schools, they had participated in actions that addressed political disenfranchisement and inhuman treatment and felt the wrath of white opposition. Prior to the waning of the Americus Movement, the punishment they faced was often experienced collectively. What made the push for desegregating public schools different was that those who decided to attend Americus High faced a heightened sense of white opposition directed at themselves. There was no National Guard to protect them, nor was there national attention or reporting on the hostility that continued to accompany desegregation. Regardless of the picture *Life* attempted to portray about desegregation in Americus, those who embodied *Brown* by personally integrating schools recount a very different experience, and those scars remain with them decades after achieving this historic feat. For example, Freeman, Sabbs, and Mansfield were early participants in the Americus Movement and were among the girls stolen and held at the Leesburg Stockade. The tragedy at the stockade, however, was less antagonistic than their experiences at Americus. Each of them recalled their years at Americus High being the most difficult of their adolescence. Freeman vividly remembered the hostility she encountered the first day she attended Americus and how it continued throughout her tenure. She recalled being labeled the "smart nigger" and how those experiences resulted in "me not speaking to anybody from the time I got dropped off at school until I returned home, unless I asked a question in class."[90] By the time Sabbs enrolled in Americus High the climate remained hostile to black bodies. Her recollection of her experiences at Americus was summed up as "that was my season in hell, and it was not a one-shot deal or a few weeks. It was nine months, every year, for four years. It was like a jail sentence. . . . When I walked into Americus High School—I turned thirteen the year I went there. I went there at thirteen years old and I didn't know the world. I never, I had never experienced that kind of racism." She went on to note that "I was one of the few that came and stayed. But a lot

of them couldn't take it. . . . It was hard getting up every morning and going into the lion's den, because you never knew what was going to happen.
It was always danger, it was always mental and physical threats. There was
always maltreatment by the teachers."[91] Sabbs witnessed her sibling being
jailed for registering people to vote and being confined for weeks in the
horrid conditions of the Leesburg Stockade, yet it was her own fight to desegregate Americus that taught her the most about racism. Sandra Mansfield, who also participated as a youth in the movement and was one of
the Stolen Girls, had a similar experience. She was one of the first to integrate the high school but did not graduate from Americus because of the
abuse: "I didn't graduate because I went through so much. . . . It took a toll
on me because I went through so much. I had to take a break because I
burned out. Being called names at school and stuff and being spat on just
did something to me."[92] These recollections are pivotal to understanding
the educational farrago that continued during desegregation. Although they
were no longer receiving their white counterparts' used materials, students
were reminded of their second-class status in other overt ways. Furthermore, they did not have the protection that came with attending segregated
black schools. The contact with constant hostility meant that desegregation in Americus was not linear, and to portray it as such does a disservice to
the painful experiences endured by Freeman, Sabbs, Mansfield, and others
in order to obtain some degree of equality. Additionally, it diminishes the
role of those who perpetuated the hostilities, which made the goal of being
treated as a human being more difficult to achieve.

CHAPTER 4

EDUCATIONAL RESOURCES ARE
NOT FOR WHITE SCHOOLS ONLY

Power concedes nothing without a demand.
It never did and it never will.
—Frederick Douglass

O n June 30, 2012, alums from Colquitt County Training School, Charlie A. Gray Elementary, Moultrie High School for Negro Youth, and William Bryant High School came from all over the state of Georgia to participate in the eighth biennial Ram Round-Up reunion. This event took place in Moultrie, Georgia, for those who attended black schools from their founding years to the time they closed or were desegregated. The attendees used this event as an opportunity to celebrate the important bonds that were established and maintained during their adolescence. Although they went to school during the legal and/or prolonged years of segregation, they spent little time, if any, discussing segregation or the accompanying dilapidated conditions. Very few conversations arose about the political and economic disenfranchisement that many of their parents experienced, or the second-class citizenship that marked their educational tenure, which undoubtedly influenced their educational experiences. Ram Round-Up was a celebration of the people and places that cultivated them socially, emotionally, spiritually, and intellectually at the time they needed it the most. The weekend was spent discussing the teachers who had a profound impact on their lives, the characteristics of their principals, the pranks they pulled, and, of course, the football state championship of 1961. Alums noted that this was an event of which the memories are fond and therapeutic.[1]

Inevitably, the conversations within some circles illuminated the social components of education. Graduates of these segregated schools remembered lovers lost and lovers gained (some of whom are still married). As they ate, drank, danced, and laughed, the recollections of the bonds established and maintained with their peers portrayed how indelible those relationships were to their educational experiences. The emphasis on friendships was not just a matter of hindsight or nostalgia. Memoirs, oral histories, and school records reinforce that students understood the relational component of education in real time. Whether it is Anne Wheeler discussing how those bonds were strengthened during students' walks through white neighborhoods or documents portraying how black youth in Moultrie supported each other during the boycott, it is clear that relationships were important.[2] The reunion is a symbol of what existed and the need for its existence. Celebrating the good times with those who helped create memorable moments revives what was and what survived.

Despite the good memories that were elevated at the reunion, the former students of black schools in Moultrie have not forgotten about the inequities and challenges they faced during the same period they now celebrate. While they talked about the teachers who nurtured them and the peers who supported them, the social, economic, and political oppression of the period has not been forgotten. In fact, in the dedication section of the reunion "yearbook" are the words, "We remember the times we shared. . . . Laughter, tears, pains. . . . These were vital parts of our day to day living."[3] This discloses that the camaraderie black students experienced with their teachers and peers was connected to an institution that comforted them through adverse conditions that resulted in painful experiences. The actions that caused tears and pain did not lessen the importance of laughter. The benediction does, however, provide an example of the ubiquitous interconnectedness. White opposition did not stop blacks from creating memories, but it was an unwelcome partner because reminiscing on what was also reveals what was not and why.

Events and conversations during Ram Round-Up remind us of the continual dialogue between what is and what was, along with the variables that shape the current moments and moments to come.[4] For example, Dr. Delores Ensley Hawkins, a representative from President Barack Obama's presidential campaign, attended the reunion. While having someone representing the first black president at the event had to be exciting, it was a natural reminder of a period when a black person could not run for president, let alone a second term. Less than fifty years ago, some of the alums were advocating for educational resources equal to those afforded their white counterparts; now they were at a reunion living something that was once inconceivable. The historical significance of Obama's election and reelection, the celebration of black schools, and the activism of alums are connected by the oppressive ideas and realities that once made these events implausible. Black youth demanding the same resources as their white classmates is analogous to occupying a political office because both such resources and such offices were viewed by many as reserved for whites. Although alums from Moultrie chose to compartmentalize their experiences for the reunion, their lived experiences took place in the context of the sullied reality of white opposition.[5]

Despite the points of juxtaposition that existed under segregation and continued during the first two decades after *Brown*, alums of Colquitt County Training School, Moultrie High for Negro Youth, Charlie A. Gray Elementary, and William Bryant High concluded that those complexities were worth preserving. The reunion and their lived experiences signify a complexity that intertwines advancement and stagnation. From the time Moultrie was founded, black Moultrians experienced an educational farrago. Black youth entered a school system where the boundaries of citizenship and equality were fixed along racial lines, which meant that whites received the best resources available whereas blacks were given the leftovers. Even within that hostile context, black Moultrians created safe havens by developing healthy relationships and demanding better resources. Once students in Moultrie began to advocate for better facilities, they realized, as did their peers in Tifton and Americus, that a new norm could be established. New customs, however, would only be formed by those willing to challenge the racial traditions of Colquitt County, particularly in Moultrie, because whites were comfortable with the current social climate. As they fought to improve their educational facilities, these activists provided a template for fairness with the purpose of giving themselves an opportunity to live as full citizens, which challenged the racial boundaries of Moultrie. Decades later, an American "with a funny name," Barack Hussein Obama, would use a similarly audacious philosophy to run for president of the United States of America.[6]

Racial History and the Economics
of Educational Opportunities

The educational experiences of black Moultrians were shaped by economic variables that extended beyond their control. Like their peers from the region, controllers of the town's purse saw an economic benefit in providing a subpar education to those they viewed as laborers. Historian Robert Zieger has discussed the interconnection between race and labor and the profound implications it had on black families dating as far back as the Civil War. British historian Adam Fairclough has noted that many white southerners ignored policies promoted by the Fair Employment Practices Committee during World War II because they believed that "blacks were only fit for certain jobs, and white workers would never stand the presence of blacks in the same grades."[7] While Zieger and Fairclough's works elevate the connection between labor, race, and education from the Civil War to the civil rights movement, most of the scholarship on labor and race illustrates the various ways white southerners confined black workers to domestic or field work. Scholarship on race and labor, however, largely ignores how this ideology negatively affected the educational experiences of black youth. This is problematic because educational opportunities were directly shaped by economics that aligned with the racial history of a geographic location. Black students' educational opportunities being linked to a cost-benefit analysis was a practice executed throughout Colquitt County. People from rural areas like Doerun were even more vulnerable than their peers in Moultrie. Although the degree varied, the economic plight created by blacks' educational realities had very real consequences, because profit margins were factored into how much schooling they received.

Moultrie was founded in 1859 and named after General William Moultrie, who was a revolutionary war hero. Known primarily for its production in agriculture, the city experienced an economic boom as the local timber supply, mostly pine, supported the expansion of sawmills and the manufacture of products derived from pine resin. According to local historian W. A. Covington, during the same period a school was established along with a newspaper, a railroad, and several businesses.[8] Moultrie experienced another economic boom in the early twentieth century with the start of World War I. Southern historian William F. Holmes states that "the outbreak of World War I in 1914 created new demands for foodstuffs, and within a short time modern meat packing plants opened in Moultrie."[9]

When the meat packing plant was established in Moultrie, according to Covington, "it revolutionized agriculture and industry," which Moultrie needed.[10] Colquitt County benefited greatly from a diversity of commerce during this period but remained largely dependent on agriculture. Moultrie, more specifically, was a farmland community with limited diversity in its commerce. The overreliance on timber negatively affected black Moultrians because in the early twentieth century their worth, as whites saw it, was only visible through their labor. Therefore, sharecropping and domestic service were the primary areas in which they were employed.[11]

The economic success that occurred in Moultrie in the late nineteenth and early twentieth centuries did not include the black community. During this time, blacks remained economically dependent on whites. As southern and political historian John Smith states, "black tenant farmers and sharecroppers . . . remained in 'slavery of debt' to white landowners and cotton factors."[12] These kinds of economic restraints made it very difficult for blacks to establish educational structures or send their children to school with any regularity. Although histories of Moultrie tends to focus on the founding of the town and how it developed economically, the race relations that were established during its founding and their subsequent development over time are equally important because they placed the educational desires of blacks in Colquitt County in direct opposition with the town's economic viability. This adversarial relationship incentivized, instead of discouraged, white antagonism.

As with Americus, the history of black Moultrians is largely ignored during the early periods of Moultrie's history, but several inferences can be made about race relations by examining the level of equality based on the type of education citizens could access. Covington notes that a rudimentary elementary school was established in Moultrie in the late 1860s, but does not say whether black children had access to formal education during the period. However, local historians of Moultrie's black education Ruth Mason and Annie Ruth Thompson note that "education was a problem for Negroes in Colquitt County. In Moultrie, there were no exceptions. Around 1907–8 Negro children attended school in the C.M.E. Methodist Church."[13] Blacks throughout Georgia experienced an increase in their educational opportunities during the early twentieth century, but their schooling was definitely not equal to that of whites.[14] Educational opportunities changed in the 1920s when Moultrie High School for Negro Youth was built and, a decade later, when more improvements were made for black youth by the addition of tenth and eleventh grades. Black Moultrians faced less than equal improvements due to the political conundrum set forth by *Cumming*.[15] This 1899 case provided permission for local governments to operate an unequal educational system and local officials in Moultrie accepted this decision without any qualms. *Cumming* left black Moultrians with limited legal recourse. The real ramifications from this decision were revealed in school attendance data. For example, in the 1930s there were "7,074 whites" enrolled in school compared to only "1,870 colored."[16] Economics aided a sociopolitical structure that essentially forced blacks to constantly choose between earning enough through their labor to acquire basic living essentials or seeking education for themselves or their children in hope of future social mobility.

Attendance disparities between black and white students were exacerbated by exploitive relationships that constantly placed black parents in precarious situations. This disparity speaks directly to the educational and economic forms of opposition that were rampant in the area. In addition to constantly having to weigh between sending their children to school or the field, black parents had to deal with white farmers who did not believe black children needed an education to fulfill their positions in life. The systematization of confining them to perpetual labor resulted in a dual struggle that grossly undermined the educational opportunities of black students while devaluing their worth. Having grown up in Doerun, Ann Wheeler and her younger brother, Johnny McBurrows, remembered how education was stressed in their community, yet also how so few of their peers had access to a formal education. Because several black families remained tied to sharecropping in the rural parts of Colquitt County, education was very unstable. McBurrows noted that this was the case mostly for males, but black females' access to education was just as problematic. They were not expected to use their education for economic mobility, but to return to their stations in life as domestic workers. Wheeler recalled that in Doerun, "Once young black men, whose fathers did not own their own farm, got big enough [which was typically around the seventh grade], that was it for their education. It was unusual for black young males out of the rural area to [attend] high school."[17] While the educational level of black students in southwest Georgia increased during this period, too many of them were barred from the chance of improving their circumstances because of the oppressive context whites were able to sustain with protection from *Plessy* and *Cumming*.

Although black parents were in a very difficult position when it came to making decisions about the educational trajectory for their children, they played an essential role in their children obtaining formal education despite economic restrictions. Wheeler and McBurrows stated that it was because of their father, Sam McBurrows, that they were able to receive a formal education. Even though their father only had a third-grade education, he was determined to see all his children graduate from high school because he believed that education was the only tool that would liberate black people from the bonds of sharecropping and domestic work.[18] McBurrows said, "My father had what we called mother wit, and he was determined to see all his children obtained an education."[19] When parents made the decision to send their children to school, concessions had to be made by both parties. For example, Sam McBurrows picked up another job at the local fertilizing plant, and the children would sometimes only go to school for half a day. Although the white landowners that McBurrows sharecropped for agreed to this arrangement, several white farmers were against it. McBurrows and Wheeler vividly remembered their bus being stopped by a white farmer to return one of their classmates back to the farm. Like in many places throughout the South, education was viewed as the great equalizer in Colquitt County, but these constant actions challenged the viability of this idea.

In addition to being viewed as a commodity for farming, those who were fortunate enough to receive a formal education remained confined to a structure that continued its racialization on a second-class basis. Even though black parents sacrificed a great deal, the educational experiences of black youth in the 1950s and 1960s continued to be in direct contrast to the *Brown* decision. Regardless of the sacrifices made by parents or the legislation passed by the federal government, which was ignored, blacks in Colquitt County were not viewed as equals. Wheeler said that, throughout her educational career, she only remembered starting school on the first day once. In addition to constantly starting school late, she remembered the arduous and often dangerous miles she and her siblings had to walk to reach school. The toll the walk took was recalled by McBurrows: when he was in the third grade, he was so tired on the walk back from school that he tried to "ride this huge turtle because [he] was so beat."[20] Besides the physical toll, the legal advance of *Brown* could do nothing to address the nature of the walk: the same danger McBurrows's older sister and her classmates encountered, he experienced too. The continuation of segregation after it was outlawed meant that in order to get to school black youth still had to walk through the white side of town, where they often encountered different levels of harassment. Wheeler recalled that white youth "would sic the dogs on you because you were black and you were coming from school and you supposed to be working. . . . It was like sport to them. . . . Back then, we really were not considered humans. . . . It was normal to be harassed and threatened and picked at."[21] Black youth having to deal with the normalcy of being harassed was difficult enough, but the type of education they had access to shortly after *Brown* reinforced the idea of their second-class status.

White farmers, who controlled the school board, believed that educating black youth was a waste of time. In areas like Doerun the bare minimum was done, which explains why Wheeler spent all her elementary years at a church school and her siblings at former military barracks: the structures spoke to the intent just as much as the lack of resources. McBurrows remembered that the barracks "had no gas and no heat." In fact, the school board would only provide coal once a month, so the students "cut wood" to heat the barracks.[22] During this same period, a white high school was built in Doerun and another in Moultrie. Restricting the resources of black schools while providing a proportionally larger amount of resources to white schools with taxpayers' dollars was practiced throughout the South. School boards justified this practice after *Brown* as part of the town's norms, with no intention of changing.

Black youth who grew up in Moultrie did not have to deal with the same type of opposition their counterparts from the rural area faced because Moultrie was a small metropolis in southwest Georgia. By the mid-twentieth century, the town did not depend on the labor of black youth as did the surrounding rural communities. Therefore, students did not have to worry about starting the school year a month later or being removed by white farmers to go work the fields. Furthermore, their educational experiences were not full of dangerous encounters with white students who considered it a sport to terrorize black youth. Nevertheless, by the time those who grew up in the city met those who grew up in the county at the segregated William Bryant High School, the educational experiences of all had been influenced by the county's economic ethos and its racial history.

To those who experienced less of the mental, physical, and psychological violence perpetuated by white opposition in Colquitt County, it may have

appeared as if local white officials were more responsive to their black constituents by the mid-twentieth century. The data show that the school board
there was not as negligent as some of the officials from neighboring counties in addressing educational issues experienced by black students in years
past. Minutes from the school board's meetings reveal that members discussed the construction of Charlie A. Gray in 1953 as part of a larger conversation about the state's 1951 School Building Authority Act. This law
gave school officials the authority to use their discretion in determining
how building funds were allocated to "provide in the immediate future ad-
ditional buildings, facilities, and improvements."[23] With the authority given
by the state, local officials decided to make a number of improvements to
existing educational facilities and to build new ones, which included, for the
entire county, a couple of black elementary schools. The decision by the
school board to address the dire situation of black education speaks more
to the malleability of white opposition than to some form of progress. As
seen in Tifton, there were different levels and degrees of hostility displayed
by the school board, so including black schools in a plan that continued to
send the majority of resources to white schools did not allow blacks the
best chance for social and economic mobility. In fact, addressing only the
most dire conditions at William Bryant High epitomizes the board's willingness to operate within the racial framework, with the intention of making sure blacks remained within their allotted caste. Yes, there were limited
resources allocated to a black school, but only of the type that kept blacks
from rural areas susceptible to field work and those who lived in small cities
tied to menial labor. Even when school boards like Colquitt County's provided what they considered aid to black schools, the aid was less than blacks
requested.

From 1951 to 1965, members of the school board refused to use the
School Building Authority Act to put forth more than a few resolutions to
improve the structures of black schools. Simultaneously, they continued
traditional practices, which included black schools remaining the deposito-
ries of used materials from white schools, well after *Brown*. Several participants recalled receiving used books and buses that had been used by their
white counterparts. McBurrows stated, "We had secondhand books, we
rode on the secondhand school bus. Even when they bused us to school our
buses were the buses that had been used two or three years by the white
school."[24] As rural blacks who were able to survive the economic entrap-

ments of Colquitt County travelled to Moultrie for high school, they found out that black students who lived in the city were susceptible to very similar educational oppression as those who lived in the county.

The continuation of racialized practices established in the nineteenth century forced black youth to develop a keen sense about society.[25] Quickly they learned the town's racial ethos, because it was a survival mechanism. The reasons for constant harassment by their white counterparts and receiving secondhand materials became clearer as they got older. Institutional forms of harassment were systematic and a denial of one's citizenship. The older black youth became, the more they understood this reality, especially as they progressed through school. Jimmy Holton, alum of William Bryant High and leader of the student movement, noted that he and his classmates were aware at a young age of the materials they did not have but did not link the lack of resources to a larger struggle for citizenship and educational equality.[26] However, as they got older and became more aware of the racial divide that created their educational conditions, black youth in Moultrie grew increasingly frustrated because the opportunities afforded to the white citizens of Moultrie and Colquitt County continued to elude them. The racial inequities in Moultrie were so engrained that even a watershed case like *Brown* did little to disrupt the norm. In fact, *Brown* received little attention in Colquitt County, according to those who attended public schools at the time.[27]

Improvements that exploited black Moultrians' vulnerability were directly linked to the lack of economic opportunities that existed throughout the area. This scheme was established and upheld by local white officials and their supporters in Colquitt County, which made it difficult for black parents. For example, several blacks throughout the county had difficulty sending their children to Moultrie, where the only black high school in the county was located, which was used to support the argument that more schools were not needed in the area due to low enrollment. Various forms of racialized barriers to equality in public education hardened after *Brown*, with the majority of whites in Colquitt County being "opposed to integration at any time, in between times, and at all times, in all forms."[28] Therefore, the racial customs that were established at the town's founding continued to influence the educational experiences of black youth during the 1950s, 1960s, and early 1970s. The second-class treatment that blacks endured for nearly a century came to a head in the mid-1960s when black students decided to challenge the very foundation of the status quo.

Activism Birthed on the Other Side of Bliss

Black youth decided to attack the racial boundaries of Moultrie in the mid-1960s. Several factors contributed to their decision to fight against social norms that had been established and maintained since the city's founding. First, the level of frustration caused by dehumanizing practices reached a point where inaction was not an option. Second, SNCC had established a presence in the area. Finally, the Albany Movement had gained national notoriety, which provided their neighbors with a template of how to respond to racial matters. These factors, like in Tifton and Americus, were interconnected because their existence dealt with unsettling ills of the black experience, which ranged from having limited economic opportunities to hazardous school conditions. Too often, blacks found themselves at the bottom of the economic order with little opportunity for advancement and a lack of essential educational resources. Historians Timothy Minchin and John Salmond state, "decades of segregation had locked African Americans into the worst jobs, while whites gained significant economic benefits from this system." Furthermore, the authors suggest that whites often coerced blacks into settling for the status quo by threatening "that they could lose their jobs or homes if they enrolled their children in white schools."[29] Consistently, the economic booms that Moultrie experienced skipped over black Moultrians, which created an economic reality that kept most black adults from using specific opportunities to thwart the customs of the city. As a result, the civil unrest that occurred in the 1960s had been brewing since the late nineteenth century.

Throughout southwest Georgia, school boards and the black communities clashed because each group had diverging purposes for black education. These clashes were not equally matched because, like in other parts of America, black Moultrians did not have the same political influence as those who found comfort in their subjugation. The political ramifications of this uneven power structure allowed school officials to operate from a minimalist framework that contrasted with the concepts of equality and citizenship adopted by black adults and black youth.[30] This resulted in black students dealing with overcrowding and lacking basic educational resources. Until 1957, William Bryant High was responsible for educating all black youth in Moultrie from first through the twelfth grade. So little maintenance was being done at the school that by the late 1950s and early 1960s, the wear and tear of housing so many students had become obvious.[31] One of the common characteristics elevated by former students was how the structure of the school was declining because of overcrowding and the lack of upkeep. These memories were so salient to them because many of them returned to William Bryant for secondary education and the problems were still there. The intentional negligence by the school board continued an oppressive context for black students that left activism as the only viable option for improvements to occur.

The building of Charlie A. Gray may have been viewed as progress by those in power, but the regress should be acknowledged as well. Creating schools for black youth was an oppositional strategy adopted by many school boards throughout the South to prolong *Plessy*. Furthermore, the construction of Charlie A. Gray did not address the erosion of resources occurring at other black schools. Like *Brown*, the new school was needed but it did not end the systematic problems that existed at William Bryant, problems that also continued at the new school. However, when Charlie A. Gray opened its doors at the beginning of the school year in 1957, there were several black students who got the opportunity to be educated in a building equipped with basic resources, and they remembered how vastly different their elementary experiences were from their high school experiences.[32] J. W. Green Jr. began his educational career at William Bryant High but spent his elementary years at Charlie A. Gray.[33] He remembered the dramatic structural improvements at Gray. He also recalled the resources being somewhat better in elementary than they were in high school, but noted that students still "had it on a different scale" than their white counterparts.[34] Dale Williams, like Green, had the opportunity to attend the newly built school. When asked what he remembered most about his experiences, he stated, "It was a new structure, so everything was new and alike."[35] The same was recalled by Jimmy Holton when asked about his transition from the overcrowded school to the recently erected institution. Those who were able to attend the new black elementary school recalled the mood as one of relief rather than of progress.

When Charlie A. Gray was built, black youth in Moultrie understood that the actions taken were done out of necessity and for the avoidance of national attention rather than a sense of fairness. They grew up during a time that reinforced racial boundaries explicitly. The perpetual cycle of black students receiving their white counterparts' used materials denotes the constant presence of white opposition. As was the case in Tifton and

Americus, young black Moultrians continued to receive secondhand materials that whites deemed no longer good enough for their children. Holton stated, "All our materials, we had to share. We had to share books, share, share, share. Sometimes two would have one book or three had one book at one time. Then it was hand-me-downs. Most of the hand-me-down books were passed down to us and there [were] a few new books here and there, but not to accommodate a whole classroom. [Whites would] get new books and [every student in the] class would get new books."[36] Holton's recollection of his experience at Charlie A. Grey mirrored Green's, a younger classmate of his. Green remembered the secondhand materials this way: "We received hand-me-down or what the [white] schools [labeled old] materials. Once they finished with them and was ready to purchase new ones, they would send the old ones to us."[37] These racial customs continued in the newly built school. This reinforced to black youth that a new building did not equate to progress or equality. Outside of conceding a new building structure, school officials refused to acknowledge that black youth were entitled to the same materials as white youth, regardless of a federal mandate.

For this reason, Holton recalled always believing Charlie A. Gray was built "because [William Bryant] did not have the space." Moreover, Green suggested it was built on a "different scale," which reinforced the ideal that when resources were funneled to them, the additions still uniquely undergirded their second-class citizenship.[38] In other words, the addition of a new black school occurred simultaneously with the strengthening of racial customs that supported the low priority given to providing black students with a well-resourced education in Colquitt County. Consequently, as some black youth escaped the hazardous conditions of William Bryant High, it seemed a temporary escape, as the racial customs of Moultrie penetrated through the newly built structure and affected their educational experiences in similar ways. The school board's refusal to make any significant investments in black education could not be wiped away with the erection of an elementary school.

The conflict over public education intensified after *Brown* as local officials became more concerned about their exposure to outside entities meddling in local affairs and as black youth became increasingly intolerant of how the school board defined educational progress.[39] Even with outside agitation being a possibility and black youth growing more intolerant, the

Colquitt County School Board remained crafty as to how to provide educational opportunities for black students that were not on par with that of whites. School officials accomplished this by using a two-pronged approach. First, concessions should not disrupt the status quo, meaning that fundamental demands to equalize the school system were often ignored. For example, the building of Charlie A. Gray was a concession by the school board. William Bryant High was already overcrowded, and with the increased enrollment of rural students attending high school, something had to be done. Although the building of a black elementary school was a concession, it fell within the racial restrictions of Colquitt County. The fact that black students who attended Charlie A. Gray received nothing more than a new facility illuminates that they still functioned within the boundaries of educational inequality.

The other approach that the Colquitt County School Board utilized to sustain the status quo was to ignore the plight of black students altogether. By the mid-twentieth century, William Bryant reached overcapacity by 50 percent and lacked basic necessities like heat. Black youth also had to deal with their school being treated like a landfill for white schools to send old goods. The fact that school officials ignored the concerns of blacks fostered a climate in which black youth were confined to a second-class education. Although the approach taken by the board was not unique, these types of actions are often discussed as a byproduct of the Jim Crow South rather than a quintessential barrier to black students accessing resources needed to compete equally with their white counterparts. Given the context of denied access, it is not surprising that young black Moultrians refused to accept second-class treatment as a way of life. They viewed the school board's minimalist and apathetic approaches to their education as an attack on their rights as citizens of Colquitt County. Ironically, these approaches by school officials ignited the social movement in Moultrie. Students who had grown weary of waiting on a school board to do the right thing by improving the conditions of their school used direct action to demand improvements. Through direct action, black youth held public officials accountable by demanding that their educational needs no longer be ignored at the expense of remaining loyal to a racist ethos.

The decision to acquire equal resources through confrontational means was audacious because of the existential threat that existed. The omnipresence of white opposition was accompanied by fear tactics, which had to be considered by those who decided to use direct action, even black youth. In

Moultrie, the fear permeated differently than in the violent history of the Mississippi Delta or Birmingham; nevertheless, the fear that black Moultrians felt was a visible reality throughout the black community.[40] Southern historian Charles Payne's assertion that "fear was so obviously a hurdle to participating in the movement that it can easily become an all-purpose explanation" was not only applicable to the movement in Mississippi.[41] Fear kept a number of black people from participating in protests for a host of reasons throughout the South, and Moultrie was no different. As in the other settings, one reason several adults were hesitant to join the movement in Colquitt County was largely economic, as mentioned earlier. When Holton recalled what caused the fear of the black community in Moultrie, he noted that people were fearful "of losing their lives [and their] livelihood. You know, jobs. Klansmen had a great influence in Colquitt County [which meant] you could lose your job. People were scared of being harmed." In addition to noting that black adults were fearful, Holton stated that their fear was passed down to the youth: "Even [people] my age [were] afraid. [In fact,] most of the youth were afraid."[42] Williams, a classmate of Holton, agreed with his assessment that fear existed among the adults, but he did not feel that youth were as fearful. In fact, Williams believed that "children didn't realize how much danger they possibly could have been in," which implies that they were not as fearful as they should have been.[43] While the two may differ regarding the degree to which fear existed among the youth, both agreed that it was one of the characteristics exhibited within the black community in Moultrie during the late 1950s and early 1960s. Moreover, both of their recollections illuminate how black youth made the decision to directly advocate for better resources at a moment when educational agony was not decreasing.

The customs that existed intentionally established and maintained fear to stifle any challenges to the status quo. The degree to which fear influenced participation in the movement may be debatable, but the fact that it made it difficult for the movement to gain traction is not. The fear that existed in Moultrie was noticed by the leaders of SNCC as well. SNCC arrived in Moultrie in the summer of 1964. Enthused by some measured success with their Southwest Georgia Project, particularly the Albany Movement, they came to Colquitt County with the intention of mobilizing the black community around a social, political, and educational issue of the community's choosing. Aware of the political disenfranchisement taking place throughout southwest Georgia, SNCC usually galvanized people around voter registration. Mukasa Dada stated that "voter registration was used to get working-class people talking, which brought up other issues that blacks were dealing with in the community."[44] However, voter registration did not take off as they hoped because of fear. A letter from James Stanley Parry to SNCC's headquarters about Moultrie stated that "SNCC has been working in Moultrie since the summer, seemingly without success."[45] Many people were afraid, with reason, of what might happen to their jobs or their homes, or what might happen to their lives, if they were to participate in the movement.

Even though Blacks in Moultrie did not invite SNCC to Colquitt County, they were not upset at their presence. Yet that did not mean they were ready to become foot soldiers for the "cause." African Americans were aware of the injustices they faced daily but had not reached a collective consensus on how to address their concerns. Parry's letter summed it up this way: "Some had taken all they could of a society in which they were called 'boy' until their hair was white, where the only places for them were the back door and back of the broom, and had escaped through drunkenness and numbness. Others felt it was futile for five or ten or a hundred people to try to challenge what's been building in the South for three hundred years."[46] Besides the fear that was so entrenched in Moultrie during the mid-1960s, pessimism also made it very difficult for a social movement to gain traction. Before an effective social movement could take place in Moultrie, SNCC had to find enough people who were not held back by fear and believed they had the power to change the racial boundaries. This was a difficult task when they could not even get people to attend mass meetings. In such a climate, the community surely would not agree to participate in a boycott. For almost a year, Herman Kitchen and Isaac Simpkins attempted with little to no success to organize a social movement in Moultrie, but they eventually found a constituency and an issue that impelled the movement in Moultrie from nonexistent to relentlessly willing to challenge white opposition.

Out Front Fighting for What Is Just

Jimmy Holton, known throughout Moultrie as being the youth leader of the student movement, portrayed Moultrie after the *Brown* decision as a typical "small southern town" where Jim Crow laws ruled and any suggestion of change was met with opposition. He also noted that blacks were passive about directly challenging this way of life, which often made the small town appear to be stuck in time.[47] The intrinsic customs of Moultrie affected the possibility of the start of a social movement. Local whites were initially successful in limiting agitation to a handful of people. In an area where blacks were a considerable percentage of the population, when SNCC began recruiting, most were not available. Faced with the reality that adults, black or white, would not join the movement in significant numbers, the movement depended in its early days primarily on black youth.

As with the Tifton movement, black youth in Moultrie were out front when the civil rights movement started in Colquitt County. Unlike Barbara Johns, the Little Rock Nine, and other black youth who excelled academically and decided to become activists, the youth who were the first to heed SNCC's call to action were not ideal candidates, according to Holton. They would not have been selected to integrate the segregated white schools nor were they held in high regard. Holton described the initial joiners of the movement this way: "We weren't that popular. We weren't the brightest. I think, more or less, we were the wrong people doing the right thing."[48] He also suggested that some of the youth who joined the movement initially were not unfamiliar with disciplinary infractions; the foundation of the Moultrie Movement hinged on students who were not likely to be voted by classmates as the most likely to succeed. Nevertheless, it was high school students like Jimmy Holton who were the initiators and sustainers of the Moultrie Movement.

Young black activists in Moultrie were somewhat optimistic, because even though they had not personally witnessed a sociopolitical and education shift in their community, other nearby movements had proved that challenging Jim Crow was not an insurmountable task.[49] While there was no definitive evidence that segregation could be completely defeated, they relied on the evidence that showed them, in other parts of southwest Georgia and throughout the South, that the traditions of Jim Crow could be severely crippled. By the time SNCC arrived in Moultrie, black students were aware of the demands being made by their peers in the region. Williams noted that they were aware of the Albany Movement and how that movement "played a major role in what was going on" in Moultrie.[50] Therefore, it is not surprising that youth leadership and participation proved very pivotal in Moultrie because of the contributions that were being made by youth to the larger civil rights movement. In addition to believing that the impossible was possible due to the social context of the period, the individual and collective frustration deeply contributed to black youth being in the forefront in Moultrie. According to Holton, youth were driven by the social context of the period, but they also were tired of the culture that denied them their inalienable rights. "We wanted to be a people, we wanted to be a race of people that just said no, no, enough of this. It's time to say no to this. I think people needed the pride. Now we could stand up. . . . We're not afraid anymore."[51] The dissatisfaction felt among the youth, along with a degree of success from their neighboring peers, catapulted them to a leadership position and persuaded a number of them to join SNCC.

The events outside of Moultrie, combined with the dissatisfaction felt by Moultrie's black youth, not only swayed them to join but also influenced them to adopt the methods used by SNCC during the period. The adoption of direct action as a form of protest proved pivotal to challenging the systematic inequities in Moultrie. In the same letter, Parry wrote to SNCC's headquarters about the fear that existed within the black community. He also stated that "the younger people, the students, looked at things differently; things were in a mess, and it was intolerable to them to live in a world that needed so much. So, after a while, they got fed up and took matters out of their parents' hands."[52] Holton reiterated this point by noting, "there were ten to twelve of us trying to do some things. . . . We were fine. We had no fear. We would challenge them [by] walking into a restaurant. We did some things off and on because we didn't have that fear. Plus, we didn't have to worry about them firing us. We were independent."[53] The use of sporadic protest by young black Moultrians signaled the challenges they would address. Oral histories along with archival data reveal that it was the youth who initially took on the dangerous task of walking into segregated public facilities knowing they could be arrested or beaten. Although the initial acts were spontaneous, they were effective because they displayed a necessary form of agitation. Furthermore, these small yet impulsive forms of protest laid the foundation for the Moultrie Movement because, without them, the school movement might not have emerged. As acknowledgment of the need for a movement remained confined to secret conversations among black adults in Moultrie, black youth brought it to the public sphere. Those black youth who started on the frontline and remained there gave SNCC a presence in a place it desperately needed. With local black youth leading the charge, white officials could not attribute the feeling of dissatisfaction to outside agitation.

Responses Informed by Reality, Not Federal Intrusion

Brown was dormant for over fifteen years in Moultrie. In all honesty, black Moultrians did not have the desire to attend white schools, but they desperately desired that their schools be equipped with the necessary resources that would allow them to compete with their white counterparts. Additionally, eradication of the daily mistreatment was a high priority. An incident that happened to Green portrays the reality that kindled black students' decision to fight for equality in Moultrie. He stated that, while at the movies,

> my Sunday school teacher wanted a fountain soda. So, they would serve fountain soda at the drug store up on the corner. I knew the rules, go to the back stand at the back door and wait until you are asked, "Can I serve you," or "What do you want?" [As I was waiting] a term was used that I never heard before. . . . A white lady was standing in front of me with a child in her arms and by her leg, so the child said, "Mama, what's that?" and she turned around and looked and she said, "A nigger." So I looked back to see what a nigger was, but wasn't no one standing behind me. I was the only one there, and so I took it as being offensive, so I left out of the pharmacy without getting the fountain soda and ran down and told my mother that the woman just called me a nigger, and mama said, "That's alright, baby."[54]

Even though he was unaware of the economic constraints his mother faced at the time, the lesson Green learned was direct and painful. An ordinary day turned into a life lesson on citizenship, and the lesson he was taught was one that would be reinforced repeatedly. Although other black youth may not have experienced the citizenship lesson Green was taught because Moultrie was a very segregated place, their educational reality at William Bryant High was another excellent teacher. Williams remembered how he first came to understand his reality in high school, stating, "When I got to William Bryant is when I really became aware that things were being handed down to us. The books were secondhand and the laboratory equipment was secondhand."[55] The hand-me-down customs practiced at William Bryant made inequality relevant to them. Thus, the struggle for equality and citizenship was not an abstract exercise or the creation of an outside force. The personal impact of being treated as a second-class citizen had little to do with the successes or failures of a landmark federal decision. These customs were localized and so, too, were the responses by young black Moultrians.

Much like the educational realities of black youth in Tifton and Americus, black youth in Moultrie understood their realities on multiple fronts. Besides dealing with the very personal reality of being given old materials, a practical component existed as well. In fact, Williams suggested that it was the practical issues that became the tipping point for their activism: "The concern at that time was, it was February, and there was not heat. . . . We had suffered through this and it was cold for a while and the conditions were just deplorable."[56] In addition to students having to learn under circumstances that were far from ideal, William Bryant lost its accreditation because of the conditions, which had very practical consequences for black youth. Although the loss of accreditation meant little to the Southern Association of Colleges and Secondary Schools, it meant a lot to those who were enrolled in the school at the time.[57] Furthermore, black youth knew that the lack of improvements to their school was not a coincidence. A letter that summarizes the activity of SNCC in Moultrie began by implying that the reality black youth faced at William Bryant was not accidental, stating that "all the Negro high school students in Colquitt County go to William Bryant. The white high school, Moultrie High, is unfilled; Bryant High has 750 students in space for 500. There are two accreditation associations in Georgia, Bryant has been taken off both accreditation lists—it's been off one for two years. The school board hasn't become noticeably aroused—after all, Moultrie High is still accredited. The state board of education supplies textbooks for only 600 students; the city-county board supplies none. Five buildings used for classes are substandard or condemned."[58] Regardless of whether a student was coming from the rural parts of Colquitt County or the city of Moultrie, black youth who attended William Bryant faced several injustices that the school board was unwilling to correct.[59]

Just as whites in southwest Georgia consistently utilized the same strategies to suppress demands for equality, SNCC had effective ways to disrupt the status quo. The strategy adopted to ignite a social movement was to show how political disenfranchisement and lack of economic mobility interconnected with the educational system, which inevitably determined the type of education black youth had access to.[60] Although the interconnectedness of inequities is theoretically and pragmatically accurate, it was nearly impossible to address all three injustices simultaneously with the same level of zeal. Therefore, SNCC chose to use voter registration as the driving force because it had been successful in galvanizing the youth in Americus. This approach was somewhat effective, but a voter registration drive did not motivate the youth to join the movement. Black youth in Moultrie already knew they wanted to focus on improving the conditions at William Bryant High. They did not disregard the importance of achieving political enfranchisement and economic mobility for their parents, but those issues did not represent what they felt was the most salient issue. Stephen Tuck's suggestion that, "in the case of Moultrie, Colquitt County, school boycotts represented the culmination rather than the beginning of local protest" is shortsighted because it views the galvanization of the movement as the climax instead of the beginning.[61] The decision by those who largely comprised the movement to center it around improving the conditions at William Bryant challenged long-held traditions in Moultrie and supplied the impetus for the movement there.

Herman Kitchen, a member of SNCC and very instrumental in the Moultrie Movement, stated that, "for the past few months, Isaac and I have been working on research and organizing the community but people wouldn't work with me at first because I had to find out what they were really interested in doing. And it turned out that the kids wanted action to improve the high school."[62] Black youth focusing on educational equality were very similar to their counterparts in Tifton because their struggle was clearly defined. While it may be somewhat of an overstatement by Tuck when he suggests that improving the conditions at William Bryant High ranked highest among priorities within the larger movement in Moultrie, he is correct about the purpose of the protest when he states that "school boycotts were increasingly in protest at the poor equipment in the overwhelmingly black schools rather than a push for full integration."[63] The origin of the movement in Moultrie may be debatable and the order in which they wanted to address problems can be contested, but those who participated in the movement and the archival data are clear about the purpose of the movement. Young black Moultrians viewed educational equality from the point of view of resources improving at their school, a fundamentally different approach than that taken by *Brown*.

It did not take long for the members of SNCC and black students at William Bryant to agree that improving school conditions would be the focus of the Moultrie Movement. Nor did they spend a lot of time deciding on an effective tactic, because they knew a school boycott would get the attention of the school board. They also felt that the school board would oppose any improvements to William Bryant, which meant the protest could potentially be drawn out, which in turn meant that media coverage was a possibility. If any disagreement took place, it appeared to be over when the boycott should occur. Although the correspondence from Kitchen and Isaac portrays the protest in stages—SNCC galvanized students around the issue of educational improvements, they discussed strategies, then the protest occurred—it was not a seamless process. According to Holton, the boycott that eventually took place at William Bryant in 1965 had been scheduled to take place in the fall of 1964.

> The summer of 1964, we continued to meet and through [spontaneous protests performed over the summer] we became a little bit more visible. I thought, especially the month of July, we were going to move. We were ready to bring things down and things like that during the summer months. Let's block out the school before school gets started in September. So we tried to meet in August and tried to get the community together, tell parents not to let their children go to school in September, let's walk out. It was a good time to do it. We had July, August, kind of planned and looked at it and tried to get the people to meet, and they would not show up. That was in September. We said, okay, no problem. We got the Thanksgiving holiday is coming up. Let's do it again. So we go to Thanksgiving holiday, we were trying to get the people to do the mass meeting so we could block out this group because of all the conditions and quality. We want equal, we want to be separate but equal. We want everything, everything we need. Thanksgiving holiday passed by, then we've got the Christmas holidays coming up, so now we're trying to meet and do the same thing. So we go back after Christmas holiday. We're going to block out. We [went] to the barber [shop talking to] the guys, we are going to block out the school. Don't go to school. First of year [came] and at the beginning of the year [1965] William Bryant was full of students.[64]

Deciding the most effective moment to begin the boycott was not the only contested issue during the early phase of the movement. Williams noted that students' hesitancy stemmed from the conundrum in which they found themselves. On one hand, they agreed that the boycott was the most effective tool they had in addressing the issues they faced. On the other hand, they did not want to skip school because they "were taught that education was the way to better [themselves]."[65] Opinions differed on how immediately to begin, but the consensus was still that the boycott was needed.

Outside of the deplorable conditions and the accreditation issues at William Bryant, Herman Kitchen suggested that there was an economic component that persuaded students to act. He noted that the students "know that the county is getting $201,934 from the federal government for use in upgrading Colquitt County schools." Therefore, the protest was seen as a way to "prohibit or stop that money from coming into the schools on [an unequal] basis."[66] Once the sense of urgency increased among the youth, organizers and leaders of the movement felt they had enough participation to have an effective protest, so they began strategizing a plan that would fundamentally change William Bryant and Moultrie.

Kitchen and Isaac organized a mass meeting on February 2, 1965, at Friendship Baptist Church. The gathering was specifically for students and parents to discuss how they would go about demanding that William Bryant be improved immediately. Kitchen recalled that "we talked about immediate action and made plans for it, to correct the deficiencies of the school."[67] Although there were only twenty students at the meeting and four adults, those in attendance decided that they would proceed with the boycott. The students in attendance were responsible for making sure that 50 percent of the students enrolled in William Bryant participated. As the meeting adjourned, twenty black youth left determined to change the status quo. By the next morning, the Moultrie Movement had grown exponentially because of SNCC's organizational skills and the peer recruitment by black students.

The recruiting strategy by SNCC and black students worked. On February 3, 1965, several students at William Bryant High agreed to participate in the boycott. With a large student population willing to participate, the protest began as a sit-in. According to Kitchen, "by 9:30, there were more than three hundred pupils in the hall, singing songs and demanding to have a general assembly so that they could really find out from the superintendent and principal the facts about why the school was off the accredited list and what could be done to get it back on."[68] After their request for the general assembly was denied, the sit-in quickly turned into a boycott. The boycott did not result in students leaving the premises immediately. In fact, students initially "marched around the school." The movement quickly moved beyond school grounds and became an illustration that, as a SNCC member wrote, "all [blacks] were not happy down here."[69] The participation of so many youth from William Bryant illustrated that the frustration they felt was not just felt by a few.

Even though they reached their quota of participants, several more students wanted to participate in the boycott but could not. In fact, many students who did not participate in the boycott were just as tired of the conditions at their school as their classmates who left the school. Green, whose mother forbade him to participate, remembered how he wanted to be involved in the protest. "I was fourteen when they began to protest in our community, so my mother wouldn't allow me to march. I did things behind her back when she was at work, but I didn't go to meetings and things like that because she didn't want me to go to jail."[70] An article published in the *Moultrie Observer* illuminated that many had the desire to participate in the boycott but were not able or willing to defy their parents: "several students stayed behind because they had been disallowed from marching by their parents."[71] Sensitive to the predicament of their peers, youth leaders of the movement did not pressure students who were told by their parents not to participate. Besides, they had enough students involved to affect operations at William Bryant. The effect was twofold. First, "the county was losing $1500 or so every day because the students were out of school"; second, the students who remained at William Bryant were disengaged from what was going on inside the school because they were "busy looking wistfully out the windows as the march passed."[72] The unintended benefit of the internal disruption was that it magnified the external disruption by eliminating the appearance of normalcy. With a significant number of students either not attending school or being distracted by those not at school, William Bryant was not operational. This combination contributed to the early success of a movement that had had its difficulties deciding when to begin.

No Turning Back despite the Fierce Opposition

An idea that started with twenty students, four parents, and a couple of members from SNCC transformed into a movement. With the clear intention of improving conditions at William Bryant, they now dealt with an oppositional school board. After several hours of unsuccessful negotiations, more than five hundred students walked out of the dilapidated and non-accredited school and vowed not to return until their demands were met. Black youth wanted the superintendent to meet them at William Bryant High, but once that request was not granted, "they decided to march to the courthouse . . . hand-in-hand, in silence, in a line three blocks long."[73] On their way to the courthouse they experienced, like others before them, racial epithets and aggressive arrests. The racial epithets came from white onlookers who believed that black youth challenging the ethos of Moultrie was unacceptable. A march to the courthouse demanding "more teachers, more books, and a better school" warranted the same verbal abuse encountered by those who attempted to integrate white schools because, in the minds of many whites, it was a direct attack on their way of life.[74]

Verbal abuse was a common method used to articulate white dissatisfaction with activism, but so, too, were aggressive arrests. Police did not simply arrest black youth in a respectful or humane manner. The arrests were done in a way that was dehumanizing and intended to send a message. Immediately after the protest began, the police and the superintendent tried to squelch the protest without addressing the students' concerns by arresting students in a manner that would discourage others from participating in the boycott. When students did not respond to the superintendent's efforts to squelch the protest, according to the *Moultrie Observer*, "the police began arresting students and Deputy Sheriff Dennis McCorvey was hit by a brick." The brick was thrown because the "police announced that the grounds would be cleared by whatever means necessary and they called in another three or four cars of city and county cops." The students' fears surely were heightened by the increased presence of the police authority and the threat escalated those fears. However, the students also believed that "this was their school and they were the only ones trying to make it better."[75] The officers were perceived as a hindrance to the goal they were trying to achieve, and once officers entered the school, the tone of the protest changed dramatically.

A student who attended William Bryant remembered the incident and stated, "As cops began to arrest us, [several of] us sat down as a way to make it more difficult for the cops. However, the cops grabbed and started dragging, aiming for doorposts, rocks, dragging us along the ground, not even trying to lift us. One cop [kicked] my head as I was pulled by. They did the same with others. Kids kept singing, though they cried. As the first girl was dragged out, one boy couldn't accept this kind of treatment, yelled 'You can't do that,' picked up a rock, and threw it at the cop. They took out after him with guns drawn, and, from their talk, would cheerfully have killed him if they could have gotten a shot. Another girl, grabbed and carried by the head, bit one cop in the side."[76] Regardless of the defensive methods used by a few students, the police were the aggressors. The aggression did not end with the arrests of three hundred students. Like those in Americus, black youth in Moultrie endured constant hostility once they arrived at the police station. Two SNCC workers were arrested and "were in a cell for eight," whereas in "cells the same size, but [that] had double-decker bunks, and so [were] 'designed for 16,' they crammed 33 girls into one, with no light, and for several hours no heat."[77] The message that the superintendent and the police were sending to the students was one their parents were afraid they would learn, which was that the status quo would be protected by any means. The protest was only in its second day, and it had faced massive opposition. However, black students had shown the authorities and the school board that they were not easily frightened and had no intention of turning back.

In the face of fierce opposition, students from Moultrie remained undeterred in their desire to see equal education, as they defined it, materialize in Moultrie. The resolve of the participants in the movement was increased by the solidarity that had developed at the beginning of the movement, and it grew stronger as the fight progressed. Students at William Bryant already had deplorable school conditions as a unifying factor and the backlash they received for demanding better conditions and accreditation strengthened their resolve. Holton stated, "The most important thing we had to do, and we stood on this, was to be united. We were united as a race of people. In other words, we came together and showed some solidarity."[78] The unity displayed by black youth was pivotal to the boycott continuing because white officials were definitely unified.

An example that illuminates the solidarity that existed among black youth and between black youth and members of SNCC was everyone's willingness to remain in jail. Twenty-four hours had not passed before the organizers, the leaders, and the participants of the movement were arrested and jailed. Despite the horrid conditions, everyone who was arrested decided to remain in jail until everyone was released, due to the necessity of keeping the protest going. This undoubtedly put the boycott in grave danger, but everyone understood the importance of filling the jail. When the bond for each youth was set at twenty-two dollars, "all were determined to stay until all got out. Five or six parents insisted on bailing their children out, but several refused to leave." The decision to stay in jail was a unifying factor, but youth only had so much autonomy. Therefore, when some were forced by their parents to be bailed out, a number of them made sure they "stopped by their colleagues' cell to tell them they didn't want to leave and that they'd be back as soon as possible."[79] Youth who were totally committed both to their peers and to being obedient to their parents faced a difficult dilemma. For example, when Robert Shield's parents forbade him to take part in any more demonstrations and ordered him to return to school, "he left home and moved in with a friend."[80] While this decision by Shields was definitely not typical, his reaction and the reactions of those forced out of jail by their parents provide insight into the solidarity that existed during the period.

Another illustration that exemplifies the unified nature of the boycott occurred days later. On February 5, 1965, nearly three hundred other students marched to the courthouse demanding the release of all parties affiliated with the William Bryant High boycott, while repeating the initial demands made by the students who were in jail. SNCC member Willie Ricks (Mukasa Dada) told the chief of police that if "they weren't out by three o'clock there would be three hundred more coming in."[81] In addition, he stated that "if equal resources were not funneled to the black high school, they would be in the white school Monday morning getting it."[82] At the time, the threat may have seemed to be an idle one, but it was not: several parents filled out applications for their children to transfer to the white high school. This tactic was employed to bring attention to the discrepancies that existed between William Bryant and Moultrie High.

Both approaches were successful because the purpose of students flooding the jail or applying for admission to white schools was the same. The protesters wanted to force white school officials to respect their right to voice their grievances and address their concerns. By Friday evening, "all of the [youth] and Herman [Kitchen] were out of jail." The chief of police attempted to hold two SNCC workers but once the students made a fuss about that they eventually released the last two.[83] Although the boycott was still in its early stages, black youth felt that they had accomplished a great feat. Parry described the mood after the release of the boycott participants: "everybody was happy. . . . The feeling was different this time, like that of a victory parade after a football game because things started to happen."[84] Besides getting the participants released from jail, the *Moultrie Observer* noted that "the Moultrie School Board of Education agreed to meet with spokesmen from William Bryant and agree[d] to certain requests."[85] The requests that school officials agreed to—to implement a desegregation plan, work on restoring William Bryant's accreditation, and pave the roads around the school—were significant but fell short of all the demands, so students remained out of school.

The concessions that students forced the school board to make were transitory because, by Sunday, school officials began diluting the seriousness of the boycott by implying that the conditions at William Bryant were not as bad as the students claimed. The superintendent stated that "some of William Bryant's facilities are among the more modern structures in the city system." He also denied the students' claim of "being housed in a condemned building."[86] Instead of the school board addressing the deplorable conditions at the black high school, they spent nearly a week dismissing the educational experiences black youth had endured for decades. In a very direct way, the superintendent attempted to deny that the school board's negligence was a legitimate reason for the protest by trivializing the boycott.

The plan to dismiss the boycott did not work because external agencies came to Moultrie and validated the claims made by black youth. One of those outside organizations was the Georgia Teacher and Education Association (GTEA). Dr. Horace Tate, executive secretary of GTEA, requested that Dr. Claude Purcell, the state school superintendent, send representatives to Moultrie to investigate the conditions at William Bryant, and Dr. Purcell granted Dr. Tate's request. Members of GTEA conducted a thorough investigation which lasted two days and found that "inadequacies exist[ed]."[87] While GTEA performed their external investigation, black youth continued to put pressure on local politicians and school officials. From February 8 through February 11, black youth marched to the local school superintendent's office demanding that the inadequacies GTEA verified be addressed. On February 9, the school board made some concessions. According to the *Moultrie Observer* and confirmed by several SNCC files, "the board approved the purchase of 157 desks and $200 worth of library books." They also "promised $4,000 to blacktop the campus," which Kitchen noted "would not pave a small room."[88] Nearly a week after the boycott began and a few days after the investigation performed by GTEA, school officials continued to refuse to address the students' core demands. The ones they did address did little to change the educational experiences of black youth or the racial climate of Moultrie.

After the investigation, school officials no longer attempted to dismiss the conditions at William Bryant. Instead of going back and forth with GTEA, they noted that students were breaking the truancy law. If they continued to boycott, parents would be fined and students who refused to attend school would be arrested. While this was another attempt to force black students back to class, it only increased their resolve. From February 10 through February 17, nearly four hundred students were arrested for truancy and the attendance at William Bryant High dropped below 10 percent. According to Parry, black Moultrians viewed the superintendent's execution of the truancy law as a way to defuse the boycott, so again black parents responded by attempting to enroll their children in the white school. He noted that "the law said that the children must be enrolled in a school," but that when black parents requested transfers, they were all denied.[89] Given the fact that every black parent was turned away, it is evident that school officials were more concerned with the boycott ending than improving the educational conditions black youth faced. However, after weeks of circumventing the demands made by black students, school officials began addressing some of the issues that caused the movement.

On February 22, most of the students returned to William Bryant High with expectations that most of their demands would be met. Holton remembered that, after the boycott ended, "they finally got some [new] books and some maintenance work done on the building."[90] Although Kitchen thought that anything apart from a new school was not good enough, other members of SNCC noted victories from the boycott. A letter discussing the Moultrie Movement noted that "improvements to a large extent occurred. The school board was forced to hire teachers, buy books, start paving roads and landscaping the grounds. [They were also forced] to file an integration plan and bring the school up to standards such that it would be reaccredited."[91] Although students had fought for weeks for so much more, the boycott forced school officials to finally address some of the concerns put forth by the students at William Bryant.

Concessions without Transformation

Forcing officials to concede certain social norms and transforming a system are not the same. The results may look similar, but concession and transformation are very different. Those who led the boycott understood the main leverage they had in transforming the system was the boycott. Holton said he tried to keep the boycott alive because he believed that, once the students reentered William Bryant, the movement in Moultrie would shift from transformational to concessional. He also witnessed the movement move from being a student-led protest to one overtaken by adults, which he believed was detrimental to their cause. He stated, "we got tricked, we were doing good. . . . The boycott was a successful tool to get what we wanted because we shut the whole system down."[92] As long as the boycott was alive, schools, black and white, did not function fully because school officials had to spend so much of their attention and resources on the students at William Bryant. Ironically, the concessions made by the school board brought some form of normalcy to Moultrie, which was not entirely beneficial to black students.

Holton was not the only participant who felt that returning to school was not in the best interests of the students. Williams noted that by the time the decision was made to return to campus, "we had not accomplished what we were after."[93] Black youth wanted equality and they were not concerned with how long it took to obtain, but school officials and a growing segment of the black community were. Although black youth could wait school officials out because the evidence sided with them, their parents did not have that luxury. Unlike the students who participated, numerous adults had an economic penalty associated with the boycott. Parents were penalized for their children's involvement, so the concessions they were willing to accept put them at odds with the younger generation, particularly Holton. Besides believing that once his classmates reentered the school, they would not come back out, he also believed that most of the parents accepted the improvements proposed by the school board because they were scared. He noted, "we got what we call bootlicking leaders" who were in charge of the talks to end the boycott. It was they who came up with the agreement that if students returned to class then the improvements to William Bryant would occur.[94]

Whether the return by students to William Bryant was due to the shift in leadership, the economic penalty, or a mixture of two is debatable. However, those who participated in the movement agree that the movement lost a lot of momentum once the students returned to school. Undoubtedly, the boycott accomplished a great deal, but one can only wonder what transformational changes could have occurred if the boycott had continued. If black youth were able to force a school system that was clinging to the customs of Jim Crow to concede on a number of traditions in a matter of only two weeks, maybe a transformation would have occurred if the boycott had gone on longer.

CHAPTER 5

WHEN DESEGREGATION
WAS NOT ENOUGH

There is no magic, either in mixed schools
or in segregated schools. A mixed school
with poor and unsympathetic teachers,
with hostile public opinion, and no teaching
of truth concerning black folk, is bad.
—W. E. B. Du Bois

In 1935, W. E. B. Du Bois concluded that a unidirectional solution for solving the educational inequities persistent throughout America did not exist. His conclusion relied on empirical data established in the late nineteenth and early twentieth centuries that analyzed the interconnectedness of inequities using a multivalent approach.[1] By the time the NAACP Legal Defense Fund team started devising a plan to chisel at legalized injustices, a sound systemic analysis of the intersectionality between white opposition and the economic, political, and educational mobility of nonwhites was established. Humanists, social scientists, legal scholars, and various laypeople from different communities were conscious of how federal decisions were often soiled by racist ideologies that shaped outcomes in real time and affected future generations as well. Therefore, Du Bois's articulation of replacing a racialized form of segregation with a racialized form of desegregation foreshadowed the limitation of using desegregation as the primary tool to achieve the type of equality hoped for. The refusal to devise a plan that addressed the enormity of segregation diluted the power of *Brown* decades before the case made it to the Supreme Court, which is why student movements were essential in southwest Georgia and in other parts of country.

Outside of *Brown*, federal decisions and government officials are often treated as nonconsequential actors in the fight for educational equality. Likewise, the ideological shift among loyal white citizens from staunch supporters of federal rulings to antagonists is either couched as a legal fight between federal and state courts and governments, or deprioritized by those who choose to elevate the experiences and responses of marginalized communities. For different reasons, both approaches leave two distinct yet fundamental questions unanswered. First, if this was primarily a federal versus state fight, why was there no backlash from whites against other federal legal decisions regarding education, such as *Plessy* and *Cumming*? Second, advocacy to improve public education has always been in close proximity to the implementation and maintaining of a racialized school system, so how did that close contact with antagonism thwart progress? The answers to these questions lie within the multifaceted nature of continued opposition and resistance, as well as from scrutinizing the sociopolitical aftermath. White opposition was just as consequential to matters of education, both before and after *Brown*, as those who are celebrated for desegregating white schools. Treating these variables as disassociated entities does not explicate why educational equality was not achieved through desegregation.

Educational Equality and the Need for a Different Lens

To understand why local officials were so staunchly opposed to a particular federal decision and why the advocacy of black youth was just as audacious as the demands made under *Plessy*, one has to fundamentally shift the lens we use to operationalize educational equality. The first step is to challenge the linearity approach to educational history. A cursory reading of the history of American education reveals that public schools were segregated and that *Brown* ruled segregation unconstitutional. However, this does not explain why each generation has dealt with similar educational inequities. The second step is to see local officials and black youth as contradictory partners who were unequally affected by federal decisions. Because the power distribution was unequal, the narrative is much more complex than the progressive agenda, often at the core of this approach, would have it. This reframing clearly shows that education for blacks remained within a spectrum ranging from totally unequal to education for their white counter-parts to less unequal than the previous generation.[2] Lawyers who worked on the landmark case, black teacher organizations, and black parents and their children understood that the elimination of legal segregation in pub-lic schools was not synonymous with educational equality. *Brown* assisted in fostering a climate that made educational equality a possibility, but the incomplete implementation of the decision continued to restrict the edu-cational experiences of black youth. The gap between what was and what should have been reinforced the spectrum instead of eliminating it.

The goal of educational equality remained elusive for black youth, even after the outlawing of segregation, primarily because the ideas and actions of those who were marginalized were ignored.[3] For example, when black youth and civil rights organizations in Tifton, Americus, and Moultrie were fighting for their humanity to be recognized and equal resources allocated to their schools, concessions often fell woefully short of their demands. Ad-ditionally, when access was granted to well-resourced schools, a significant number of white officials, white administrators, white teachers, white par-ents, and white students often went out of their way to show black stu-dents they were not welcome.[4] The toxicity that accompanied desegrega-tion moved black youth further away from the educational equality they sought. Lorena Sabbs remembered how the barriers she and her peers faced shaped their understanding of what it meant to have rights without enforcement.[5]

Black youth attending public schools in southwest Georgia after *Brown* were not the only ones who understood the difference between having rights and having those rights fulfilled. In fact, the most powerful per-son in America during the most disputatious years of the implementation of *Brown*, Lyndon B. Johnson, agreed with black youth. In 1964, Presi-dent Johnson gave the commencement address at Howard University, en-titled "To Fulfill These Rights," where he noted that passing laws was not enough. He stated, "Freedom is not enough, you do not wipe away the scars of centuries by saying: Now you are free to go where you want, and do as you desire, and choose the leaders you please." The president explained why solely granting someone freedom was not enough by stating, "You do not take a person who, for years, has been hobbled by chains and liberate him, bring him up to the starting line of a race and then say, 'you are free to compete with all the others,' and still justly believe that you have been com-pletely fair."[6] This articulation by President Johnson was not a revelation to black youth like Sabbs, or to members of civil rights organizations. Still, having someone occupying the highest office in the land point to the limitations of solely placing people within the same spaces as the singular strategy to solving problems created by centuries of oppression, without addressing other issues, such as real-time hostilities, elevated the matter to national importance.

Even with Johnson's illumination of the limitations of the legislative process, he adopted the philosophy of being able to legislate fairness. Passing federal laws to correct the racial injustices that plagued the United States of America was common during this period. Johnson's predecessors—John F. Kennedy and Dwight Eisenhower—also believed federal legislation could address the systematic unfairness caused by centuries of racism—hence, both administrations' work on voter rights. While federal acts are often overly criticized for not going far enough or overpraised for ending racial inequities, the commonality of the actions was that they fostered opportunities for new possibilities in regard to equality and citizenship. Prior to these actions, for the most part, blacks were legally segregated and barred from the decision-making process regarding education, politics, and economics. Their separation and disenfranchisement had real consequences that federal laws and statutes were intended to address.[7]

Meanwhile, each legal decision that went against segregation faced fierce opposition from local officials and a large segment of the white population because several of them saw the decisions, primarily *Brown*, as an infringement on their way of life. Jason Sokol states, "As whites clung to discriminatory ideas and practices, their 'problem' gained depth and intensity. . . . Blacks decided to risk all for freedom, and whites had to respond."[8] So as whites responded locally, the degree to which federal rulings could cure centuries of injustice was invariably affected. Instead of the rulings becoming a basis for partnership between federal and local officials, they became points of contention. Throughout the period, federal rulings rarely fulfilled their purpose, but most of that can be attributed to the opposition they faced. Regardless of how sincere judges were when they handed down landmark rulings, the implementation of the decisions usually had to be carried out by local officials. Therefore, federal actions cannot be examined exclusively through a national lens. Although the implementation of and the opposition to *Brown* occurred on different levels throughout the South, leaders and their white constituents in each state were determined to maintain a system in which the ideals of Jim Crow prevailed, even when the system was forced to compromise. An in-depth analysis reveals that white opposition was not isolated to a few states. In fact, it has been noted, "Not long after the Supreme Court . . . outlawed segregated schools, the job of racially integrating those schools proved not only politically unpopular but difficult in a practical sense as well."[9] When segregation, discrimination, and political disenfranchisement were ruled unconstitutional, state officials, particularly those in the South, attempted to ignore, circumvent, or meet the minimum requirements of the rulings. Unfortunately, state officials and local white populations were not as concerned about addressing the injustices that were rampant throughout the country. Their lack of concern had profound consequences for the educational experiences of black youth, the economic and social mobility of the black community, and blacks' political influence.

Many who hoped federal rulings would bring new opportunities quickly realized that decisions were one thing and implementation was something totally different. This was on display in Georgia. Stephen Tuck notes, "The history of Georgia sheds light on how local movements emerged and developed."[10] From Herman Talmadge to Carl E. Sanders, state officials made it clear that Georgia officials had no intention of willfully doing away with practices President Johnson deemed counter to his vision of the Great Society.[11] Furthermore, state and local leaders made it painfully clear that they had no intention of accepting federal mandates to aid in the equalization of American or Georgian society. Invariably, this created a conundrum because federal rulings granted blacks access to arenas into which they had been denied entry for centuries, but states like Georgia disregarded those rulings for decades. Prior to the 1960s, most black Georgians remained confined to the margins of society. Second-class education, segregation, economic stagnation, and political disenfranchisement were too common, particularly in smaller metropolises like Albany, Tifton, Americus, and Moultrie. Federal rulings did very little to move blacks away from the margins because the landmark decisions and civil rights legislation were often ignored or diluted to the point where the effect was limited. Georgia, a very influential southern state, made it clear that it had very little intention of desegregating public schools, providing blacks access to public facilities, or removing the barriers that made it difficult for blacks to exercise their right to vote. White Georgians—politicians, leaders, parents, students, and administrators—were loyal to the customs of Jim Crow, and it would take more than court decisions or legislative exercises for them to be persuaded that there was life after Jim Crow.

The Desire to Be Included and
the Power of Systemic Exclusion

At the crux of the educational farrago are the dynamics of blacks' desire and limited power to transform public schooling into a democratic institution versus whites' desire and unchecked power to continue a racialized school system after *Brown*. This continued tension meant that placing people in proximity to one another did not alleviate the fundamental disagreements that had existed since the creation of public schools in America. Blacks always had a greater desire for education than whites did for blacks being educated.[12] Furthermore, the unequal distribution of power favored the desires of whites, but blacks were not totally powerless. In fact, it was the desire and power wielded by young black people and civil rights organizations that took judicial and legislative exercises from the courtroom and the legislature to local institutions, most notably public schools. As Lorena Sabbs stated, "The rule of law is only something on paper until it's challenged, until people are made to get it right. If that means overflowing their jails, if it means boycotting their retail establishments or whatever, something has to be done."[13] Her distinction between what was legal and what was lived encapsulates the educational experiences of black youth attending public schools during this period. By acting feverishly to close this gap, Sabbs and her peers, knowingly or unknowingly, carried on a tradition that existed within the long black freedom struggle since the seventeenth century to embody what was being fought for. Placing deeds with words accompanied the struggle for equality for blacks because the legislative process repeatedly showed equality could not be achieved through mere reliance on the law.[14] The birth of Jim Crow, sanctioned by *Plessy*, came after the ratification of the Fourteenth Amendment, which amplifies Sabbs's articulation of why she and her peers felt obligated to fight. Adopting direct action as a tactic to achieve equality conveys the lack of confidence that existed within black communities throughout southwest Georgia that they could rely on the legal process to obtain equality. Because their sociopolitical experiences were linked to a legal history that either contributed to inequities or ignored their plight, relying on the legal process to achieve their desired goals was a nonstarter. Despite the disadvantages, black youth, along with the organizations that agreed with their ideas, felt obligated to become the actual people needed for legal decisions addressing inequities to be effective. It was one thing to demand freedom, equality, justice, and citizenship, but it was another thing to become the tangible symbol of what was being demanded. Their audaciousness in embodying the variables of equality directly challenged exclusionary practices targeting black youth and contributed to the functionality of society and public schools, writ large.

Despite the federal actions, blacks remained the burden-bearers for various forms of fairness to be implemented. Although this responsibility did not originate during the mid-twentieth century, the role changed dramatically during this period. Prior to the mid-1900s, blacks, for the most part, advocated for equality and citizenship using legal avenues, gradualism, and self-help. However, those who took up the mantle during the mid-twentieth century accepted the responsibility of being the ones who would make sure fairness occurred, but the characteristics changed considerably. Blacks, particularly the youth, continued to use the courts and self-help as means to achieve equality, but gradualism was rarely accepted. As more young people became involved in the struggle, urgency replaced gradualism as the approach to achieving equality. Consequently, direct action became the most prevalent form of protest toward the end of the 1950s and throughout the 1960s and early 1970s, which inevitably changed the tenor of the period. The change in tone can be directly attributed to the frustration several black communities felt because federal rulings and federal legislation made little local impact. As more black youth felt compelled to respond to the social and political ills they faced, the movement became less about what federal rulings were not doing and more about what local officials were not allowing to occur. Youth, along with organizations like SNCC and the SCLC, indicted local leaders and local citizens as perpetrators of a system that promoted inequality. Therefore, black students did not spend an inordinate amount of time critiquing national politicians or federal officials, because the legal arena was no longer the problem. By the time most youth decided to join the freedom struggle, blacks legally had the right to vote and to attend the school of their choosing. However, the social norms that were practiced locally made attaining these rights all but impossible. This dynamic essentially transformed a top-down movement where the federal government and national organizations used legislation to achieve equality into a bottom-up localized movement where equality would be gained through various degrees of protest.[15]

This is not to say that local blacks, particularly black youth, excused national leaders for their inaction and their often passive compromises. For example, the second year of the national event "Youth March for Integrated Schools" shows how federal officials were not immune to criticism. A. Phillip Randolph and several youth participants criticized President Eisenhower for not appearing at the event. Later on, President Kennedy was criticized for his refusal to protect the Freedom Riders, and President Johnson was criticized for not aiding the marchers crossing the Edmund Pettus Bridge in Selma, Alabama.[16] So by no means was the federal government excused by blacks for them being left to largely fend for themselves. However, the reality of the period was that the federal government assumed the position of legislator and occasionally provided protection, as was the case in Little Rock. Although several blacks took issue with this arrangement, they took solace in the fact that most of the federal actions during this period sided with the cause for equality.

Events that transpired throughout the South, particularly in Tifton, Americus, and Moultrie, during the mid-twentieth century illustrate that desire and power were unfairly distributed, but they were not solely dominated by those in power. While local officials and the constituents they prioritized largely contributed to the delay of desegregation and its one-way implementation, those who were marginalized by this relationship had the zeal to gain enough power to improve certain elements of public education (i.e., treatment, resources, and access). Although their achievements were aided by legal decisions, elements of white opposition remained constant during the same period, and that powerful variable altered the results of the demands being made by black youth and civil rights organizations throughout southwest Georgia. The ability of white opposition to weaken the legislative process and the advocacy of those pushing for equality provide insight into why educational inequality remained more than a vestige of segregation. Because this duality remained uneven, what public schools became continued to be primarily shaped by those who were invested in socioeconomic and sociopolitical inequities. Instead of using *Brown* as an opportunity to improve race relations through democratizing public education, a significant number of those with power chose to remain wedded to ideologies that weaponized public schools as an institution in which black minds were viewed as inferior, black bodies were seen as those of laborers, and the allocation of resources remained in the hands of whites.[17] The infusion of racialized ideologies and the implementation of desegregation illuminate how components of *Plessy* persevered at a pivotal moment in American history when social activism was so rapid.[18]

The increased participation of youth fighting for educational equality did not lend itself to greater cooperation from those who had power or those affiliated with the powerful. In fact, youth activists like Juanita Wilson (Bynum) of Americus, Georgia, saw the correlation between youth advocating for their constitutional rights and the increase in white opposition in real time. She stated, "Let me tell something about white men, baby. Whatever it is that's going to give you equality, they are always skimming to minimize that equality."[19] Examples of this lived reality were found in the complexities of implementing desegregation, the rampant voter disenfranchisement, and the resource gap between white and black schools. The constant attempt to weaken legal decisions explains why Wilson's generation felt obligated to go into segregated primary and secondary schools and public universities to make *Brown* somewhat of a reality, which provided a degree of measurable progress. Furthermore, their sense of obligation pushed them and organizations like SNCC to register people to vote, which fortified the usefulness and the effectiveness of the Voting Rights Act. And it was these same youth who picketed and marched for better housing, better jobs, and access to public facilities. While federal rulings and legislation gave blacks the legal high ground, it was largely left up to blacks to see those rulings implemented. In addition to being responsible for the implementation of the rulings, blacks were also responsible for changing the minds and hearts of local whites. Examining the activism of black youth through a national and local context illuminates how they constantly pushed federal rulings further and pushed back against opposition they felt denied any component of their citizenship.

Young people who lived through the passage and implementation of *Brown* experienced a myriad of emotions that shaped their interaction with public school. For example, Fran Kitchen of Tifton remembered desegregation not being discussed much until freedom of choice requirements came about. When black Tiftonians were given the choice to attend formerly segregated white schools, Kitchen recalled the fear that permeated the community. She stated, "A lot of the parents [were] just afraid, they didn't want their children hurt."[20] Her recollection of fear was not isolated to Tifton. Her counterparts in Americus and Moultrie remembered the fear of black students being hurt, demoted, and treated unfairly as a fundamental part of the desegregation story in southwest Georgia. The fear that existed throughout the region can be largely attributed to the unfair way desegregation was enforced. Black students who were academically astute and well-behaved were often chosen to desegregate, but they were often treated as if they were inferior.[21] The continuation of white opposition being the context after desegregation is a sobering reminder of the limitations of proximity. Desegregation placed black students in more well-resourced schools and simultaneously exposed them to hostility that previous generations did not encounter. This is not to suggest that segregation was better, but it does force us to recognize what occurred when "second-class" desegregation was implemented.[22] Dr. Horace Tate, executive secretary of the Georgia Teachers and Education Association, referred to "second-class" integration as evil because it presented a facade of progress while remaining tied to the ideals that created the need for progress. The inherent contradictions in the implementation of desegregation provide enough evidence that desegregation alone was not going to alleviate a large amount of the educational, social, economic, and political suffering experienced by black youth and their parents. In fact, desegregation was only one of many elements local white Georgians opposed. They opposed voting rights for blacks, economic mobility, better treatment for blacks, and improving the conditions of black schools. An examination of Tifton, Americus, and Moultrie illuminates why desegregation was not enough and how educational inequities, voter suppression, and economic stagnation were interconnected struggles that played out throughout southwest Georgia.

Lessons Learned from a Moment in Time

The story of black youth refusing to accept inequality, specifically unequal education, in the aftermath of *Brown* is as much an indictment of America's public school system and those who wanted to preserve an antiquated system as it is a means to examine the ways in which black students advocated for equal education. Unfortunately, black youth faced a matrix of educational inequities from 1954 to 1972 because whites refused to accept a number of legal decisions and laws meant to improve the lives of blacks. Archival data as well as scholarship depict how white resistance was instrumental in creating an educational climate that was not beneficial to black students.[23] They were often met with hostility from white students, parents, and administrators. Too often, black youth experienced prevailing educational conditions that sought to subordinate and not educate. Ironically, the hostile nature of public schools, particularly in the South, influenced the activism of countless black youth. Gael Graham notes that "high school students absorbed the lessons and messages drawn from outside societal conflicts at the same time that local conditions galvanized them to respond to specific issues."[24] She is correct in that tension created opportunities for youth to articulate their concerns. The implication, however, that it was "outside conflicts" that contributed to the activism of black youth is not entirely accurate. Black students were immensely intimate with one of the societal sectors creating conflict. Public schools in southwest Georgia maintained an adversarial educational climate for black students, and students routinely responded to the inequities that they found most egregious. This resulted in black youth not being able to fully enjoy their adolescence because the educational system, along with societal norms, reinforced that they were different, less than human, and did not have the same rights as white Americans. Therefore, the primary indictment of public schools during the post-*Brown* era was their failure to create a climate in which the intellectual, cultural, and creative skills of black youth were cultivated. Black students, however, emphatically rejected this arrangement by unapologetically becoming warriors for freedom.[25]

The energy and activism of black youth within the context of white opposition reveal that public schools aided in creating gaps that were racialized.[26] After *Brown* established that segregation violated the Fourteenth Amendment, public schools continued operating under the guise of gradualism without intending that the majority of black students would have access to the type of education afforded to whites.[27] It is important to return to Marshall Frady's article "Discovering One Another in a Georgia Town" to illuminate that the public schools were not neutral. While public schools in the South, particularly in Americus, were receiving kudos for their implementation of desegregation, they were simultaneously mistreating black students, overdisciplining them, and beginning a trend of black students being overrepresented in special needs courses.[28] These early phenomena were racialized, and they allowed the farrago of public schools to continue after the *Brown* decision. It is difficult to conclude that black youth, with their focus on equal treatment, were foreshadowing, but their prioritization of equal treatment provides a keen lesson on why it needs to be elevated.

When equal treatment of students is not intentionally prioritized, then formerly segregated schools regress to the default, which *Brown* declared and black students knew was problematic. Treating students with a certain level of dignity is essential to creating learning institutions that work for all parties involved.

The other lesson learned was how black students spent a lot of energy on improving the educational conditions in their schools. When the movement reached Tifton, leaders were able to galvanize the students around getting better resources for their school. While there were federal actions trying to enforce desegregation after *Brown*, one of the earliest forms of activism that took place in southwest Georgia focused mainly on improving the resources that were being funneled into black schools. Alton Pertilla, Walter Dykes, Johnny Terrell, and Major Wright all noted that what made them get involved in the movement was the personal connection they had with their school and how it was important to see the conditions improve. They also noted how black students interpreted the secondhand materials and the lack of resources as a reflection of how the local school board viewed them as citizens. As youth, they all noted how limited resources along with the inequities their parents faced meant that they were not viewed as citizens. Given the fact that students equated comparable resources with equality and full citizenship, it is not surprising that the demands made by young black Tiftonians during this period focused primarily on improving the resources at their school. Of course, their fight for better educational facilities also improved life in other areas, such as voter participation. The Tifton experience is one example of how youth forced local officials to concede on some of the practices of Jim Crow, and it illuminates how progress and regress continued to occupy the same space up until the early 1970s.

Researching the activism of black youth reveals the way they defined equal education. The data suggest that through their activism they operationalized and conceptualized what equal education meant. Oral histories and archival data are clear about what black youth, post-*Brown*, expected. They did not seek the implementation of the *Brown* decision as much as they sought equality itself, whether they were attending a white school or a black school. Furthermore, they were motivated by the larger civil rights movement and the inability of their parents to act. More than that, they did not separate educational ideas from other forms of inequality. These points were illuminated in Tifton, Americus, and Moultrie.

This study also reveals the complex relationship between civil rights or-

ganizations and student activism. We have heard the story of black youth
being influenced by organizations or just mimicking organizations; however, exploring the relationship between black students and organizations
in southwest Georgia reveals a more complex narrative. Black youth were
indeed influenced by organizations and mirrored some of their ways, but
they also influenced organizations. Scott Baker discusses how the energy
and perseverance of the youth motivated organizations to stay involved
when morale in the local community was low.[29] Just as black youth gave national organizations a jolt when needed, SNCC and the SCLC gave students a place where their ideas were cultivated and appreciated, as educational historians David Cecelski and Dionne Danns have pointed out.[30]
Thus, the relationship that existed between black youth and national organizations was essential to shaping the struggle for equality. Their mutual interest in fighting against an oppressive system created a relationship that
was connected through circumstances and shared ideologies. As a result of
that relationship, black youth knew that when they fought against educational injustices, they could depend on SNCC and the SCLC for physical
and emotional support. Likewise, national organizations recognized they
could count on black youth when they needed people to protest any form
of segregation. Although student leaders like Major Wright and leaders of
organizations like Willie Ricks faced a different set of obstacles, they recognized that those obstacles were caused by the same oppressive system. The
common objective of defeating inequities caused by white oppression made
the decision to join forces beneficial to both parties.

Elevating the ideas and activism of black youth cannot be done without simultaneously analyzing the somber reality of how the innocence of
youth, embodied in havens of childhood, was altered for black students by
an oppressive educational system. The literature too often elevates the heroism of black youth without exploring the pain and damage that accompanied their struggle. As Lorena Sabbs recalled when reflecting on the pain
she endured as a youth activist, "the fourteen-year-old girl is in there some-
where."[31] The scars from those struggles affected the childhood of black
youth because they were interconnected with their educational experiences. Capturing the conundrum of fighting for what was just while simultaneously experiencing the pain of fighting provides a more accurate
description of what young activists experienced, which helps extend the literature of American education in general and black education specifically.
Additionally, elevating the pain that accompanied the different ways black

youth participated in the struggle for equal education reflects more accurately the totality of white opposition.

The nationally known stories of black youth such as the Little Rock Nine entering white schools and being treated in a hostile manner but persevering reflect the experience of countless black students throughout the South. We need to broaden our narrative of the black youth who are recognized for their bravery—in particular, to recognize the bravery of black youth whose fight for educational equality had little or nothing to do with desegregation per se. Unfortunately, these activists are too often ignored in the literature and during our commemorations. Ignoring their ideas and contributions to the struggle to make public schools more equitable skews the definition of educational equality in a way that lends itself to a definition and practice of equal education that allows forms of marginalization to continue.

EPILOGUE

THE ELUSIVE NATURE OF
EDUCATIONAL EQUALITY

I see only one face—the face of the future. . . .
I cannot help thinking—that a hundred years from
now the historians will be calling this not the beat
generation, but the generation of integration.
—Dr. Martin Luther King Jr.

O ver sixty years ago, Dr. Martin Luther King Jr. prophesied that the generation attending public schools after *Brown* would accomplish a feat, to live in a racially integrated society, that generations before them could not. Embedded in his prophesy was an accepted ideology that separation fueled racial hostility and racial anxiety that integration could quell.[1] Public schools amplified the hope of ending systemic racism through people occupying the same public spaces. Utilizing educational institutions as laboratories to cure societal ills ignored how those institutions contributed to those ills. King did not have to wait a hundred years to see if the generation attending public schools after *Brown* would live up to the tumultuous task of eradicating racism because whites used schools to announce their forthright opposition to desegregation. Within a decade, King went from having unequivocal hope in the possibilities of integration to calling for a "genuine equality" that demanded federal and local governments go beyond proximity.[2] The evolution in his thinking coincided with events that were occurring in real time, explaining why integration remained elusive for the majority of black students decades after *Brown*. Persistent rejection of various calls for improvement made it difficult to keep hope that public schools would positively contribute to the fight for educational equality.

Academic institutions did not become transformative because there were not enough whites willing to share the burden. At the foundation of King's hope was the belief that a partnership would form, but when the moment came for members of the "integration generation" to decide if they would be different, a number of whites adamantly opposed transformation while others remained silent. Thus, assessing if the generation attending public schools after *Brown* would become the "generation of integration" did not take a century to determine. Although some degree of racial intermingling occurred, the limited extent to which integration was systematically implemented did not compare to that of segregation.[3] Unfortunately, by the late 1960s and early 1970s, there were enough data to distinguish between the rhetoric of equality and the reality of continued segregation and other forms of inequality. Widespread realities challenged the idea that whites wanted to assist in placing public education on a unidirectional path toward equality. Too often the educational experiences of black students were the opposite of inclusive, tolerant, or equal. Historian Rebecca de Schweinitz argues that educational gains were made but that black students still felt inequalities persisted daily. She states, "young people expressed dissatisfaction with better but nevertheless inadequate and inferior schools and educational programs."[4] The opposition that black youth experienced well into the late 1960s was also documented by the Civil Rights Commission.[5] A statement given by the commission in 1969 noted that "the Attorney General and the Secretary of Health, Education, and Welfare had urged that no action be taken to slow the pace of school desegregation."[6] The commission referred to states asking the federal government to slow down the plans to desegregate America's public schools and requesting that federal monies not be withheld from states that refused to desegregate. The only power that the federal government had over the states was the ability to withhold educational dollars from states that refused a federal mandate. The commission went on to state, "the statistics purporting to show the present extent of school desegregation . . . give an overly optimistic, misleading and inaccurate picture of the scope of desegregation actually achieved."[7] The commission's statement provides insight not necessarily on the success or failure of desegregation but more about people who were opposed to implementing real educational changes. The fact that a fight remained against desegregation nearly twenty years after the passage of *Brown* unveils the political and social climate that prevailed in counties where local officials were actively advocating against the pursuit of correcting historical wrongs.

The Civil Rights Commission statement revealed that southern states were more concerned with being able to control their educational policies than making education more inclusive and equal for black students.[8] One of the issues the commission saw with the way desegregation was being implemented was that "white students and teachers frequently harass and punish the black children whose parents have chosen to send their children to formerly white-attended schools." The commission concluded, "we are deeply concerned over the directions recently being taken in Federal efforts to desegregate elementary and secondary schools."[9] Even though the commission mainly focused on the status of desegregation in public schools, their concerns were analogous to the problems black students articulated. Lived experiences along with commissioned reports articulate how the circuitous route chosen by those in power to implement a diluted form of educational equality consistently resulted in black students being placed within the constitutionality of fairness without experiencing the totality of educational equality.

The begrudging approach to educational changes has not prevented this historical moment from being viewed and elevated as progress, despite the reluctance that continued to motivate the marginalization of black students. Ironically, even though the educational farrago continued decades after the outlawing of segregation, the mid-twentieth century is consistently pointed to by politicians, scholars, philanthropists, and citizens as the watershed period that placed us on the pathway to educational equality. It is very difficult to have a conversation about public schooling and educational equality and not discuss *Brown*. The natural progression of this conversation, intentionally or unintentionally, links educational equality with *Brown*, which implies that the goals have been achieved. Unfortunately, this has led to a false sense of accomplishment that the data do not support. Although blacks and other marginalized students have made gains since the passage of *Brown*, there have also been regressions—public schools remain largely segregated, black students remain overdisciplined and underrepresented in advanced courses—that should concern every American citizen.[10]

A desire to believe that public schools are fundamentally better today than they were sixty-five years ago prevents us from understanding the intimacy between the past and the present, which aids in explaining continued inequities. The disconnect between what we think we have achieved versus what we have achieved can be explained by Toni Morrison's caution against abstract history: "The past is something that has to be confronted. [History] is a relationship between our personal history and our racial history that sometimes gets made distant."[11] Morrison subsequently notes that in looking at a distant phase of history, we often fail to elevate the complications of a period in time and instead infuse it with what is comforting to us. Her articulation is apropos when reflecting on the desegregation era: that history is often viewed through a lens that detaches the personal history from the racial history, which makes the narrative more palatable. Additionally, this historical detachment promotes a false sense of progress, because in the present there is no governor standing in the schoolhouse door and there are no black students being escorted into school by the national guard. But if this is the standard to measure progress, then "equality" existed within a short time after the *Brown* decision in those places where violence did not erupt and federal assistance was not needed.[12] We know, however, that progress is more than the removal of hostility, and the path toward equality is more than placing people together in physical proximity. We must reject an abstract history that falsely portrays we were closer to achieving educational equality because of a single occurrence sixty-five years ago.

Lessons Learned in Real Time
That Continue to Be Ignored

There are numerous events that illustrate the continued reluctance within public schools in America to learn lessons from the past. The sixty-fifth anniversary commemoration of *Brown* and a legal decision in California, where a school district agreed to desegregate "segregated programs for separate communities," elucidate why the twenty-first century has yielded similar results for black students as the mid-twentieth century. Monumental anniversaries encourage reflection on a collective period rather than year-to-year analysis to measure change. Sentiments such as "we refuse to believe that separate is inherently unequal" and "the federal government contributed to racial segregation, so [it] must be part of the solution" are not new, but the ongoing relevancy of these views sixty-five years later is sobering.[13] Coupled with the relevancy of these ideas is the continued practice of school systems creating advantages and disadvantages for students along racial lines. For example, the school district of Sausalito, located near

San Francisco, settled a case that acknowledged schools were segregated along racial lines. According to one report, the district set up two charter schools—Willow Creek Academy and Bayside–Martin Luther King Jr. Academy—with the deliberate intent "by school district officials to set up a separate and unequal system that would keep low-income children of color out of a white enclave." The report also noted that the district established and maintained this scheme by directing most of the resources to Willow Creek while underfunding Bayside-Martin. The state attorney general noted that "the district had systematically starved the school it ran of resources."[14] There is a long history of officials operating school systems within a racial hierarchy, with predictable outcomes. The justifications used by political officials and their white constituents to support segregation mirror the reasons used in Georgia's Glenn Bill and in school districts throughout southwest Georgia during the 1960s and early 1970s. The willingness to racialize public education offers a stark account as to why educational inequality has remained persistent for over a century.

The ability of school systems to operate without considering the needs of those they believed unworthy has been challenged in different ways. One of the ways is continued agitation. Nearly forty-five years after the protest at William Bryant High School in Moultrie, Georgia, black students in Baltimore, Maryland, walked out of their school protesting against educational inequalities. Reports tell us that the protest began with an African American male starting up the chant, "We don't want your pity. We want funding for our city." Students, primarily black, were protesting the funding disparities between the Baltimore school system and the nearby Fairfax County school system, populated predominantly by white students. One female student stated, "Last year it was hard for us to get toilet paper and soap in the bathroom. We would get it at the beginning of the week, but, like, Wednesday, no more for you."[15] Political scientist Avis Jones-DeWeever, who was the executive director of the National Council of Negro Women at the time, asserted that these inequities stem from a racialized tax policy that produces racialized results.[16] The lack of funding that fueled the protest in Baltimore was akin to the frustration black Moultrians felt along with black communities throughout the South in the early twentieth century, a frustration that led them to double-tax themselves in order to fund their schools.[17] The linkage of these periods elucidates the agony and the determination of each generation to make themselves visible to school systems that attempted to ignore them.

The other way by which those who were marginalized continued to challenge the inherent racism in school districts and other sociopolitical systems was to correct the system from within. Several youth activists from southwest Georgia and in other parts of the South continued their activism through service work. Walter Dykes and Alton Pertilla joined the armed forces, which enhanced the leadership skills they entered with. After leaving the military, they each returned to their communities and used those enhanced skills by being "heavily involved in local politics."[18] Serving their communities reinforced the belief that citizenship equated to equal treatment, which was a lesson they learned before enlisting. In addition to military service as a tool to continue their fight for equality, former youth activists became educators, entrepreneurs, and politicians. Juanita Wilson spent thirty years teaching in the Sumter County public school system. Jimmy Holton spent most of his career working for the postal service, but he was also an educator in the Colquitt County school system. Sam Mahone continued his activist's work by using art to portray the elusive struggle for equality. At the time of our interviews, he had worked fifteen years for the High Museum of Art in Atlanta, Georgia, and in retirement has continued his long involvement in the fight to create—and, finally, the plans to actually establish—a civil rights museum in Americus. Lorena Sabbs spent decades diversifying corporate America before returning to Americus to run the family business, Barnum Funeral Home. Like Charles Sherrod, Sabbs uses her entrepreneurial spirit to benefit black communities in greater southwest Georgia by hosting community engagement events such as Black Women and the Vote. Dale Williams spent decades as the director of human resources for the city of Moultrie and Johnny Terrell served as vice mayor of Tifton and is on the city council. Like Linda Brown, Melba Pattillo Beals, John Lewis, and so many other former black youth activists, participants in the southwest Georgia student movements chose professions and/or citizen involvement in public service with the intent of continuing the fight for full participation, equal treatment, and equal resources.

Looking at the continued commitment to achieving educational equality that blacks and other marginalized groups have shown for over a century, one has to wonder, what are the effects of pretending we do not have the answers to implementing an educational system that is inclusive, and what must be done? The answer is rather simple. One possible result of ignoring the lessons learned is a significant number of black students in every generation still never experiencing full equality in public schools. The elusiveness of equality, according to American pedagogical theorist Gloria Ladson-Billings, has resulted in a "historical debt."[19] Similar to what Du Bois articulated about desegregation in the 1930s, Ladson-Billings reminds us that there is no comfortable way to move forward without acknowledging these results. In that process, there must be admission of the primary factors that engineered this debt, which are that "we can point to little evidence that we really gave *Brown* a chance" and that continuing funding disparities have put certain groups at seismic disadvantages.[20] Without collectively acknowledging these truths, the public education that will be available to future generations will be the racialized one their predecessors endured. It will be impossible to begin answering the question of what must be done until we admit and accept historical failures

Fortunately (or unfortunately), the answer, as to what must be done to make public education more inclusive, has been provided throughout history. Whether from former enslaved blacks at the turn of the twentieth century linking education to their rights as citizens, or black youth in southwest Georgia demanding equal treatment and resources, the answer to securing educational equality lies within the ideas and actions of the marginalized themselves. We must collectively imagine that public education can and should be equal. When Joanne Jordan, alumna of William Bryant in Moultrie, recalled the advocacy that occurred at her school, she remembered that she and her fellow students imagined that things could get better. "We all knew that problems existed. . . . That gave me a desire. It was to the point that we are willing to die as children, but did what was right."[21] The audaciousness displayed by young black Moultrians and others provides a blueprint of what needs to be included when there is an attempt to do what appears to many to be impossible. The inability to implement an educational system that is imaginative in this sense has resulted in a perpetual cycle of foreshadowing and enacting what public schools became toward the latter half of the twentieth century and what they continue to be. This is a far cry from what black youth imagined.

In addition to imagining, there must be collective efforts working uniformly to create an educational system that centralizes equality. The actions of black youth in the 1960s and early 1970s provided an opportunity for public schools to transform from racialized institutions into equitable ones. Unfortunately, that opportunity was missed, by and large. What public schools became in southwest Georgia in the early 1970s followed a path similar to what they became throughout the South due to the actions of local politicians and their white constituents. White flight to more segregated areas to seek schools that were outside the reach of *Brown* decreased the number of white people who had to interact with public education in mixed-race communities.[22] As whites sought enclaves, those who continued to send their children to public schools often managed to create intra-segregation within desegregated schools that influenced placement in advanced courses, special education courses, and extracurricular activities, which included sports and club participation.[23] White loyalty to the status quo maintained various forms of mistreatment when a harmonious partnership was needed. Choosing white flight and intrasegregation meant that black youth had limited allies at a time when black schools were being closed at a rapid pace and black teachers and black principals were being fired or demoted.

With the divisions that remained in public schools after desegregation, one might think that the efforts of black youth were in vain, but that would be an inaccurate assessment. Black youth were presented a historical moment to transform an institution and they gave their maximum effort. The joy of meeting that challenge is encapsulated by Joanne Jordan, who participated in the boycott at William Bryant in Moultrie, in her recollection of students' response. "It was an exciting day, it had been planned. And I think we expected it to get as big—I wouldn't use the word out of 'proportion,' because—it was just an exciting day, it was an exciting day. They even called the police. And we did some things . . . some fighting and stuff like that, but it's an experience that I will always live my life through, and it's an experience that I think everybody—and I don't want to just say the black race, but everybody should have experience [like] that. To see that there's, like—there's another life, there's another way to live. Why are we living like this, and why don't we have this?"[24]

NOTES

Preface. The Invisibility of the Activists' Scars

1. Myles interview.

2. Rosalind Bentley, "Girls Imprisoned in Leesburg Stockade to Get State Historical Marker," *Atlanta Journal-Constitution*, July 23, 2019, https://www.ajc.com /news/state—regional/girls-imprisoned-leesburg-stockade-get-state-historical -marker/uGgSuxRrOxw6LANKGmuHpK; Nedra Rhone and Rosalind Bentley, "Leesburg's Legacy," *Atlanta Journal-Constitution*, March 21, 2019, https://www .ajc.com/news/state—regional/leesburg-legacy/VJ665jMdNmoTkeaZiKF9kM.

3. Lichtman and French, *Historians and the Living Past*, xv.

4. Paul E. Johnson, "Reflections," 381.

5. Todd-Breland, *Political Education*, 2–6.

6. Nikole Hannah-Jones, "America Wasn't a Democracy, Until Black Americans Made It One," *New York Times*, August 14, 2019, https://www.nytimes.com /interactive/2019/08/14/magazine/black-history-american-democracy.html; Hannah-Jones, "The 1619 Project," *New York Times*, August 14, 2019, https:// www.nytimes.com/interactive/2019/08/14/magazine/1619-america-slavery.html; Kelley and Lewis, *To Make Our World Anew*; Dante James, *Slavery*.

7. Hannah-Jones, "1619 Project."

Introduction. A Unique Divorce between Federal
Decisions and Loyal White Local Southern Officials

1. "Georgia's Schools: The Color-Line Disturbance—The Glenn Bill—Some Interviews—What a Georgia Newspaper Says," *Hartford (Conn.) Courant*, July 27, 1887, 2; Pinder and Hanson, "De Jure, De Facto," 165; Link, *Atlanta, Cradle*; Jewell, *Race, Social Reform*.

2. "Some Southern Ideas," *San Francisco Chronicle*, August 22, 1887; "Mixed Schools: The Georgia Legislature Wrestling with the Question of the Co-education of the Whites and Blacks," *Louisville (Ky.) Courier-Journal*, September 23, 1887, 2.

3. "The Color Line: Passage by the Georgia Legislature of the Glenn Bill—Argument on Both Sides," *Louisville Courier-Journal*, August 3, 1887, 5; "Georgia's Schools."

4. For more about the political life in Georgia after Reconstruction, see Grant, *Way It Was*; Lipsitz, *Possessive Investment*.

5. James D. Anderson, *Education of Blacks*; Heather Andrea Williams, *Self-Taught*; Green, *Educational Reconstruction*; Thuesen, *Greater than Equal*.

6. The ways in which resources for public education were disproportionately allocated have been articulated in scholarship like Tyack, *One Best System*; Kaestle, *Pillars of the Republic*; Urban, *American Education*; Green, *Educational Reconstruction*; Mondale, *School*; Ravitch, *Great School Wars*; David Wallace Adams, *Education for Extinction*; Irons, *People's History*.

7. James D. Anderson, *Education of Blacks*; Tamura, *History of Discrimination*; Urban, *American Education*; Mondale, *School*.

8. Several seminal works have noted how the creation of race aided in shaping social norms and the effect whiteness had on public schooling. See Mills, *Racial Contract*; Grace Elizabeth Hale, *Making Whiteness*; Watkins, *White Architects of Black Education*; Haney López, *White by Law*; David Wallace Adams, *Education for Extinction*; Kendi, *Stamped from the Beginning*; Carol Anderson, *White Rage*.

9. For more on the unlimited power white southern local officials had in shaping educational policies that affected black education in the South, see Ritterhouse, *Growing Up Jim Crow*; Ward, *Defending White Democracy*; Carol Anderson, *White Rage*; Watkins, *White Architects of Black Education*; Kluger, *Simple Justice*; Tyack and Cuban, *Tinkering toward Utopia*; de Schweinitz, *If We Could Change*; Haney López, *White by Law*.

10. The law was not neutral when it came to issues of race in the United States. See Crooms-Robinson, "African American Legal Status from Reconstruction Law"; Crooms-Robinson, "African American Legal Status from the Harlem Renaissance"; Fireside, *Separate and Unequal*; Irons, *People's History*; Tushnet, *NAACP's Legal Strategy*; Bartley, "Race Relations and the Quest"; Grace Elizabeth Hale, *Making Whiteness*.

11. For information on the politicization of precedent, see the seminal works Kendrick and Kendrick, *Sarah's Long Walk*; Tushnet, *NAACP's Legal Strategy*; Kluger, *Simple Justice*; Bell, *Silent Covenants*; Sokol, *There Goes My Everything*; Webb, *Massive Resistance*; Irons, *People's History*; Fireside, *Separate and Unequal*; Goldstone, *Inherently Unequal*.

12. Local school boards in the South had the ability to reinforce educational inequities because of federal decisions. Tamura, *History of Discrimination*; Tushnet, *NAACP's Legal Strategy*; Thuesen, *Greater than Equal*; Kluger, *Simple Justice*.

13. It is important to note that federal decisions were not stagnant. Legal decisions' ability to morph should not be interpreted as progress. For more on how federal decisions adjusted without substantially changing, see Endersby and Horner, *Lloyd Gaines and the Fight*; McNeil and Higginbotham, *Groundwork*; Crooms-Robinson, "African American Legal Status from the Harlem Renaissance"; Tushnet, *NAACP's Legal Strategy*.

14. Endersby and Horner, *Lloyd Gaines and the Fight*; Kluger, *Simple Justice*, 155–314.

15. Although the Fourteenth Amendment granted nonwhite citizens equal protection under the law, *Plessy* and *Cumming* underscored the contradictions that existed. This contradiction had profound educational consequences. See David Wallace Adams, *Education for Extinction*; James D. Anderson, *Education of Blacks*; Anderson and Kharem, *Education as Freedom*; Webb, *Massive Resistance*; Kluger, *Simple Justice*; Tamura, *History of Discrimination*; Williamson-Lott, Darling-Hammond, and Hyler, "Education and the Quest"; Woodson, "Fifty Years of Negro Citizenship."

16. Sweatt v. Painter, 339 U.S. 629 (1950).

17. The Supreme Court tended to define equality within a limited scope. Several scholars have illuminated the way *Sweatt v. Painter* expanded the limited definition of educational equality. See Lavergne, *Before Brown*; Shabazz, *Advancing Democracy*; Sweatt v. Painter (1950).

18. Carol Anderson, *White Rage*; James D. Anderson, *Education of Blacks*; Baker, *Paradoxes of Desegregation*; Bell, *Silent Covenants*; Cecelski, *Along Freedom Road*.

19. Carol Anderson, *White Rage*, 68–70.

20. Tushnet, *NAACP's Legal Strategy*, 136 (ellipsis in original).

21. For more regarding the long legal strategy that led to a direct attack on segregation and how several legal scholars have complicated the legal history of the path from segregation to desegregation, see Kluger, *Simple Justice*; McNeil and Higginbotham, *Groundwork*; Rawn James, *Root and Branch*; Tushnet, *NAACP's Legal Strategy*; Juan Williams, *Thurgood Marshall*; Bryan K. Fair, "Still Standing"; Cox, "Reflections of One"; Carter, *"Brown's Legacy."*

22. *Brown I* refers to the original lawsuit and the Supreme Court's 1954 decision. *Brown II* refers to the Supreme Court's enforcement decree issued a year later. Scholars have investigated *Brown* from various perspectives. See Carter, "Brown's Legacy"; Kluger, *Simple Justice*; Titus, *Brown's Battleground*; Byrne, *Brown v. Board of Education*; Ball, *With More Deliberate Speed*; Burton and O'Brien, *Remembering Brown at Fifty*; Willis, "'Let Me In'"; Brown-Nagin, *Courage to Dissent*; Anderson and Byrne, *Unfinished Agenda of Brown*; Klarman, *Brown v. Board of Education*; Patterson, *Brown v. Board of Education*; Philipsen, "Second Promise of Brown"; Daugherity and Bolton, *With All Deliberate Speed*; Ogletree, *All Deliberate Speed*.

23. Earl Warren and Supreme Court of the United States, *U.S. Reports: Brown v. Board of Education, 347 U.S. 483* (1954), https://www.loc.gov/item/usrep347483; Kluger, *Simple Justice*; Patterson, *Brown v. Board of Education*.

24. For a detailed portrayal of how and why white local southern officials responded in various ways to *Brown*, see Sokol, *There Goes My Everything*; Webb, *Massive Resistance*; Roche, *Restructured Resistance*; Carol Anderson, *White Rage*; Ward, *Defending White Democracy*.

25. The climate that was created by the refusal to accept *Brown* as the law of the land has profoundly shaped the theoretical framework of this study. The fol-

lowing works have contributed greatly: Sokol, *There Goes My Everything*; Klarman, *Unfinished Business*; Kendi, *Stamped from the Beginning*; Carol Anderson, *White Rage*; Kimberley Johnson, *Reforming Jim Crow*; Ritterhouse, *Growing Up Jim Crow*; Woodward, *Strange Career of Jim Crow*; Hoffer, *Plessy v. Ferguson*.

26. "'With Deliberate Speed' Is the Coming Phrase," *New York Times*, June 1, 1955, 28; Ward, *Defending White Democracy*; Erickson, *Making the Unequal Metropolis*; Klarman, *Unfinished Business*; Orfield, Eaton, and Harvard Project, *Dismantling Desegregation*; Daugherity and Bolton, *With All Deliberate Speed*; Ogletree, *All Deliberate Speed*; Ball, *With More Deliberate Speed*; Kluger, *Simple Justice*; Kruse, *White Flight*.

27. Brown v. Board of Education of Topeka, 349 U.S. 294 (1955).

28. Bell, *Silent Covenants*; Patterson, *Brown v. Board of Education*; Ogletree, *All Deliberate Speed*; Titus, *Brown's Battleground*; Anderson and Byrne, *Unfinished Agenda of Brown*; Jacoway, "Not Anger But Sorrow"; Willis, "'Let Me In.'"

29. Carol Anderson, *White Rage*; Willis, "'Let Me In'"; Danns, Purdy, and Span, *Using Past as Prologue*; Anderson and Kharem, *Education as Freedom*; K'Meyer, *From Brown to Meredith*; Klarman, *Brown v. Board of Education*; Kluger, *Simple Justice*; Brown-Nagin, *Courage to Dissent*; Titus, *Brown's Battleground*; Sokol, *There Goes My Everything*; Ladson-Billings, "From the Achievement Gap."

30. For more on the similarities between black students attending public schools before and after *Brown*, see Holloway, *Jim Crow Wisdom*; Carol Anderson, *White Rage*; Kendi, *Stamped from the Beginning*; Baker, *Paradoxes of Desegregation*; Jon Hale, *Freedom Schools*; Thuesen, *Greater than Equal*.

31. Cecelski, *Along Freedom Road*; Huntley and McKerley, *Foot Soldiers for Democracy*; Thuesen, *Greater than Equal*; Baker, *Paradoxes of Desegregation*; Jon Hale, *Freedom Schools*; Willis, "'Let Me In.'"

32. The historiography of American education reveals the long history of contestation that existed around public education. See James D. Anderson, *Education of Blacks*; Donohue, Heckman, and Todd, "Schooling of Southern Blacks"; Haney López, *White by Law*; Mills, *Racial Contract*; Ravitch, *Great School Wars*; Urban, *American Education*; Heather Andrea Williams, *Self-Taught*; Williamson-Lott, Darling-Hammond, and Hyler, "Education and the Quest."

33. Other theoretical frameworks utilized in this book are social movement theory and the rhetoric of social protest. In *Social Movements: The Key Concepts*, the authors—Graeme Chesters and Ian Welsh—conceptualize social movement theory as an interdisciplinary study that seeks to explain why social mobilization occurs, the forms under which it manifests, as well as potential social, cultural, and political consequences (see 1–43). Furthermore, they explain key concepts of social movement theories, including collective identity, which explains cohesion within a particular movement, and direct-action, which "is an intervention to achieve change by means that lie outside the normal channels of social or political engagement" (61). See also Willis, "'Let Me In'"; Rosenberg, *Hollow Hope*; Morris and Browne, *Readings on the Rhetoric*. Using rhetoric of social protest as a theo-

retical framework is useful to my study because language is pivotal to social movements. According to Charles E. Morris III and Stephen Browne, authors of *Readings on the Rhetoric of Social Protest*, examining rhetoric of social protest as a theory allows one to study how symbols—words, signs, images, music, even bodies—shape our perceptions of reality and invite us to act accordingly. Rhetoric applies to any situation in which persuasion occurs or intended to occur.

34. Urban and Wagoner, *American Education*; Kluger, *Simple Justice*; Blackmon, *Slavery by Another Name*.

35. The justification used to perpetuate black subjugation is articulated in the following works: Heather Andrea Williams, *Self-Taught*; Blackmon, *Slavery by Another Name*; Anderson, *White Rage*; Kendi, *Stamped from the Beginning*; Watkins, *White Architects of Black Education*; Kluger, *Simple Justice*; Klarman, *From Jim Crow*.

36. "Roosevelt Urges Negroes to Work," *New York Times*, August 20, 1910, 2.

37. "Blacks Can't Rule, Taft Tells South: Present Election Laws, Squaring with Federal Constitution, an Adequate Prevention," *New York Times*, December 8, 1908, 2; Meier, "Negro and the Democratic Party."

38. "Blacks Can't Rule, Taft Tells South," 2; Grantham, "Georgia Politics and the Disfranchisement."

39. "Taft to Keep Out of New York Fight: Will Have Nothing to Say as to Candidates or Platform—Makes Address on Negro Education," *Hartford Courant*, August 27, 1910; "Hoke Smith Takes Helm: Inaugurated Governor of Georgia," *Baltimore Sun*, June 30, 1907.

40. James D. Anderson, *Education of Blacks*; Bullock, *History of Negro Education*; Thuesen, *Greater than Equal*; Jerome E. Morris, "Forgotten Voices of Black Educators."

41. For how segregation continued to create circumstances of opposition for blacks and how federal politicians responded, see Lisio, *Hoover, Blacks, and Lily-Whites*; Troy, *Leading from the Center*; Lewis, *W. E. B. Du Bois*; Kluger, *Simple Justice*.

42. Frederickson, *Dixiecrat Revolt and the End*; Webb, *Massive Resistance*.

43. For how blacks challenged public schools that perpetuated their subjugation, see Heather Andrea Williams, *Self-Taught*; Williamson-Lott, Darling-Hammond, and Hyler, "Education and the Quest"; James D. Anderson, *Education of Blacks*; David Wallace Adams, *Education for Extinction*; Ravitch, *Great School Wars*; Thuesen, *Greater than Equal*; Bullock, *History of Negro Education*; Walker, "Second-Class Integration"; Anderson and Kharem, *Education as Freedom*; Shabazz, *Advancing Democracy*; Urban, *American Education*.

44. Anderson and Kharem, *Education as Freedom*; James D. Anderson, *Education of Blacks*; Heather Andrea Williams, *Self-Taught*; Green, *Educational Reconstruction*; Walker, *Their Highest Potential*; Walker, *Hello Professor*; Walker, "Second-Class Integration"; Cecelski, *Along Freedom Road*; Baker, *Paradoxes of Desegregation*; Grace Elizabeth Hale, *Making Whiteness*; Thuesen, *Greater than Equal*; Danns, Purdy, and Span, *Using Past as Prologue*; Titus, *Brown's Battle-*

ground; Huntley and McKerley, *Foot Soldiers for Democracy*; de Schweinitz, *If We Could Change*; Willis, "'Let Me In.'"

45. Several scholars have illuminated the various experiences that existed during segregation and during desegregation. See Cecelski, *Along Freedom Road*; Grady-Willis, *Challenging U.S. Apartheid*; Walker, *Their Highest Potential*; Williamson-Lott, Darling-Hammond, and Hyler, "Education and the Quest"; Jon Hale, *Freedom Schools*; Thuesen, *Greater than Equal*; Danns, Purdy, and Span, *Using Past as Prologue*.

46. For more on works that challenge the linearity narrative of public schooling, see James D. Anderson, *Education of Blacks*; Cecelski, *Along Freedom Road*; Walker, *Their Highest Potential*; Baker, *Paradoxes of Desegregation*; Fairclough, *Better Day Coming*; Robert Collins Smith, *They Closed Their Schools*; Bullock, *History of Negro Education*; Beals, *Warriors Don't Cry*; Jacoway, "Not Anger But Sorrow"; McCluskey, *Forgotten Sisterhood*.

47. A number of scholars have discussed how desegregation flowed unidirectionally, which negatively impacted black principals, black teachers, and black students. For more on the negative consequences of one-way desegregation, see Foster, *Black Teachers on Teaching*; Morris and Morris, *Price They Paid*; Jerome E. Morris, *Troubling the Waters*; Cecelski, *Along Freedom Road*; Baker, *Paradoxes of Desegregation*; Walker, *Hello Professor*; Milner and Howard, "Black Teachers, Black Students"; Dougherty, "That's When We Were Marching"; Span and Rivers, "Reassessing the Achievement Gap"; Danns, *Something Better for Our Children*; Danns, Purdy, and Span, *Using Past as Prologue*.

48. Garraghan, *Guide to Historical Method*; Gottschalk, *Understanding History*; Ruane, *Introducing Social Research Methods*; Baum, *Transcribing and Editing Oral History*; Sommer, *Oral History Manual*; Valerie Raleigh Yow, *Recording Oral History*; Gracy, *Introduction to Archives and Manuscripts*; Creswell, *Qualitative Inquiry and Research Design*; Gerring, *Case Study Research*; Huberman and Miles, *Qualitative Researcher's Companion*.

49. For how whites viewed *Brown*, see Sokol, *There Goes My Everything*; Klarman, *From Jim Crow*; Rosenberg, *Hollow Hope*; Kruse, *White Flight*.

50. Bynum, "We Must March Forward!"; Franklin, *After the Rebellion*; Mitra, *Student Voice in School Reform*; Willis, "'Let Me In'"; Burrow, *Child Shall Lead Them*; Chamberlain, "'And a Child Shall Lead'"; Huntley and McKerley, *Foot Soldiers for Democracy*; de Schweinitz, *If We Could Change*.

Chapter 1. *Brown* and the Muddled Realities of Public Education

1. Wheeler interview.

2. Blackmon, *Slavery by Another Name*; Alexander, *New Jim Crow*; Rothstein, *Color of Law*; Trounstine, *Segregation by Design*.

3. Crooms-Robinson, "African American Legal Status from Reconstruction Law"; Green, *Educational Reconstruction*; Richardson, *How the South Won*.

4. Wheeler interview.

5. Juan Williams, *Thurgood Marshall*, 229.

6. To gain fuller insight into the philosophies of the lawyers who fought to dismantle segregation, see Williams, *Thurgood Marshall*; Kluger, *Simple Justice*; Tushnet, *NAACP's Legal Strategy*; Cox, "Reflections of One," xvii–xxiv; Rawn James, *Root and Branch*.

7. Juan Williams, *Thurgood Marshall*, 2000, 226.

8. For more regarding the meticulous nature of Justice Thurgood Marshall, see Rawn James, *Root and Branch*; Juan Williams, *Thurgood Marshall*; Lavergne, *Before Brown*; Kluger, *Simple Justice*.

9. For more on the various narratives about the *Brown* decision, see Patterson, *Brown v. Board of Education*; Anderson and Byrne, *Unfinished Agenda of Brown*; Bell, *Silent Covenants*; Burton and O'Brien, *Remembering Brown at Fifty*; Byrne, *Brown v. Board of Education*; Daugherity and Bolton, *With All Deliberate Speed*; Milner and Howard, "Black Teachers, Black Students"; Klarman, *Brown v. Board of Education*; Philipsen, "Second Promise of Brown"; Kluger, *Simple Justice*.

10. Ruth Carbonette Yow, *Students of the Dream*; Erickson, *Making the Unequal Metropolis*.

11. For the different responses to desegregation, see Kirk, *Redefining the Color Line*; Robert Collins Smith, *They Closed Their Schools*; Titus, *Brown's Battleground*.

12. Carter, "*Brown's* Legacy"; Ashenfelter, Collins, and Yoon, "Evaluating the Role of *Brown*"; Bell, *Silent Covenants*; Bryan K. Fair, "Still Standing"; Kluger, *Simple Justice*.

13. Klarman, *Unfinished Business*; Bullock, *History of Negro Education*.

14. Mondale, *School*.

15. Patterson, *Brown v. Board of Education*, xiv.

16. For more on how *Brown II* allowed southern states to circumvent *Brown I*, see Ball, *With More Deliberate Speed*; Daugherity and Bolton, *With All Deliberate Speed*; "'With Deliberate Speed' Is the Coming Phrase," *New York Times*, June 1, 1955, 28; Ogletree, *All Deliberate Speed*; Kluger, *Simple Justice*; Walker, *Their Highest Potential*; Cox, "Reflections of One."

17. For more on the need to complicate the legal history of *Brown*, see Brown-Nagin, *Courage to Dissent*.

18. Cox, "Reflections of One," xxiv.

19. Walker, *Their Highest Potential*, 184.

20. In Rustin, *Bayard Rustin Papers*.

21. Klarman, *Unfinished Business*, 7–8.

22. Sokol, *There Goes My Everything*, 48.

23. Purdy, *Transforming the Elite*.

24. Ibid.; Danns, Purdy, and Span, *Using Past as Prologue*; Walker, "Second-Class Integration"; Williamson-Lott, Darling-Hammond, and Hyler, "Education and the Quest."

25. "500 Schools Desegregated Year after Court Ruling," *Atlanta Daily World*, April 30, 1955.

26. Ibid.

27. Ibid.

28. "Baltimore Crowd Attacks 4 Pupils: Negro Boy Punched in Fight Over Integration—Schools Resume in Milford," *New York Times*, October 2, 1954, 18.

29. Bess Furman, "Student 'Strikes' Widen in Capital," *New York Times*, October 6, 1954, 20. While A. Philip Randolph does not defend the effectiveness of *Brown*, he does downplay white students' role in opposing integration. In a letter sent to Sergeant William Bracey—president of the Guardians Association—he stated, "Negro and white youth are giving to the implementing of the Supreme Court decisions. American youth has taken initiative and we all have an obligation to back them up. . . . In the South white youth are reveling against the irresponsible behavior of publicity hungry politicians." Based on archival data and secondary sources, Randolph portraying white youth as proponents of integration is a stretch. Randolph, *The Papers of A. Philip Randolph*. See also Webb, *Massive Resistance*.

30. "Washington School Demonstrators Admit 'We Accomplished Nothing': Students Return to Classes after School Leaders' Plea," *Atlanta Daily World*, October 7, 1954, 1.

31. "Baltimore Crowd Attacks 4 Pupils."

32. Jacoway, "Not Anger But Sorrow," 4–5. See also Willis, "'Let Me In.'"

33. Beals, *I Will Not Fear*.

34. Jack Fox, "Students Ask for Orderly Mixing: 3 Va. Cities Set for Integration," *Chicago Daily Defender*, February 2, 1959.

35. Ibid.

36. An article published in the *Daily Defender* portrayed how the responses of white students living in Colp, Illinois, were parallel to those of the white students living in Baltimore, Washington, and Little Rock toward integration. See "White Pupils Boycott New Integrated School in Colp," *Chicago Daily Defender*, August 28, 1957.

37. Randolph, *Papers of A. Philip Randolph*.

38. "Mass Youth Rally May 26 to Honor 'Freedom Fighters,'" *New York Amsterdam News*, May 25, 1957.

39. Bullock, *History of Negro Education*; Grady-Willis, *Challenging U.S. Apartheid*; Willis, "'Let Me In'"; Jon Hale, *Freedom Schools*.

40. Ellen Levine, *Freedom's Children*, xi–xii. See also "Youth Tell of Fight for Freedom in South," *Atlanta Daily World*, June 4, 1957; "Mass Youth Rally May 26 to Honor 'Freedom Fighters,'" *New York Amsterdam News*, May 25, 1957.

41. "Mass Youth Rally May 26."

42. For more on how black youth sought to transform public schools immediately after the *Brown* decision, see Thuesen, *Greater than Equal*.

43. "Pupils Boycott 6 Jim Crow Schools," *Chicago Daily Defender*, February 11, 1959; "School Officials to Discipline High School Student 'Marchers,'" *Atlanta Daily World*, January 10, 1964, 1.

44. Prior to this event, the NAACP held a campaign meeting on April 17th to discuss several projects the organization wanted to host. One of the projects was a National Youth Conference on Desegregation. The purpose of the conference

would be "to stimulate and inform outstanding teen-age youth leaders and win their influence and active support for our Civil Rights program. To advise National Office on what youth want and need to effectively participate in the campaign to end segregation. To find out what youth are doing and what they feel they can do to help advance our Civil Rights objectives." NAACP, "NAACP Youth File: General Department File: Form Letters," sec. 2:001.

45. Although the NAACP Youth Council participated in the event, the Brotherhood of Sleeping Car Porters was the organization that spearheaded it. Roy Wilkins did not participate in the first Youth March for Integrated Schools because it did not follow the typical procedural guidelines of the NAACP. He believed in the purpose and mission of the event but felt that A. Philip Randolph did not have enough time to plan an effective march. In fairness to Roy Wilkins, the event was hurriedly planned, and he was told about the event only weeks before the march was to take place. Although the NAACP helped sponsor the 1958 march, they played a more pivotal role in the 1959 march. NAACP, "NAACP Youth File: General Department File: Career Conference."

46. Some scholars have elevated the importance of this event in their work. See Kersten, *A. Philip Randolph*; Pfeffer, *A. Philip Randolph, Pioneer*; Jervis Anderson, *Bayard Rustin*; Daniel Levine, *Bayard Rustin*.

47. When Randolph was asked why the march had to happen, he responded by stating, "While the courts are handing down favorable decisions on the desegregation and integration of public schools, we must remember that the South is not accepting these decisions and is waging a nationwide campaign for their evasion and nullification. Moreover, the courts can change their position on the question. They have changed before, and they can change again. It was the Supreme Court which handed down the decision involving the case *Plessy vs. Ferguson.* . . . But today it has handed down the decision reversing its position on this question." Randolph, *Papers of A. Philip Randolph*, reel 27.

48. Jervis Anderson, *Bayard Rustin*, 100–101.

49. Rustin, *Bayard Rustin Papers*.

50. Although the delegation did not meet with President Eisenhower, they did leave with his staff some recommendations that relate to this study. One of them, which reinforces their support of *Brown*, was, "The Chief Executive should place his weight behind the passage of a truly effective Civil Rights Bill in the present session of Congress. As far as school integration is concerned, we believe that the Douglas-Javits-Celler Bill is by far the most far-sighted and constructive piece of legislation before Congress. . . . The Douglas-Javits-Cellar Bill is an historic and statesmanlike proposal. It empowers the Federal Government to move into the center of the school picture and to undertake, on a nationwide basis, careful and constructive planning of the nation's march toward integration." Another suggestion was "to call a White House Conference of youth and student leaders, chosen from national and regional organizations, both North and South, to discuss ways in which youth may participate in the implementation of the 1954 Supreme Court decision." Randolph, *Papers of A. Philip Randolph*.

51. NAACP, "NAACP Administrative File."

52. Ibid.

53. Randolph, *Papers of A. Philip Randolph*, l, reel 27.

54. Randolph's letter to Frost reveals that she was not the only parent who felt this way. He stated, "Thank you for your kind letter . . . expressing your appreciation. I think your letter was very splendid in indicating the value of democratic participation in mass demonstration. . . . I have received many encouraging letters indicating the tremendous value of the experience to the youth through participation in the March." Randolph, *Papers of A. Philip Randolph*.

55. Ibid., reel 27.

56. Ibid.

57. Pfeffer, *A. Philip Randolph, Pioneer*, 182.

58. Randolph, *Papers of A. Philip Randolph*, reel 27.

59. Randolph, *Papers of A. Philip Randolph*, reel 27. Randolph connects the injustices taking place in America to injustices taking place in other parts of the world. He wrote (ibid.), "When Faubus of Little Rock is encouraged and supported in this flagrant attack upon little Negro children[s]' right to attend integrated schools in Little Rock, aid, comfort and support are being given to the horrors committed by the Russian communists in Hungary against the people of Hungary and the tragedy visited upon the people of Tibet by Chinese communist barbarianism. Because liberty is indivisible, one cannot support colonialism in Africa and racism in the United States without strengthening the hands of communism in its march for world-wide conquest."

60. "Integration Will Bring 'Knowledge of Each Other,' Wilkins Says as 26,000 Youth March," *Los Angeles Tribune*, April 24, 1959, 7. See also Randolph, *Papers of A. Philip Randolph*.

61. "Integration Will Bring 'Knowledge.'"

62. Lloyd Weaver, "A Teen Viewpoint," *New York Amsterdam News*, November 8, 1958, 34.

63. There is no report on the youth marching for integrated schools after 1959, which implies that the marches did not continue, or that the number of participants decreased so dramatically that newspapers decided not to cover the event. The latter is unlikely, especially for black newspapers, because integration/desegregation was such an important topic during this period. The inability to continue the Youth March for Integrated Schools substantiates the claim that there was a pragmatic shift among some in the black community about *Brown* in the 1960s. See "Integration Will Bring 'Knowledge,'"; Bullock, *History of Negro Education*; Willis, "'Let Me In'"; Grady-Willis, *Challenging U.S. Apartheid*.

64. Randolph, *Papers of A. Philip Randolph*, reel 27.

65. Daugherity and Bolton, *With All Deliberate Speed*.

66. Donohue, Heckman, and Todd, "Schooling of Southern Blacks," 233. The measures used in this study were attendance-based pupil/teacher ratio, term length, and per-diem teacher salary.

67. Orfield, Eaton, and Harvard Project, *Dismantling Desegregation*; Walker, *Their Highest Potential*.

68. Synnott, "Desegregation in South Carolina," 61.

69. For more on how the civil rights movement became a combination of localized movements taking place throughout the South, see Payne, *I've Got the Light*; Garrow, *Bearing the Cross*; Tuck, *Beyond Atlanta*.

70. Carol Anderson, *White Rage*; Jeffries, *Bloody Lowndes*; Titus, *Brown's Battleground*.

71. Tuck, *Beyond Atlanta*; Hornsby, "Black Public Education"; Coleman, *History of Georgia*; Meyers, *Empire State of the South*; Grady-Willis, *Challenging U.S. Apartheid*; Brown-Nagin, *Courage to Dissent*; McGrath, "Great Expectations."

72. Baker, *Paradoxes of Desegregation*; Cecelski, *Along Freedom Road*; Jon Hale, *Freedom Schools*.

73. Brinson, "Second Look."

74. "Southern School Desegregation Bogged Down in 'Tokenism': Fourth of a Series," *Pittsburgh Courier*, March 3, 1962, sec. 2, p. 3.

75. "College Students Issue Their Manifesto," *Atlanta Daily World*, March 10, 1960.

76. Grady-Willis, *Challenging U.S. Apartheid*, xv.

77. "Ga Pupil Asks for Better School Equipment, Expelled," *Cleveland Call and Post*, January 27, 1962, 5B; "County High School Closed after Protest," *Atlanta Daily World*, January 18, 1962, 2.

78. "Rural Ga. Area Pupils Walk Out for Better School," *Daily Defender*, October 23, 1962, 8. The *Atlanta Daily World* also covered this story. Black schools in the South were not the only black schools in the country that dealt with poor conditions and overcrowding. Several articles give examples of the overcrowding that took place in Chicago and Milwaukee and how black students responded. See "Big Boycott Drummed Up by Students," *Chicago Defender*, December 3, 1966, col. 3, p. 1; "2,500 Students Stay Out in May-Spencer Boycott," *Daily Defender*, February 15, 1968, col. 3, p. 2; "Students Plan City Schools Boycott," *Daily Defender*, February 26, 1968, 9.

79. Kenneth Temple, "High School Students March to City Hall: Officials Set Probe," *Atlanta Daily World*, January 8, 1964, 1; "Efforts Being Made to Keep High Schoolers in Classes," *Atlanta Daily World*, January 9, 1964, 1; "Florida Schools Boycotted," *New York Times*, October 25, 1966, 31.

80. "Improve Crane High, Students Demand," *Daily Defender*, September 13, 1965, 5.

81. Croft, Pogue, and Walker, *Living the Legacy*; Walker, *Lost Education of Horace Tate*.

82. Croft, Pogue, and Walker, *Living the Legacy*; Walker, *Lost Education of Horace Tate*; Carol Anderson, *White Rage*; James D. Anderson, *Education of Blacks*; McCluskey, *Forgotten Sisterhood*.

83. "Students Attempt to Get Principal Back in Savannah," *Atlanta Daily*

World, March 22, 1961, 1; "School Crisis in Savannah Spreads," *Atlanta Daily World*, March 23, 1961, 1; "Walkout Wave in Savannah Slows," *Atlanta Daily World*, March 24, 1961, 1.

84. Tuck, *Beyond Atlanta*, 108. See also Garrow, *Bearing the Cross*; Branch, *Parting the Waters*.

85. Charles Sherrod, interview with author, audio recording, Albany, Georgia, July 23, 2012. See also Harris, "SNCC Papers," n.d., King Center.

86. Sherrod interview.

87. Henrietta Fuller, "SNCC Papers," September 13, 1963, King Center, SNCC Papers; Harris, "SNCC Papers."

88. McBurrows interview.

Chapter 2. The Insatiable Appetite of Jim Crow and Black Tiftonians' Desire for Full Citizenship

1. Huntley and McKerley, *Foot Soldiers for Democracy*; Wilma King, *African American Childhoods*; de Schweinitz, *If We Could Change*; Thuesen, *Greater than Equal*.

2. Cumming v. Richmond County of Board of Education, 175 U.S. 528 (December 18, 1899). The Supreme Court has rarely been neutral when it came to matters of legal segregation. On the political ramifications of the court's decision, see Connally, "Justice Harlan's 'Great Betrayal'?"; Goldstone, *Inherently Unequal*; Klarman, *From Jim Crow*.

3. Sokol, *There Goes My Everything*, 3.

4. Southern states did their best to reestablish political, educational, and social norms that resembled life before the Civil War. On the related laws and the justification for those laws, see Blackmon, *Slavery by Another Name*; Anderson, *White Rage*; Crooms-Robinson, "African American Legal Status from Reconstruction Law."

5. Quote from John D. Fair, *Tifts of Georgia*, 245.

6. Ibid.

7. On image-conscious cities like Atlanta using business as a way to maintain racial hierarchy, see Hobson, *Legend of the Black Mecca*; Purdy, *Transforming the Elite*.

8. John D. Fair, *Tifts of Georgia*, 248. Fair's omission is not isolated in the historical narrative of Tifton. The town's brochure and the *Georgia Encyclopedia* also fail to show how white hegemony was attacked by black Tiftonians.

9. For how pivotal Ella and Daughtry Melton were to the foundation of the civil rights movement in Tifton, see "Legendary Figures Remembered," *Tifton Gazette*, February 18, 2011, https://www.tiftongazette.com/archives/legendary-figures -remembered/article_4b68caa7-4281-5f38-89fd-39b8a17723aa.html.

10. "Museum Celebrates 1st Anniversary," *Tifton Gazette*, February 27, 2012, https://www.tiftongazette.com/archives/museum-celebrates-1st-anniversary/article _0b9123a7-792d-54ef-9439-9833165c549c.html.

11. Thuesen, *Greater than Equal*; Pat Watters, "Why the Negro Children March," *New York Times Sunday Magazine*, March 21, 1965, 109; Willis, "'Let Me In'"; Adams and Adams, *Just Trying to Have School*.

12. Tuck, *Beyond Atlanta*, 3.

13. Terrell interview.

14. Kitchen interview.

15. Roche, *Restructured Resistance*, 138.

16. Hornsby, "Black Public Education," 23.

17. For more on how other southern states adopted school closing as a way to avoid desegregation, see Titus, *Brown's Battleground*; Daugherity, *Keep on Keeping On*.

18. Walker, *Their Highest Potential*; Cecelski, *Along Freedom Road*. Although both these studies took place in North Carolina, the pride and philosophy reflected in them were similar to attitudes and beliefs found among black educators in Tifton.

19. It is not surprising that public school officials did not place a premium on educating black children, particularly in the early 1900s. As Tifton experienced phenomenal growth in the first decade of the twentieth century, a public high school was built for whites. However, a school for blacks was not built until 1917. See Kayla L. Tillman, "Tifton: From Indian Trails to I-75," *Tifton Magazine*, December 1990; *Tiger Alumni Reunion, 1930–1975*. I could not find any evidence that suggests whites had to fight for a school, but there is evidence that the school board delayed providing education for black children for over a decade. According to *The Tiger*, Johnny Wilson, a black pioneer of education in Tifton, strongly promoted learning for black schoolchildren. He appeared before the county and city boards of education to seek assistance in constructing a decent school building and always received a vote of sympathy and promise of financial aid as soon as funds were available. After receiving assistance from Mrs. H. H. Tift and Mrs. N. Peterson and six acres of land from Captain Tift's cousin, Industrial Elementary was built in 1917; the high school was added in 1929.

20. Kitchen interview; Terrell interview; "Legendary Figures Remembered."

21. For more on what black schools were doing exceptionally well before and after *Brown*, see Thuesen, *Greater than Equal*; Walker, *Their Highest Potential*; Cecelski, *Along Freedom Road*; McCluskey, *Forgotten Sisterhood*.

22. *Tiger Alumni Reunion, 1930–1975*, 15–16.

23. Ibid., 17–18.

24. Tillman, "Tifton." Walker describes in *Hello Professor* a similar relationship between Caswell County Training School and the larger black community. Thus, the relationship between black Tiftonians and the two black schools is a continuation of the partnership between institution and community which existed before and remained intact after *Brown*.

25. What Walker dubs "no poverty of spirit" was the goal in Tifton as well. She states that although most blacks in Caswell County were poor, "they forged a system of schooling that emphasized the importance of teacher/student relationships,

valued activities as a key means of developing the students' many talents, and believed in the children's ability to learn and their own ability to teach." Walker, *Their Highest Potential*, 200.

26. Pertilla interview.

27. Dykes interview.

28. Douglass, "Frederick Douglass Project Writings."

29. For insight on the various theories scholars have adopted to investigate white behavior, historically and contemporarily, see Feagin, *White Racial Frame*; Fine, *Off White*; DiAngelo, *White Fragility*.

30. DiAngelo, *White Fragility*, 103.

31. *Brown* deserves various critiques, but it explicitly stated that segregation was unconstitutional. Earl Warren and Supreme Court of the United States, U.S. Reports: Brown v. Board of Education, 347 U.S. 483 (1954), https://www.loc.gov /item/usrep347483; Kluger, *Simple Justice*.

32. Ignoring the federal decision was a strategy adopted by most southern states. For more, see Byrne, *Brown v. Board of Education*; Bell, *Silent Covenants*; Kluger, *Simple Justice*; Klarman, *Brown v. Board of Education*; Daugherity and Bolton, *With All Deliberate Speed*.

33. Dykes interview.

34. Pertilla interview.

35. Terrell interview; Kitchen interview.

36. It is important to note that the *Tifton Gazette*, the town's local newspaper, did not cover *Brown I* or *Brown II*. See also Tillman, "Tifton: From Indian Trails to I-75," for more on the three-step desegregation plan Tifton passed to meet federal guidelines in 1968.

37. Terrell interview.

38. Pertilla interview; Dykes interview; Terrell interview.

39. Pertilla interview.

40. Ibid.

41. Terrell interview.

42. Dykes interview.

43. See James D. Anderson, *The Education of Blacks in the South*, for more on the racialization of taxation. Anderson notes how the practice of taking tax dollars from black schools to fund white schools was commonplace. He also states that "since the Reconstruction era black southerners had adapted to a structure of oppressive education by practicing double taxation" (156). Although there is no evidence that suggests black Tiftonians double-taxed themselves, we do know that, because of the laws of Jim Crow, black tax dollars were funding facilities that they could not use or that they could not use as freely as whites.

44. Dykes interview. Dykes also said that black students were barred from the county library as well. According to him, "If you wanted to check out a book, [black students] had to tell our teacher to check out a book and she would have to go down to the white library 'cause our library was minimal. She would go check out the book for you because that was the policy in Tifton."

45. For a firsthand account of the bombing at 16th Street Baptist Church, see McKinstry and George, *While the World Watched*.

46. Jeffries, *Bloody Lowndes*, 40. See also Payne, *I've Got the Light*.

47. *Tiger*, 1962, 6.

48. J. K. Obatala, "Was the Civil-Rights Struggle Worth It?: Back Home in Tifton," *New York Times*, December 2, 1973, 37. Mr. Major Wright later changed his name to J. K. Obatala.

49. Dykes interview. It is important to note that the friction that existed between youth and adults was somewhat fluid. Yes, there were several adults who felt the youth movement brought unnecessary trouble and disagreed with the movement publicly. Privately, however, they often fully supported the youth. Dykes remembered a private conversation he had with an older black lady that really inspired him. "She said, look son, I cannot express myself [publicly] about this but I am so glad that you guys are doing something because these white people [don't plan on changing the status quo]. She told me that she could not join [the movement] because they [would] have fired her . . . but she said 'I see what y'all young people are doing' and she said 'keep on doing it.'"

50. Dykes interview. Solomon Nixon was the co-owner of Frank and Solomon Nixon Funeral Home in Tifton. The funeral home was founded in 1925 by his father, Frank Thomas "Pa Frank" Nixon.

51. Ibid.

52. Terrell interview.

53. Obatala, "Was the Civil-Rights Struggle," 37.

54. NAACP, "NAACP Youth File: General Department File: Membership Campaign"; NAACP, "NAACP Youth File: General Department File: Form Letters." Dykes said that although King was not at the event, other prominent members of the SCLC were. After he returned from Macon, he took a trip with other students to Albany, where they were advised by C. B. King on how to start a movement. According to Dykes, "C. B. King gave us the particulars on organizing around nonviolent principles. If we started a student movement, this is what you do, how if someone gets violent, you cover your head up" (Dykes interview). He also recalled that by the time they started the movement in Tifton he had already graduated from Wilson.

55. Dykes interview. When asked why the youth chose voter registration as the issue to address, Dykes stated, "That was the going thing then. You know, you get involved in the movement, you registered people to vote. We went through that experience of registering black people to vote."

56. Ibid.

57. Ibid. Dykes recalled posing these questions to Principal Mack, but those questions were not well received, according to Dykes. "When I was finishing, he told me, 'Y'all started all this mess. We know how to deal with white people. Y'all don't know what y'all doing.' I said, 'Mr. Mack, they have a county pool over there.' I said, 'That is Tift County. Why can't we go to the county pool? Mr. Mack, I don't accept that. My grandma sends her taxes, why can't we go to the county pool?'"

58. For more on how miscegenation was used to justify segregation, see "Mixed Schools: The Georgia Legislature Wrestling with the Question of the Co-education of the Whites and Blacks," *Louisville Courier-Journal*, September 23, 1887, 2; Kruse, *White Flight*; DiAngelo, *White Fragility*.

59. Dykes interview; Obatala, "Was the Civil-Rights Struggle."

60. Dykes interview. Dykes recalled that his approach was an aberration for the youth movement in Tifton, since he had been elected president by members of the organization. As justification for choosing to bypass the bylaws, he told the group that Major Wright was the best person for the position. I did not find any data to suggest this decision was questioned.

61. Dykes interview; Obatala, "Was the Civil-Rights Struggle," 38. As Wright/ Obatala reflected back on this same event, he summed it up this way: "One night a few weeks before, at Allen Temple A.M.E. Church, Walter Dykes . . . put his hands on my shoulders and told the audience that I would be the new president [of the Tifton Youth Chapter of the SCLC] because he was going off to college. There were no votes, no protests and no questions asked from the floor; just applause" (37, 90).

62. Dykes interview. Dykes also noted, "I thought that people were logical people and they would say, well, if you have been paying taxes and you got a county facility, you can use it. Even if they only [pay a percentage of the cost of the building], you can only use one quarter of this building, I can understand that, but I never could understand [not being able to use a county building]. It's a county building."

63. Quoted in Burns, *To the Mountaintop*, 343.

64. Terrell interview.

65. Burns, *To the Mountaintop*, 343.

66. For more on the reasons why direct action was the preferred strategy during the 1960s, see Hobson, *Legend of the Black Mecca*; Ogbar, *Black Power*; Carson, *In Struggle*; Payne, *I've Got the Light*.

67. Dykes and Terrell interview.

68. Terrell interview.

69. Dykes and Terrell interview.

70. Dykes, in Dykes and Terrell interview, during which Terrell echoed these sentiments. In her interview, Pertilla made similar points.

71. See Martin Luther King Jr., *Where Do We Go from Here?*, to understand how King differentiated between concession and systemic change.

72. Obatala, "Was the Civil-Rights Struggle," 37.

73. Terrell interview.

74. "Georgia Students Appeal Unequal Facilities," *Atlanta Daily World*, October 28, 1962, A1.

75. "King Warns Negroes of Token Integration Move," *Tifton Gazette*, April 3, 1962, 4.

76. Obatala, "Was the Civil-Rights Struggle," 37.

77. "Georgia Students Appeal Unequal Facilities"; "Rural Ga. Area Pupils Walk

Out for Better School," *Daily Defender*, October 23, 1962, 8. Lack of resources was not confined to Georgia. There were other protests that occurred years later outside of Georgia. See "2,500 Students Stay Out in May-Spencer Boycott," *Daily Defender*, February 15, 1968; "Students Plan City School's Boycott," *Daily Defender*, February 26, 1968, 9. Black schools in the South were not the only schools that dealt with poor conditions and overcrowding. Several articles discussed how the lack of resources led to issues like overcrowding and how black youth responded to the issues using very similar methods.

78. "Georgia Students Appeal Unequal Facilities."

79. For more on the types of activism adopted by students during the 1960s, see Willis, "'Let Me In'"; de Schweinitz, *If We Could Change*; Graham, *Young Activists*; Baker, *Paradoxes of Desegregation*; Thuesen, *Greater than Equal*.

80. "35 at Wilson High Protest Inequality," *Atlanta Daily World*, October 9, 1962, 3.

81. Ibid.

82. Obatala, "Was the Civil-Rights Struggle," 38.

83. Terrell interview with author.

84. Dykes and Terrell interview.

85. During the twentieth century, the employment security of blacks was constantly threatened when they demanded first-class participation. For more on how whites responded to participatory citizenship, see Gates et al., *Oxford Handbook*; Willis, "'Let Me In'"; Feagin, *White Racial Frame*; Carol Anderson, *White Rage*; Kendi, *Stamped from the Beginning*.

86. Terrell interview.

87. Beals, *I Will Not Fear*; Titus, *Brown's Battleground*; Daugherity, *Keep on Keeping On*; Jeffries, *Bloody Lowndes*.

88. "Georgia Students Appeal Unequal Facilities."

89. Ibid.

90. Obatala, "Was the Civil-Rights Struggle," 90.

Chapter 3. A Heavy Tax Levied
for Demanding Equality

1. "Americus and Sumter Schools Are First in Georgia to Refuse to Follow Federal Guidelines," *Tifton Gazette*, April 13, 1966, 46C.

2. Todd-Breland, *Political Education*; Podair, *Strike That Changed New York*; Formisano, *Boston against Busing*.

3. Frady, "Discovering One Another," 46D.

4. On desegregation outside the South, see Todd-Breland, *Political Education*; Formisano, *Boston against Busing*; Danns, *Something Better for Our Children*; Podair, *Strike That Changed New York*.

5. Frady, "Discovering One Another," 46D.

6. Ibid.

7. Frady noted, "When it was obvious that total school integration was at hand

for these citizens, there was a minor but noticeable evacuation of some administrators and teachers out of the Americus School System, and they were accompanied by about 375 students. Private schools multiplied over the area like an overnight backyard visitation of mushrooms" (ibid.) On how whites used flight as a response to integration, see Kruse, *White Flight*.

8. Frady, "Discovering One Another," 52D.

9. For more on the historical racial tensions in Americus, see Auchmutey, *Class of '65*; "Americus and Sumter Schools."

10. For more examples of whites being oppositional to change outside of Georgia, see Adams and Adams, *Just Trying to Have School*; Willis, "'Let Me In'"; Jon Hale, *Freedom Schools*; McKinstry and George, *While the World Watched*.

11. White opposition was displayed in various forms with varying degrees of hostility. The common goal was to prevent fundamental changes to the social and political ethos established under *Plessy*. See Carol Anderson, *White Rage*; Auchmutey, *Class of '65*; Kruse, *White Flight*.

12. "Americus and Sumter Schools."

13. Wilma King, *African American Childhoods*, 6.

14. Alan Anderson, *Remembering Americus, Georgia*; Alan Anderson interview; Williford, *Americus through the Years*.

15. Alan Anderson, "Americus School History."

16. See Watkins, *White Architects of Black Education*; James D. Anderson, *Education of Blacks*.

17. Alan Anderson, "Americus School History." Anderson notes that the funds to build Staley came from the Federal Emergency Relief Act, with preliminary construction work performed under the Works Progress Administration.

18. Ibid.

19. K'Meyer, *Interracialism and Christian Community*, 6. For more on the historical significance of Koinonia Farm, see Holley, "75-Year (and Counting)"; Fuller, *Briars in the Cotton Patch*.

20. K'Meyer, *Interracialism and Christian Community*, 81–82.

21. Tuck, *Beyond Atlanta*, 177. See also K'Meyer, *Interracialism and Christian Community*; Thelma Hunt Shirley, "How It All Started in Americus, Ga.: Part 1," *Chicago Daily Defender*, August 9, 1965, 6; Bartley, "Race Relations and the Quest." Numan Bartley suggests that the increased violence at Koinonia Farm was in large part due to the passage of *Brown*. Similarly, K'Meyer states that "in the late 1950s Koinonians became the target of violence, legal harassment, intimidation, and economic boycott. As civil rights became more of a national issue, Koinonia's interracial activity drew attention and anger" (81). According to Shirley, the farm was labeled as being "run by people with 'up-North Communistic ideas.'" Her article went on to note that the farm was established by "a group from Ridgewood, [New Jersey, as a place] where whites and blacks lived together and as quickly as this was discovered, bullets began flying through the night and a roadside pecan stand operated by the group was blown to bits."

22. NAACP, "NAACP Youth File: General Department File: Wright, Herbert L.," 1–2.

23. K'Meyer, *Interracialism and Christian Community*.

24. Tuck, *Beyond Atlanta*, 177. See also Wilson interview. Juanita Wilson is the daughter of Reverend R. L. Freeman, and she vividly remembers her father's church being used during civil rights activities. She also noted that her father was originally from Atlanta and a graduate of Morehouse College. Reverend Freeman was heavily influenced by Martin Luther King Sr., which gives some insight into why he was receptive to civil rights organizations coming to Americus.

25. For more on how white opposition shaped social movements, see Tuck, *Beyond Atlanta*; Grady-Willis, *Challenging U.S. Apartheid*.

26. Robert E. Baker, "4 Jailed in Georgia to Face 'Insurrection Trial,'" *Washington Post*, October 22, 1963, A7.

27. Ibid. See also Branch, *Parting the Waters*, 865–75. Branch's work details the origins of the law and why the district attorney in Sumter County chose to charge the four SNCC leaders with insurrection. He stated, "the charges were grounded in what was known as the 'Angelo Herndon statute' after the famous communism/integration show trial of the 1930s, which started Herndon's lawyer, Ben Davis, toward his career in the Communist Party. The state made sedition a capital crime, and the Sumter County solicitor all but openly declared that he filed these particular charges in order to jail the demonstration leaders indefinitely by fiat, as Georgia law permitted no pretrial release in capital cases.

28. "SNCC Head Hits Alleged Brutality in Americus, Ga.," *Atlanta Daily World*, August 17, 1963, 5; "5 in Georgia Jail Fight Case Today," *New York Times*, October 31, 1963, 23.

29. Mahone interview.

30. WSB-TV, "WSB-TV News Film Clip of Lawyers for Civil Rights Workers Charged with the Capital Offense of Insurrection, Police and Trial Bystanders in Americus, Georgia, 1963" (Americus, Georgia, October 31, 1963), WSB-TV News Film Collection, Walter J. Brown Media Archives and Peabody Awards Collection; Mahone, interview; Baker, "4 Jailed in Georgia."

31. "SNCC Papers," box 42, folder 14, King Center. A detailed letter written by Bell and Mants to the headquarters of SNCC discusses the issues they had with finding quality leadership in Americus. They stated, "Deacon Lonnie Evans was chosen president of the Movement. This is perhaps the grossest error ever committed. He is a weak, unimpressive, shy, sheeplike man without the self-confidence to disagree with a four-year-old. He is a man in his sixties who will address a puny little twenty-year-old like me as sir. . . . To put it short and sweet, he just doesn't have the dynamic leadership characteristics so badly needed here."

32. Mahone interview. See also Branch, *Parting the Waters*.

33. Mahone interview.

34. Tuck, *Beyond Atlanta*, 178.

35. "SNCC Head Hits Alleged Brutality," 5.

36. For more on how local law enforcement served as antagonists to local movements, see Huntley and McKerley, *Foot Soldiers for Democracy*; Mayer, *When the Children Marched*; Baker, *Paradoxes of Desegregation*; Thuesen, *Greater than Equal*; Adams and Adams, *Just Trying to Have School*.

37. Dada interview. It is important to note that, as Dada observed, a number of local blacks had a problem with the increased number of black youth participating in the movement, because they felt that young people "were too militant, brash, reckless, and disorganized."

38. Wilson interview.

39. Mahone interview.

40. "SNCC Papers," box 42, folder 14.

41. Dada interview; Sherrod interview; Mahone interview; Harris, "SNCC Papers."

42. Harris, "SNCC Papers"; Jon Hale, "Student as a Force."

43. Mahone interview. See also Harris, "SNCC Papers." For more on SNCC and freedom schools, see Jon Hale, *Freedom Schools*.

44. "SNCC Papers." The letter also notes that "due to the high illiteracy rate in Americus [they] propose to set up citizenship schools throughout the city. Literacy and voter registration workshops will be the subject of the schools. The classes will be taught by local citizens."

45. Roche, *Restructured Resistance*, 99–108. Roche states that "businessmen, farmers, educators, and top school administrators one by one came to the witness stand [before the Sibley Commission] and testified that the third district would educate its own children before it backed down from massive resistance" (102).

46. Walker interview.

47. Mansfield interview.

48. See Morris and Morris, *Price They Paid*.

49. Walker interview.

50. Mansfield interview.

51. Wilson interview.

52. Mahone interview.

53. Walker interview.

54. Mansfield interview. In her interview, Sabbs remembered "always [being] number six, seven, or eight down the line of having owned this book."

55. Wilson interview.

56. Ibid.

57. Sabbs interview.

58. Harris, "SNCC Papers," box 96, folder 10.

59. Mansfield interview.

60. For more on this incident and the Stolen Girls, see Owens, "Stolen Girls"; Westbrooks-Griffin, *Freedom Is Not Free*.

61. Fuller, "SNCC Papers," box 95, folder 11.

62. Owens, "Stolen Girls," 166. One of the girls interviewed for the piece offered chilling insight into how cruelly the girls were treated, saying, "They told us

that we'd be taken out one by one and killed" (165). Owens provides many more details on the inhumane conditions at Leesburg, including the following: "Several of the girls began throwing up or suffering from diarrhea. The only toilet was a broken commode in the corner that couldn't be flushed. It was soon clogged to the top. With no other options to relieve themselves, the girls took to squatting over the shower drain, which quickly developed a suffocating stench. . . . When their menstrual cycles came, they tore strips off their dresses and fashioned them into napkins. Bathing wasn't an option" (165–66).

63. Sabbs interview.

64. "32 Children Stay Out of School: Apparent Protest," *Atlanta Daily World*, August 31, 1963, 1.

65. Sabbs interview.

66. "Arrests Made This Morning," *Americus Times-Recorder*, August 31, 1963, 1A. See also Walker interview. The increase in arrests of black youth persuaded some teachers at Staley, although very few, to participate in the boycott. One of the teachers was Thelma Barnum and the other was Ms. Walker, who was an alumna of Staley. When asked why she decided to participate in the boycott and risk her job, she cited the treatment of the students.

67. Tuck, *Beyond Atlanta*, 176.

68. Owens, "Stolen Girls," 218.

69. Mahone interview.

70. Sokol, *There Goes My Everything*, 56. The different ways in which blacks and whites in the South, and specifically in Americus, viewed reality informed their views of the movement. Sokol argued that "whites were shocked when African Americans rose up in defiance in the 1960s. Black rebellion clashed so sharply with white perceptions that many disbelieved their own eyes" (56–57).

71. Shirley, "How It All Started," 6.

72. Mahone interview.

73. Sabbs interview.

74. Ibid.

75. For more about the hostility met by the black students who desegregated Americus High School, see Fletcher, "Brown Bag Lecture."

76. Beals, *I Will Not Fear*; Anderson and Byrne, *Unfinished Agenda of Brown*.

77. Mahone interview.

78. Wilson interview.

79. Harris, "SNCC Papers"; Fletcher, "Brown Bag Lecture."

80. Harris, "SNCC Papers."

81. Ibid.

82. Fuller, "SNCC Papers."

83. Tuck, *Beyond Atlanta*, 181.

84. Gene Roberts, "U.S. Judge Frees Four in Americus: Jailed Negro Women Out—Demonstrations Resume," *New York Times*, July 31, 1965, 50.

85. In *Beyond Atlanta*, Tuck argues that "in some ways the Americus Movement provided a case study in the argument raging within SNCC by 1965 over the

efficacy of nonviolence. Although nonviolence had failed to force significant progress, racial violence . . . provoked a reaction unprecedented even in southwest
Georgia" (184).

86. Jack Nelson, "Well-Armed Americus Gripped by Racial Fear," *Los Angeles
Times*, August 1, 1965, F 14; Tuck, *Beyond Atlanta*, 184.

87. "Klansmen March in Georgia: Negroes Counter with One of Their Own,"
Chicago Tribune, August 9, 1965, 5.

88. See Martin Luther King Jr., *Gift of Love*; Burrow, *Child Shall Lead Them*;
Grady-Willis, *Challenging U.S. Apartheid*.

89. Tuck, *Beyond Atlanta*, 185.

90. Fletcher, "Brown Bag Lecture."

91. Sabbs interview.

92. Mansfield interview. Mansfield did note that she eventually graduated and
furthered her education in child development and nursing.

Chapter 4. Educational Resources
Are Not for White Schools Only

1. McBurrows interview; Williams interview; Jordan interview; Holton interview.

2. Wheeler interview; Nina Banister, "Pride in Color," *Moultrie Observer*, February 12, 1993; Ruth Mason and Annie Ruth Thompson, "History of Public Education for Negro Children in Moultrie, Georgia," paper distributed at Ram
Round-Up, [June 2012].

3. Mason and Thompson, "History of Public Education."

4. See Carr, *What Is History?*

5. Banister, "Pride in Color"; Denegall, "History."

6. Obama, *Audacity of Hope*.

7. Zieger, *For Jobs and Freedom*; Fairclough, *Better Day Coming*, 186.

8. Covington, *History of Colquitt County*.

9. Holmes, "Economic Developments," 270.

10. Covington, *History of Colquitt County*, 223.

11. A letter in the SNCC files notes that the distinction between the black
neighborhood in Moultrie and the white neighborhood was clear: "Like all southern towns, you can tell when you pass into the Negro section. It's often as tangible
as crossing the railroad tracks. The paved roads stop, and red mud or red dust, de-
pending on the weather, takes over. The houses are poorer, unpainted, because the
people who live in them aren't allowed to hold decent jobs." SNCC Papers, King
Center, box 96, folder 11.

12. John David Smith, *Old Creed*, 210.

13. Mason and Thompson, "History of Public Education."

14. Denegall, "History." Mildred Daniels is given credit for examining the early
years of Colquitt County school board documents and, according to her, "during

the early years of black children school years [*sic*], there were two buildings. One in Moultrie and the other in Norman Park." She also suggested "that classes were housed in churches with no transportation or lunchrooms."

15. Cumming v. Richmond County of Board of Education; Connally, "Justice Harlan's 'Great Betrayal'?"

16. Roche, *Restructured Resistance*, 145.

17. Wheeler interview.

18. Reverend McBurrows noted that his father was not the only black parent in rural Colquitt County who made sure his children had access to a formal education. "There were some strong black parents who were determined, and they fought against all odds. However, most parents could not fight for their children to go to school because they started a crop, and if they raised any opposition the landlord ran them away. So they had no compensation for all the work they put in. I saw a number of black farmers who were chased out of town because they tried to change the educational conditions of their children." McBurrows interview.

19. Ibid. Reverend McBurrows also stated that "ninety-five percent of the young kids I grew up with never finished high school, and only one percent worked on a job that paid benefits and retirement."

20. Ibid.

21. Wheeler interview.

22. McBurrows interview.

23. "Minutes of Meetings of the Colquitt County School Board," Colquitt County School Board, Moultrie, Ga., March 1, 1955. Minutes from a school board meeting in 1953 also show that the same type of resolution was considered in regard to facilities for black students who lived in Doerun. The minutes noted that "the resolution of acceptance of this board adopted on April 10, 1953, and described as a Doerun Colored Elementary School have been completed and submitted. . . . The architects estimate [the project] will cost $127,777.00."

24. McBurrows interview.

25. Wilma King, *African American Childhoods*; Bernstein, *Racial Innocence*.

26. Holton interview.

27. Wheeler interview; McBurrows interview; Williams interview; Green interview; Holton interview; Herman Kitchen, "The School Boycott, Moultrie, Georgia," n.d., King Center, SNCC Papers; Banister, "Pride in Color"; Harris, "SNCC Papers."

28. Roche, *Restructured Resistance*, 145.

29. Minchin and Salmond, *After the Dream*, 47, 38.

30. Willis, "'Let Me In'"; Williamson-Lott, Darling-Hammond, and Hyler, "Education and the Quest"; Armstrong and Mason, "Introduction."

31. Williams interview; Green interview. It is important to note that Williams and Green stated that improvements were made to William Bryant High during the late 1950s and early 1960s.

32. Denegall, "History." Charlie A. Gray was a renowned educator who taught

at Moultrie High for Negro Youth. The elementary school was named in honor of him.

33. Green interview.

34. Ibid.

35. Williams interview.

36. Holton interview.

37. Green interview.

38. Holton interview; Green interview.

39. Sokol, *There Goes My Everything*; Klarman, *Unfinished Business*; Webb, *Massive Resistance*.

40. Huntley and McKerley, *Foot Soldiers for Democracy*; Payne, *I've Got the Light*; Whitfield, *Death in the Delta*; Hampton, Fayer, and Flynn, *Voices of Freedom*.

41. Payne, *I've Got the Light*, 283.

42. Holton interview.

43. Williams interview.

44. Dada interview.

45. James Parry, "SNCC Papers," March 8, 1965, King Center.

46. Parry, "SNCC Papers."

47. Holton interview.

48. Ibid.

49. Fletcher, "Brown Bag Lecture"; Tuck, *Beyond Atlanta*.

50. Williams interview.

51. Holton interview.

52. Parry, "SNCC Papers."

53. Holton interview.

54. Green interview.

55. Williams interview.

56. Ibid.

57. For a detailed discussion on SACS, accreditation, and black schools, see Walker, *Hello Professor*, 81. Walker notes that "the Southern Association was the accrediting agency that established standards for white schools and colleges throughout the South." She goes on to discuss how the organization accredited white schools while labeling black schools that met the criteria for accreditation as merely "approved." Even when the Southern Association began to accredit black schools, the organization was still noncommittal regarding the plight black schools faced daily.

58. "SNCC Papers," box 96, folder 11.

59. Herman Kitchen stated, "The county is getting $201,934 from the federal government for use in upgrading Colquitt County schools, and they are now trying to get a legal block to prohibit or stop that money from coming into the schools on a segregated basis. The 1964 Civil Rights Act outlaws such discrimination in the application of federal funds." Kitchen, "School Boycott, Moultrie, Georgia."

60. Dada interview.

61. Tuck, *Beyond Atlanta*, 188.

62. Kitchen, "School Boycott, Moultrie, Georgia."

63. Tuck, *Beyond Atlanta*, 188.

64. Holton interview.

65. Banister, "Pride in Color," 18.

66. Kitchen, "School Boycott, Moultrie, Georgia."

67. Kitchen interview.

68. Ibid.

69. "SNCC Papers."

70. Green interview.

71. Banister, "Pride in Color," 14.

72. Parry, "SNCC Papers."

73. Ibid.

74. Sokol, *There Goes My Everything*; Klarman, *Unfinished Business*; Webb, *Massive Resistance*; Kruse, *White Flight*.

75. Banister, "Pride in Color"; "SNCC Papers." Although the students were taught nonviolence by SNCC, those who remembered the incident noted that the limited violence used was out of fear and not a change in strategy. A letter from a member of SNCC explained why the student threw a brick.

76. Banister, "Pride in Color."

77. Parry, "SNCC Papers." On the treatment of youth protesters in Americus, see Owens, "Stolen Girls." Parry's letter also reveals that Herman Kitchen, another member of SNCC, was placed in a cell called the "Buzzard Roost, solitary confinement, not large enough to stand up in. . . . He was also fed only bread and water."

78. Holton interview.

79. Parry, "SNCC Papers."

80. Ibid.

81. Dada interview. See also Parry, "SNCC Papers."

82. Harris, "SNCC Papers." See also Dada interview; Banister, "Pride in Color."

83. Parry, "SNCC Papers"; Banister, "Pride in Color."

84. Parry, "SNCC Papers."

85. "Local Officials Agree to Some Negro Requests," *Moultrie Observer*, February 5, 1965.

86. Banister, "Pride in Color."

87. Banister, "Pride in Color"; "Local Officials Agree."

88. Banister, "Pride in Color"; Harris, "SNCC Papers"; Kitchen, "School Boycott, Moultrie, Georgia."

89. Parry, "SNCC Papers."

90. Holton interview.

91. "SNCC Papers." See also Kitchen, "School Boycott, Moultrie, Georgia."

92. Holton interview.

93. Williams interview.

94. Holton interview.

Chapter 5. When Desegregation Was Not Enough

1. Du Bois, *Philadelphia Negro*; Du Bois, *Souls of Black Folk*; Du Bois, "Does the Negro Need"; Heather Andrea Williams, *Self-Taught*; Carol Anderson, *Eyes off the Prize*.

2. Span and Rivers, "Reassessing the Achievement Gap"; James D. Anderson, *Education of Blacks*; Green, *Educational Reconstruction*; Walker, *Lost Education of Horace Tate*.

3. Beals, *Warriors Don't Cry*; Jacoway, "Not Anger But Sorrow"; Purdy, *Transforming the Elite*; Jon Hale, *Freedom Schools*; Willis, "'Let Me In.'"

4. Fletcher, "Brown Bag Lecture"; Sabbs interview; Kitchen interview.

5. Sabbs interview.

6. "President Lyndon B. Johnson's Commencement Address at Howard University: 'To Fulfill These Rights,' June 4, 1965," accessed February 13, 2013, http://www.lbjlib.utexas.edu/johnson/archives.hom/speeches.hom/650604.asp.

7. Gates et al., *Oxford Handbook*.

8. Sokol, *There Goes My Everything*, 350.

9. Eaton, Feldman, and Kirby, "Still Separate, Still Unequal," 143.

10. Tuck, *Beyond Atlanta*, 245.

11. Joiner et al., *History of Public Education*; Coleman, *History of Georgia*; Hornsby, "Black Public Education."

12. McCluskey, *Forgotten Sisterhood*; James D. Anderson, *Education of Blacks*; Todd-Breland, *Political Education*; Carol Anderson, *White Rage*.

13. Sabbs interview.

14. There is a wealth of scholarship that analyzes the limitations of achieving equality solely by legal means. Irons, *People's History*; Crooms-Robinson, "African American Legal Status from Reconstruction Law"; Bryan K. Fair, "Still Standing"; Goldstone, *Inherently Unequal*; Pinder and Hanson, "De Jure, De Facto," 165.

15. Jeffries, *Bloody Lowndes*; Payne, *I've Got the Light*; de Schweinitz, "'Proper Age for Suffrage.'"

16. Arsenault, *Freedom Riders*; NAACP, "NAACP Administrative File: General Office File"; Payne, *I've Got the Light*; Jeffries, *Bloody Lowndes*.

17. Carruthers and Wanamaker, "Separate and Unequal"; Ashenfelter, Collins, and Yoon, "Evaluating the Role of *Brown*."

18. Graham, *Young Activists*; de Schweinitz, *If We Could Change*; Jon Hale, *Freedom Schools*; Stoper, *Student Nonviolent Coordinating Committee*; Franklin, *After the Rebellion*.

19. Wilson interview.

20. Kitchen interview.

21. Kitchen interview; Jordan interview; Fletcher, "Brown Bag Lecture"; Jacoway, "Not Anger But Sorrow"; Beals, *I Will Not Fear*.

22. Walker, *Lost Education of Horace Tate*; Walker, "Second-Class Integration."

23. "Georgia Students Appeal Unequal Facilities," *Atlanta Daily World*, October 28, 1962, A1; Roche, *Restructured Resistance*; Carol Anderson, *White Rage*;

"32 Children Stay Out Of School: Apparent Protest," *Atlanta Daily World*, August 31, 1963, 1; "35 at Wilson High Protest Inequality," *Atlanta Daily World*, October 9, 1962, 3.

24. Graham, *Young Activists*, 198.

25. Beals, *I Will Not Fear*; Beals, *Warriors Don't Cry*; Owens, "Stolen Girls."

26. Ladson-Billings, "From the Achievement Gap"; Span and Rivers, "Reassessing the Achievement Gap"; Kendi, *Stamped from the Beginning*; Walker, *Lost Education of Horace Tate*.

27. Pinder and Hanson, "De Jure, De Facto"; Carol Anderson, *White Rage*.

28. Frady, "Discovering One Another"; Alan Anderson, *Remembering Americus, Georgia*.

29. Baker, *Paradoxes of Desegregation*.

30. Cecelski, *Along Freedom Road*; Danns, *Something Better for Our Children*.

31. Sabbs interview.

Epilogue. The Elusive Nature of Educational Equality

1. Burrow, *Child Shall Lead Them*; Wells, *Both Sides Now*; "Integration Will Bring 'Knowledge of Each Other,' Wilkins Says as 26,000 Youth March," *Los Angeles Tribune*, April 24, 1959, 7; "Editorial Excerpts from the Nation's Press on Segregation Ruling," *New York Times*, May 18, 1954, 19.

2. Ewing, "King Wanted More."

3. Diem and Brooks, "Introduction to the Issue"; Nevas, "Factors in Desegregation and Integration"; Moody, "Race, School Integration, and Friendship"; Walker, "Second-Class Integration."

4. De Schweinitz, *If We Could Change*, 231–32.

5. For more on the purpose of the United States Commission, see Grua, "Citizen[s] with a Difference."

6. "Text of Civil Rights Commission Statement on School Desegregation," *New York Times*, September 13, 1969, 28.

7. Ibid.

8. Baker, *Paradoxes of Desegregation*, 148.

9. "Text of Civil Rights Commission Statement."

10. Donnor and Dixson, *Resegregation of Schools*; Ruth Carbonette Yow, *Students of the Dream*; Monroe, "Why Are 'Bad Boys' Always Black?"; Welsh and Little, "School Discipline Dilemma"; Orfield, Eaton, and Harvard Project, *Dismantling Desegregation*.

11. "Toni Morrison on Capturing a Mother's 'Compulsion.'"

12. Margaret Anderson, *Children of the South*; "500 Schools Desegregated Year after Court Ruling," *Atlanta Daily World*, April 30, 1955, 1.

13. Richards, Ellis, and Candiotti, "65 Years since Brown"; Joe Davidson, "Brown v. Board of Education: After 65 Years, Still Seeking to Make a Promise a Reality," *Washington Post*, May 3, 2019, https://www.washingtonpost.com/politics

/2019/05/03/brown-v-board-education-after-years-still-seeking-make-promise
-reality; Lockhart, "65 Years after Brown."

14. Dana Goldstein and Anemona Hartocollis, "'Separate Programs for Separate Communities': California School District Agrees to Desegregate," New York
Times, August 9, 2019, https://www.nytimes.com/2019/08/09/us/sausalito-school
-segregation.html.

15. "U.S. Students Fight for Education Rights," YouTube post by Al Jazeera
English, February 17, 2009, http://www.youtube.com/watch?v=tGElD9srKmU.
For more on the racial inequities in the Baltimore County school system, see Ro-
sette, "School Board for the People."

16. "U.S. Students Fight for Education Rights."

17. James D. Anderson, *Education of Blacks*.

18. Pertilla interview; Dykes and Terrell interview.

19. Ladson-Billings, "From the Achievement Gap."

20. Ibid., 9.

21. Jordan interview.

22. Kruse, *White Flight*; Sokol, *There Goes My Everything*; DiAngelo, *White
Fragility*; Purdy, *Transforming the Elite*; Danns, Purdy, and Span, *Using Past as
Prologue*.

23. Adams and Adams, "We All Came Together."

24. Jordan interview.

BIBLIOGRAPHY

Archival and Manuscript Collections

Atlanta Student Movement Papers, Archives Research Center, Atlanta University Center. Atlanta, Georgia

Colquitt County School Board Minutes, Colquitt County Board of Education. Moultrie, Georgia

Ellen Payne Odom Genealogy Library Collection, Moultrie-Colquitt County Library System. Moultrie, Georgia

Genealogy and Local History Research, Lack Blackshear Regional Library System. Americus, Georgia

National Association for the Advancement of Colored People Papers (Microfilm), Emory University. Atlanta, Georgia

National Association for the Advancement of Colored People Papers (Microfilm), Collections of the Manuscript Division, Library of Congress. Washington, D.C.

Special Collections and Genealogy Room, Tifton-Tift County Public Library. Tifton, Georgia

Student Non-Violent Coordinating Committee Papers, King Center. Atlanta, Georgia

Voters Education Project, Archives Research Center, Atlanta University Center. Atlanta, Georgia

Interviews and Oral Histories

Anderson, Alan. Interview with author, audio recording, Americus, Georgia, March 15, 2012.

Dada, Mukasa. Interview with author, audio recording, Atlanta, Georgia, February 1, 2012.

———. Interview with author, audio recording, Moultrie, Georgia, March 8, 2012.

Dykes, Walter. Interview with author, audio recording, Tifton, Georgia, March 16, 2012.

Dykes, Walter, and Johnny Terrell. Interview with author, audio recording, Tifton, Georgia, January 29, 2015.

Green, J. W., Jr. Interview with author, audio recording, Moultrie, Georgia, March 15, 2012.

Holton, Jimmy. Interview with author, audio recording, Moultrie, Georgia, July 20, 2012.

Jordan, Joanne. Interview with author, audio recording, Moultrie, Georgia, January 28, 2015.

Kitchen, Fran. Interview with Author, audio recording, Tifton, Georgia, January 29, 2015.

Mahone, Sam. Interview with author, audio recording, Atlanta, Georgia, July 29, 2012.

Mansfield, Sandra. Interview with author, audio recording, Americus, Georgia, March 17, 2012.

McBurrows, Rev. Johnny. Interview with author, audio recording, Moultrie, Georgia, February 17, 2012.

Myles, David. Interview with author, audio recording, Rockdale, Maryland, September 4, 2019.

Pertilla, Alton. Interview with author, audio recording, Tifton, Georgia, March 16, 2012.

Sabbs, Lorena. Interview with author, audio recording, Americus, Georgia, March 5, 2012.

————. Interview with author, audio recording, Americus, Georgia, July 23, 2012.

Sherrod, Charles. Interview with author, audio recording, Albany, Georgia, July 23, 2012.

Terrell, Johnny. Interview with author, audio recording, Tifton, Georgia, July 21, 2012.

Walker, Ann Whea. Interview with author, audio recording, Americus, Georgia, March 16, 2012.

Wheeler, Ann. Interview with author, audio recording, Moultrie, Georgia, March 15, 2012.

Williams, Dale. Interview with author, audio recording, Moultrie, Georgia, July 20, 2012.

————. Interview with author, audio recording, Moultrie, Georgia, March 18, 2012.

Wilson, Juanita. Interview with author, audio recording, Americus, Georgia, March 17, 2012.

Newspapers

Americus Times-Recorder	*Chicago Defender*
Atlanta Daily World	*Chicago Tribune*
Atlanta Inquirer	*Hartford (Conn.) Courant*
Atlanta Journal-Constitution	*Life Magazine*
Chicago Daily Defender	*Los Angeles Times*

Los Angeles Tribune
Louisville (Ky.) Courier-Journal
Moultrie (Ga.) Observer
New York Amsterdam News
New York Times

New Pittsburgh Courier
San Francisco Chronicle
Student Voice (SNCC weekly)
Tifton (Ga.) Gazette
Washington Post

Unpublished Works and Government Documents

Anderson, Alan. "Americus School History." N.d. Accessed August 13, 2012. http://www.sumtercountyhistory.com/history/AmSchHx.htm.
Denegall, Rev. Jerry. "A History of the First Avenue Box: Rat Row and Its Neighborhood." Unpublished manuscript.
"Minutes of Meetings of the Colquitt County School Board" Colquitt County School Board, Moultrie, Georgia, March 1, 1955.
The Tiger. Tifton, Ga.: Wilson High School, 1962.
The Tiger Alumni Reunion, 1930–1975. Tifton, Ga.: Tift County Industrial/Wilson High Schools Alumni Reunion Coalition, 2005.

Films and Videos

Fuller, Faith, dir. Briars in the Cotton Patch: The Story of Koinonia Farm. 10th anniversary edition. Americus, Ga.: Cotton Patch Productions, 2012. DVD, 57 min.
James, Dante, prod. Slavery and the Making of America. Four-part series originally aired February 9 and 16, 2005, on WNET. New York: Ambrose DVD, 2005. DVD, 4 discs, 188 min.
Mondale, Sarah, dir. School: The Story of American Public Education. Four-part series originally aired September 3–4, 2001, on PBS. Produced by Stone Lantern Films and KCET Hollywood. Princeton, N.J.: Films for the Humanities and Sciences, 2000. DVD, 4 discs, 220 min.
"Toni Morrison on Capturing a Mother's 'Compulsion' to Nurture in 'Beloved.'" YouTube post by PBS NewsHour, August 6, 2019. Interview segment originally aired on MacNeil/Lehrer NewsHour, September 29, 1987. https://www.youtube.com/watch?v=pLQ6ipVRfrE.
WSB-TV. "Series of WSB-TV newsfilm clips of lawyers for civil rights workers charged with the capital offense of insurrection, police, and trial bystanders in Americus, Georgia, 1963 October 31." WSB-TV Newsfilm Collection. Walter J. Brown Media Archives and Peabody Awards Collection, University of Georgia Libraries, Athens, Georgia.

Articles and Books

Adams, David Wallace. Education for Extinction: American Indians and the Boarding School Experience, 1875–1928. Lawrence: University Press of Kansas, 1997.
Adams, Natalie, and James Adams. "'We All Came Together on the Football Field':

Unpacking the Blissful Clarity of a Popular Southern Sports Story." In *Critical Studies of Southern Place: A Reader*, edited by William Reynolds, 337–47. New York: Peter Lang, 2014.

Adams, Natalie G., and James H. Adams. *Just Trying to Have School: The Struggle for Desegregation in Mississippi*. Jackson: University Press of Mississippi, 2018.

Alexander, Michelle. *The New Jim Crow: Mass Incarceration in the Age of Colorblindness*. Rev. ed., with a new foreword by Cornel West. New York: New Press, 2012.

Anderson, Alan. *Remembering Americus, Georgia: Essays on Southern Life*. Charleston, S.C.: History Press, 2006.

Anderson, Carol. *Eyes off the Prize: The United Nations and the African American Struggle for Human Rights, 1944–1955*. New York: Cambridge University Press, 2003.

———. *White Rage: The Unspoken Truth of Our Racial Divide*. New York: Bloomsbury, 2016.

Anderson, James, and Dara N. Byrne, eds. *The Unfinished Agenda of Brown v. Board of Education*. Hoboken, N.J.: J. Wiley & Sons, 2004.

Anderson, James D. *The Education of Blacks in the South, 1860–1935*. Chapel Hill: University of North Carolina Press, 1988.

Anderson, Jervis. *Bayard Rustin: Troubles I've Seen: A Biography*. New York: HarperCollins, 1997.

Anderson, Margaret. *The Children of the South*. New York: Farrar, Straus and Giroux, 1966.

Anderson, Noel S., and Haroon Kharem. *Education as Freedom: African American Educational Thought and Activism*. Lanham, Md.: Lexington Books, 2009.

Armstrong, Chris, and Andrew Mason. "Introduction: Democratic Citizenship and Its Futures." *Critical Review of International Social and Political Philosophy* 14, no. 5 (December 2011): 553–60. https://doi.org/10.1080/13698230.2011.617118.

Arsenault, Raymond. *Freedom Riders: 1961 and the Struggle for Racial Justice*. 2nd ed. New York: Oxford University Press, 2011.

Ashenfelter, Orley, William J. Collins, and Albert H. Yoon. "Evaluating the Role of *Brown v. Board of Education* in School Equalization, Desegregation, and the Income of African Americans." *American Law and Economics Review* 8, no. 2 (Summer 2006): 213–48.

Auchmutey, Jim. *The Class of '65: A Student, a Divided Town, and the Long Road to Forgiveness*. New York: PublicAffairs, 2015.

Baker, R. Scott. *Paradoxes of Desegregation: African American Struggles for Educational Equity in Charleston, South Carolina, 1926–1972*. Columbia: University of South Carolina Press, 2006.

Ball, Arnetha, ed. *With More Deliberate Speed: Achieving Equity and Excellence in Education*. Malden, Mass.: Blackwell, 2006.

Bartley, Numan V. "Race Relations and the Quest for Equality." In Coleman, *A History of Georgia*, 361–74.

Baum, Willa K. *Transcribing and Editing Oral History*. Nashville, Tenn.: American Association for State and Local History, 1977.

Beals, Melba Pattillo. *I Will Not Fear: My Story of a Lifetime of Building Faith under Fire*. Grand Rapids, Mich.: Revell, 2018.

———. *Warriors Don't Cry: The Searing Memoir of the Battle to Integrate Little Rock's Central High*. New York: Simon Pulse, 2007.

Bell, Derrick A. *Silent Covenants: Brown v. Board of Education and the Unfulfilled Hopes for Racial Reform*. New York: Oxford University Press, 2004.

Bernstein, Robin. *Racial Innocence: Performing American Childhood from Slavery to Civil Rights*. New York: New York University Press, 2011.

Blackmon, Douglas A. *Slavery by Another Name: The Re-enslavement of Black Americans from the Civil War to World War II*. New York: Anchor, 2009.

Branch, Taylor. *Parting the Waters: America in the King Years 1954–63*. New York: Simon & Schuster, 1989.

Brinson, Albert Paul. "A Second Look: The Negro Citizen in Atlanta." Atlanta Student Movement Collection, January 1960. Robert W. Woodruff Library, Atlanta University Center.

Brown-Nagin, Tomiko. *Courage to Dissent: Atlanta and the Long History of the Civil Rights Movement*. New York: Oxford University Press, 2011.

Bullock, Henry Allen. *A History of Negro Education in the South: From 1619 to the Present*. Cambridge, Mass.: Harvard University Press, 1967.

Burns, Stewart. *To the Mountaintop: Martin Luther King Jr.'s Sacred Mission to Save America, 1955–1968*. New York: HarperSanFrancisco, 2004.

Burrow, Rufus, Jr. *A Child Shall Lead Them: Martin Luther King Jr., Young People, and the Movement*. Minneapolis, Minn.: Fortress, 2014.

Burton, Orville Vernon, and David O'Brien, eds. *Remembering Brown at Fifty: The University of Illinois Commemorates Brown v. Board of Education*. Urbana: University of Illinois Press, 2009.

Bynum, Thomas L. "'We Must March Forward!': Juanita Jackson and the Origins of the NAACP Youth Movement." *Journal of African American History* 94, no. 4 (Fall 2009): 487–508.

Byrne, Dara N., ed. *Brown v. Board of Education: Its Impact on Public Education, 1954–2004*. New York: Word for Word, 2005.

Carr, Edward Hallet. *What Is History?* New York: Vintage, 1967.

Carruthers, Celeste K., and Marianne H. Wanamaker. "Separate and Unequal in the Labor Market: Human Capital and the Jim Crow Wage Gap." Working Paper, National Bureau of Economic Research, January 2016. https://doi.org/10.3386/w21947.

Carson, Clayborne. *In Struggle: SNCC and the Black Awakening of the 1960s*. 2nd rev. ed. Cambridge, Mass.: Harvard University Press, 1995.

Carter, Robert L. "*Brown's* Legacy: Fulfilling the Promise of Equal Education." *Journal of Negro Education* 76, no. 3 (2007): 240–49. http://www.jstor.org/stable/40034568.

Cecelski, David S. *Along Freedom Road: Hyde County, North Carolina, and the*

Fate of Black Schools in the South. Chapel Hill: University of North Carolina Press, 1994.

Chamberlain, Daphne Rochelle. "'And a Child Shall Lead the Way': Children's Participation in the Jackson, Mississippi, Black Freedom Struggle, 1946–1970." PhD Diss., University of Mississippi, 2009.

Chesters, Graeme, and Ian Welsh, eds. *Social Movements: The Key Concepts.* New York: Routledge, 2010.

Coleman, Kenneth, ed. *A History of Georgia.* 2nd ed. Athens: University of Georgia Press, 1991.

Connally, C. Ellen. "Justice Harlan's 'Great Betrayal'? A Reconsideration of *Cumming v. Richmond County Board of Education.*" *Journal of Supreme Court History* 25, no. 1 (March 2000): 72–92.

Covington, W. A. *History of Colquitt County [Georgia].* 1937; Markham, Va.: Apple Manor Press, 2011.

Cox, William. "Reflections of One Who Was There." In Anderson and Byrne, *Unfinished Agenda of Brown,* xvii–xxiv.

Creswell, John W. *Qualitative Inquiry and Research Design: Choosing among Five Approaches.* 2nd ed. Thousand Oaks, Calif.: Sage Publications, 2006.

Croft, Sheryl J., Tiffany D. Pogue, and Vanessa Siddle Walker. *Living the Legacy of African American Education: A Model for University and School Engagement.* Lanham, Md.: Rowman & Littlefield, 2018.

Crooms-Robinson, Lisa. "African American Legal Status from Reconstruction Law to the Nadir of Jim Crow: 1865–1919." In Gates et al., *Oxford Handbook,* 522–38.

———. "African American Legal Status from the Harlem Renaissance through World War II." In Gates et al., *Oxford Handbook,* 539–49.

Danns, Dionne. *Something Better for Our Children: Black Organization in the Chicago Public Schools, 1963–1971.* New York: Routledge, 2003.

Danns, Dionne, Michelle A. Purdy, and Christopher M. Span, eds. *Using Past as Prologue: Contemporary Perspectives on African American Educational History.* Charlotte, N.C.: Information Age, 2015.

Daugherity, Brian J. *Keep on Keeping On: The NAACP and the Implementation of Brown v. Board of Education in Virginia.* Charlottesville: University of Virginia Press, 2016.

Daugherity, Brian J., and Charles C Bolton. *With All Deliberate Speed: Implementing Brown v. Board of Education.* Fayetteville: University of Arkansas Press, 2008.

de Schweinitz, Rebecca. *If We Could Change the World: Young People and America's Long Struggle for Racial Equality.* Chapel Hill: University of North Carolina Press, 2009.

———. "'The Proper Age for Suffrage': Vote 18 and the Politics of Age from World War II to the Age of Aquarius." In *Age in America: The Colonial Era to the Present,* edited by Corinne T. Field and Nicholas L. Syrett 209–36. New York: New York University Press, 2015.

DiAngelo, Robin. *White Fragility: Why It's So Hard for White People to Talk About Racism*. Boston: Beacon Press, 2018.

Diem, Sarah, and Jeffrey Brooks. "Introduction to the Issue on Segregation, Desegregation, and Integration: From History, to Policy, to Practice." *Teachers College Record* 115, no. 11 (2013): 1–6.

Donnor, Jamel K., and Adrienne D. Dixson, eds. *The Resegregation of Schools: Education and Race in the Twenty-First Century*. New York: Routledge, 2013.

Donohue, John J., III, James J. Heckman, and Petra E. Todd. "The Schooling of Southern Blacks: The Roles of Legal Activism and Private Philanthropy, 1910–1960." *Quarterly Journal of Economics* 117, no. 1 (February 2002): 225–68. https://doi.org/10.1162/003355302753399490.

Dougherty, Jack. "'That's When We Were Marching for Jobs': Black Teachers and the Early Civil Rights Movement in Milwaukee." *History of Education Quarterly* 38, no. 2 (Summer 1998): 121–41.

Douglass, Frederick. "Frederick Douglass Project Writings: West India Emancipation." University of Rochester Frederick Douglass Project. Accessed February 20, 2013. http://www.lib.rochester.edu/index.cfm?PAGE=4398.

Du Bois, W. E. B. "Does the Negro Need Separate Schools?" In "The Courts and the Negro Separate Schools," special issue, *Journal of Negro Education* 4, no. 3 (July 1935): 328–35.

———. *The Philadelphia Negro: A Social Study*. ATLA Monograph Preservation Program; ATLA Fiche 1988–2167. Philadelphia: published for the University of Pennsylvania, 1899.

———. *The Souls of Black Folk*. New York: Library of America, 2009.

Eaton, Susan E., Joseph Feldman, and Edward Kirby. "Still Separate, Still Unequal: The Limits of *Milliken II*'s Monetary Compensation to Segregated Schools." In Orfield, Eaton, and Harvard Project, *Dismantling Desegregation*, 143–78.

Endersby, James W., and William T. Horner. *Lloyd Gaines and the Fight to End Segregation*. Columbia: University of Missouri Press, 2016.

Erickson, Ansley T. *Making the Unequal Metropolis: School Desegregation and Its Limits*. Chicago: University of Chicago Press, 2017.

Ewing, Eve L. "King Wanted More Than Just Desegregation." *Atlantic*, March 22, 2018. https://www.theatlantic.com/magazine/archive/2018/02/still-separate-and-unequal/552515/.

Fair, Bryan K. "Still Standing in the Schoolhouse Door: Deconstructing Brown's Bias and Reconstructing Its Remedy." *Indiana Journal of Law and Social Equality* 2, no. 1 (2013): 137–65.

Fair, John D. *The Tifts of Georgia: Connecticut Yankees in King Cotton's Court*. Macon, Ga.: Mercer University Press, 2010.

Fairclough, Adam. *Better Day Coming: Blacks and Equality, 1890–2000*. New York: Viking, 2001.

Feagin, Joe R. *The White Racial Frame: Centuries of Racial Framing and Counter-framing*. New York: Routledge, 2009.

Fine, Michelle. *Off White: Readings on Race, Power, and Society*. New York: Routledge, 1996.

Fireside, Harvey. *Separate and Unequal: Homer Plessy and the Supreme Court Decision That Legalized Racism*. New York: Basic Books, 2005.

Fletcher, Robertina [Freeman]. "Brown Bag Lecture: Robertina Fletcher, Albany State University." Presentation as part of the Teacher Education Brown Bag Lecture Series, Albany, Georgia, March 27, 2019.

Formisano, Ronald P. *Boston against Busing: Race, Class, and Ethnicity in the 1960s and 1970s*. 2nd rev. ed. Chapel Hill: University of North Carolina Press, 2004.

Foster, Michèle. *Black Teachers on Teaching*. New York: New Press, 1997.

Frady, Marshall. "Discovering One Another in a Georgia Town." *Life*, February 12, 1971.

Franklin, Sekou M. *After the Rebellion: Black Youth, Social Movement Activism, and the Post–Civil Rights Generation*. New York: New York University Press, 2014.

Frederickson, Kari. *The Dixiecrat Revolt and the End of the Solid South, 1932–1968*. Chapel Hill: University of North Carolina Press, 2001.

Garraghan, Gilbert J. *A Guide to Historical Method*. Bronx, N.Y.: Fordham University Press, 1946.

Garrow, David. *Bearing the Cross: Martin Luther King, Jr., and the Southern Christian Leadership Conference*. New York: Perennial Classics, 2004.

Gates, Henry Louis, Jr., Claude Steele, Lawrence Bobo, Michael Dawson, Gerald Jaynes, Lisa Crooms-Robinson, and Linda Darling-Hammond, eds. *The Oxford Handbook of African American Citizenship, 1865–Present*. New York: Oxford University Press, 2012.

Gerring, John. *Case Study Research: Principles and Practices*. Cambridge: Cambridge University Press, 2007.

Goldstone, Lawrence. *Inherently Unequal: The Betrayal of Equal Rights by the Supreme Court, 1865–1903*. New York: Walker, 2012.

Gottschalk, Louis Reichenthal. *Understanding History; a Primer of Historical Method*. Knopf, 1969.

Gracy, David B. *An Introduction to Archives and Manuscripts*. (Professional Development Series; v.2). Special Libraries Association, 1981.

Grady-Willis, Winston A. *Challenging U.S. Apartheid: Atlanta and Black Struggles for Human Rights, 1960–1977*. Durham, N.C.: Duke University Press, 2006.

Graham, Gael. *Young Activists: American High School Students in the Age of Protest*. Dekalb: Northern Illinois University Press, 2006.

Grant, Donald L. *The Way It Was in the South: The Black Experience in Georgia*. Athens: University of Georgia Press, 2001.

Grantham, Dewey W. "Georgia Politics and the Disfranchisement of the Negro." *Georgia Historical Quarterly* 32, no. 1 (March 1948): 1–21. http://www.jstor.org/stable/40577090.

Green, Hilary. *Educational Reconstruction: African American Schools in the Urban South, 1865–1890*. New York: Fordham University Press, 2016.

Grua, David W. "'Citizen[s] with a Difference': The U.S. Commission on Civil Rights and Native Americans, 1961–1981." *Federal History*, no. 3 (2011): 33–50.

Hale, Grace Elizabeth. *Making Whiteness: The Culture of Segregation in the South, 1890–1940*. New York: Vintage, 1999.

Hale, Jon. *The Freedom Schools: Student Activists in the Mississippi Civil Rights Movement*. New York: Columbia University Press, 2016.

———. "'The Student as a Force for Social Change': The Mississippi Freedom Schools and Student Engagement." *Journal of African American History* 96, no. 3 (Summer 2011): 325–47.

Hampton, Henry, Steve Fayer, and Sarah Flynn. *Voices of Freedom: An Oral History of the Civil Rights Movement from the 1950s through the 1980s*. New York: Bantam, 1991.

Haney López, Ian. *White by Law: The Legal Construction of Race*. Rev. ed. New York: New York University Press, 2006.

Hobson, Maurice J. *The Legend of the Black Mecca: Politics and Class in the Making of Modern Atlanta*. Chapel Hill: University of North Carolina Press, 2017.

Hoffer, William James Hull. *Plessy v. Ferguson: Race and Inequality in Jim Crow America*. Lawrence: University Press of Kansas, 2012.

Holley, Santi Elijah. "The 75-Year (and Counting) Christian Interracial Farm Experiment." *Topic*, February 2018. https://www.topic.com/the-75-year-and-counting-christian-interracial-farm-experiment.

Holloway, Jonathan Scott. *Jim Crow Wisdom: Memory and Identity in Black America since 1940*. Chapel Hill: University of North Carolina Press, 2013.

Holmes, William F. "Economic Developments, 1890–1940." In Coleman, *A History of Georgia*, 257–76.

Hornsby, Alton, Jr. "Black Public Education in Atlanta, Georgia, 1954–1973: From Segregation to Segregation." *Journal of Negro History* 76, no. 1/4 (Winter–Autumn 1991): 21–47. http://www.jstor.org/stable/2717407.

Huberman, A. Michael, and Matthew B. Miles. *The Qualitative Researcher's Companion*. Thousand Oaks, Calif.: Sage Publications, 2002.

Huntley, Horace, and John W. McKerley. *Foot Soldiers for Democracy: The Men, Women, and Children of the Birmingham Civil Rights Movement*. Urbana: University of Illinois Press, 2009.

Irons, Peter. *A People's History of the Supreme Court: The Men and Women Whose Cases and Decisions Have Shaped Our Constitution*. Rev. ed. New York: Penguin, 2006.

Jacoway, Elizabeth. "Not Anger But Sorrow: Minnijean Brown Trickey Remembers the Little Rock Crisis." *Arkansas Historical Quarterly* 64, no. 1 (Spring 2005): 1–26. https://doi.org/10.2307/40018557.

James, Rawn, Jr. *Root and Branch: Charles Hamilton Houston, Thurgood Marshall, and the Struggle to End Segregation*. New York: Bloomsbury, 2013.

Jeffries, Hasan Kwame. *Bloody Lowndes: Civil Rights and Black Power in Alabama's Black Belt*. New York: New York University Press, 2009.

Jewell, Joseph O. *Race, Social Reform, and the Making of a Middle Class: The American Missionary Association and Black Atlanta, 1870–1900*. Lanham, Md.: Rowman & Littlefield, 2007.

Johnson, Kimberley. *Reforming Jim Crow: Southern Politics and State in the Age before Brown*. New York: Oxford University Press, 2010.

Johnson, Paul E. "Reflections: Looking Back at Social History." *Reviews in American History* 39, no. 2 (June 2011): 379–88. https://doi.org/10.1353/rah.2011.0059.

Joiner, Oscar H., James C. Bonner, H. S. Shearouse, and T. E. Smith, eds. *A History of Public Education in Georgia, 1734–1976*. Columbia, S.C.: R. L. Bryan, 1979.

Kaestle, Carl F. *Pillars of the Republic: Common Schools and American Society, 1780–1860*. New York: Hill and Wang, 1983.

Kelley, Robin D. G., and Earl Lewis, eds. *To Make Our World Anew: A History of African Americans*. New York: Oxford University Press, 2000.

Kendi, Ibram X. *Stamped from the Beginning: The Definitive History of Racist Ideas in America*. New York: Nation Books, 2016.

Kendrick, Stephen, and Paul Kendrick. *Sarah's Long Walk: The Free Blacks of Boston and How Their Struggle for Equality Changed America*. Boston: Beacon, 2004.

Kersten, Andrew Edmund. *A. Philip Randolph: A Life in the Vanguard*. Lanham, Md.: Rowman & Littlefield, 2007.

King, Martin Luther, Jr. *A Gift of Love: Sermons from Strength to Love and Other Preaching*. Boston: Beacon, 2012.

———. *Where Do We Go from Here: Chaos or Community?* Boston: Beacon, 2010.

King, Wilma. *African American Childhoods: Historical Perspectives from Slavery to Civil Rights*. New York: Palgrave Macmillan, 2005.

Kirk, John A. *Redefining the Color Line: Black Activism in Little Rock, Arkansas, 1940–1970*. Gainesville: University Press of Florida, 2002.

Klarman, Michael J. *Brown v. Board of Education and the Civil Rights Movement*. New York: Oxford University Press, 2007. Abridged ed. of Klarman, *From Jim Crow to Civil Rights*.

———. *From Jim Crow to Civil Rights: The Supreme Court and the Struggle for Racial Equality*. New York: Oxford University Press, 2006.

———. *Unfinished Business: Racial Equality in American History*. New York: Oxford University Press, 2007.

Kluger, Richard. *Simple Justice: The History of Brown v. Board of Education and Black America's Struggle for Equality*. New York: Vintage, 2004.

K'Meyer, Tracy E. *From Brown to Meredith: The Long Struggle for School Desegregation in Louisville, Kentucky, 1954–2007*. Chapel Hill: University of North Carolina Press, 2016.

———. *Interracialism and Christian Community in the Postwar South: The Story of Koinonia Farm*. Charlottesville: University Press of Virginia, 1997.

Kruse, Kevin M. *White Flight: Atlanta and the Making of Modern Conservatism.* Princeton, N.J.: Princeton University Press, 2007.

Ladson-Billings, Gloria. "From the Achievement Gap to the Education Debt: Understanding Achievement in U.S. Schools." *Educational Researcher* 35, no. 7 (October 2006): 3–12.

Lavergne, Gary M. *Before Brown: Herman Marion Sweatt, Thurgood Marshall, and the Long Road to Justice.* Austin: University of Texas Press, 2010.

Levine, Daniel. *Bayard Rustin and the Civil Rights Movement.* New Brunswick, N.J.: Rutgers University Press, 1999.

Levine, Ellen. *Freedom's Children: Young Civil Rights Activists Tell Their Own Stories.* Puffin, 2000.

Lewis, David Levering. *W. E. B. Du Bois: The Fight for Equality and the American Century, 1919–1963.* New York: Henry Holt, 2001.

Lichtman, Allan J., and Valerie French. *Historians and the Living Past: The Theory and Practice of Historical Study.* Wheeling, Ill.: Harlan Davidson, 1978.

Link, William A. *Atlanta, Cradle of the New South: Race and Remembering in the Civil War's Aftermath.* Chapel Hill: University of North Carolina Press, 2013.

Lipsitz, George. *The Possessive Investment in Whiteness: How White People Profit from Identity Politics.* 20th anniv. ed. Philadelphia, Pa,: Temple University Press, 2018.

Lisio, Donald J. *Hoover, Blacks, and Lily-Whites: A Study of Southern Strategies.* Chapel Hill: University of North Carolina Press, 2012.

Lockhart, P. R. "65 Years after Brown v. Board of Education, School Segregation Is Getting Worse." *Vox*, May 10, 2019. https://www.vox.com/identities/2019/5/10/18566052/school-segregation-brown-board-education-report.

Mayer, Robert H. *When the Children Marched: The Birmingham Civil Rights Movement.* Berkeley Heights, N.J.: Enslow, 2008.

McCluskey, Audrey Thomas. *A Forgotten Sisterhood: Pioneering Black Women Educators and Activists in the Jim Crow South.* Lanham, Md.: Rowman & Littlefield, 2014.

McGrath, Susan Margaret. "Great Expectations: The History of School Desegregation in Atlanta and Boston, 1954–1990." PhD diss., Emory University, 1992.

McKinstry, Carolyn Maull, with Denise George. *While the World Watched: A Birmingham Bombing Survivor Comes of Age during the Civil Rights Movement.* Carol Stream, Ill.: Tyndale House, 2011.

McNeil, Genna Rae, and A. Leon Higginbotham Jr. *Groundwork: Charles Hamilton Houston and the Struggle for Civil Rights.* Philadelphia: University of Pennsylvania Press, 1984.

Meier, August. "The Negro and the Democratic Party, 1875–1915." *Phylon* 17, no. 2 (2nd Qtr, 1956): 173–91. https://doi.org/10.2307/272592.

Meyers, Christopher C., ed. *The Empire State of the South: Georgia History in Documents and Essays.* Macon, Ga.: Mercer University Press, 2008.

Mills, Charles W. *The Racial Contract.* Ithaca, N.Y.: Cornell University Press, 1999.

Milner, H. Richard, and Tyrone C. Howard. "Black Teachers, Black Students, Black Communities, and Brown: Perspectives and Insights from Experts." *Journal of Negro Education* 73, no. 3 (Summer 2004): 285–97. https://doi.org/10.2307/4129612.

Minchin, Timothy J., and John A. Salmond. *After the Dream: Black and White Southerners since 1965.* Lexington: University Press of Kentucky, 2011.

Mitra, Dana L. *Student Voice in School Reform: Building Youth-Adult Partnerships That Strengthen Schools and Empower Youth.* Albany: State University of New York Press, 2008.

Monroe, Carla R. "Why Are 'Bad Boys' Always Black? Causes of Disproportionality in School Discipline and Recommendations for Change." *Clearing House* 79, no. 1 (September–October 2005): 45–50.

Moody, James. "Race, School Integration, and Friendship Segregation in America." *American Journal of Sociology* 107, no. 3 (November 2001): 679–716. https://doi.org/10.1086/338954.

Morris, Charles E., III, and Stephen Howard Browne. *Readings on the Rhetoric of Social Protest.* State College, Pa.: Strata, 2001.

Morris, Jerome E. "Forgotten Voices of Black Educators: Critical Race Perspectives on the Implementation of a Desegregation Plan." *Educational Policy* 15, no. 4 (September 2001): 575–600. https://doi.org/10.1177/0895904801015004004.

———. *Troubling the Waters: Fulfilling the Promise of Quality Public Schooling for Black Children.* New York: Teachers College Press, 2009.

Morris, Vivian Gunn, and Curtis L. Morris. *The Price They Paid: Desegregation in an African American Community.* New York: Teachers College Press, 2002.

NAACP. "NAACP Administrative File: General Office File: Youth March on Washington, 1958–September 1959." In NAACP, *Papers of the NAACP, Part 24,* reel 41, 0448–0682.

———. "NAACP Youth File: General Department File: Career Conference, 1956–1961." In NAACP, *Papers of the NAACP, Part 19,* reel 7, 0420–0785.

———. "NAACP Youth File: General Department File: Form Letters, 1956–1957, 1960–1965." In NAACP, *Papers of the NAACP, Part 19,* reel 10, 0255–0567.

———. "NAACP Youth File: General Department File: Membership Campaign, 1956–1960." In NAACP, *Papers of the NAACP, Part 19,* reel 13, 0491–0606.

———. "NAACP Youth File: General Department File: Wright, Herbert L." In NAACP, *Papers of the NAACP, Part 19: Youth File, Series C,* reel 19, fr. 0001, reel 21, fr. 0479.

———. *Papers of the NAACP, Part 19: Youth File, Series C: 1940–1955, NAACP—Youthbuilders.* Bethesda, Md.: University Publications of America, 2014.

———. *Papers of the NAACP, Part 19: Youth File, Series D: Youth Department Files, 1956–1965.* Bethesda, Md.: University Publications of America, 2014.

———. *Papers of the NAACP, Part 24: Special Subjects, 1956–1965, Series C: Life*

Memberships—Zangrando. Bethesda, Md.: University Publications of America, 2014.

Nevas, Susan R. "Factors in Desegregation and Integration." *Equal Opportunity Review* (Fall 1977). New York: ERIC Clearinghouse on Urban Education, 1977.

Obama, Barack. *The Audacity of Hope: Thoughts on Reclaiming the American Dream*. New York: Crown, 2006.

Ogbar, Jeffrey O. G. *Black Power: Radical Politics and African American Identity*. Baltimore: Johns Hopkins University Press, 2005.

Ogletree, Charles J., Jr. *All Deliberate Speed: Reflections on the First Half-Century of Brown v. Board of Education*. New York: W. W. Norton, 2005.

Orfield, Gary, Susan E. Eaton, and Harvard Project on School Desegregation, eds. *Dismantling Desegregation: The Quiet Reversal of Brown v. Board of Education*. New York: New Press, 1996.

Owens, Donna. "Stolen Girls." *Essence*, June 2006.

Patterson, James T. *Brown v. Board of Education: A Civil Rights Milestone and Its Troubled Legacy*. New York: Oxford University Press, 2001.

Payne, Charles M. *I've Got the Light of Freedom: The Organizing Tradition and the Mississippi Freedom Struggle*. Berkeley: University of California Press, 1996.

Pfeffer, Paula F. *A. Philip Randolph, Pioneer of the Civil Rights Movement*. Baton Rouge: Louisiana State University Press, 1990.

Philipsen, Maike. "The Second Promise of Brown." *Urban Review* 26, no. 4 (December 1994): 257–72.

Pinder, Kamina A., and Evan R. Hanson. "De Jure, De Facto, & Déjà Vu All Over Again: A Historical Perspective of Georgia's Segregation-Era School Equalization Program." *John Marshall Law Journal* 3, no. 2 (2009): 165.

Podair, Jerald E. *The Strike That Changed New York: Blacks, Whites, and the Ocean Hill–Brownsville Crisis*. New Haven, Conn. Formisano: Yale University Press, 2004.

Purdy, Michelle A. *Transforming the Elite: Black Students and the Desegregation of Private Schools*. Chapel Hill: University of North Carolina Press, 2018.

Randolph, A. Philip. *The Papers of A. Philip Randolph*. Compiled by David H. Werning. Bethesda, Md.: University Publications of America, 1990.

Ravitch, Diane. *The Great School Wars: A History of the New York City Public Schools*. Baltimore: Johns Hopkins University Press, 2000.

Richards, Janelle, Rehema Ellis, and Elissa Candiotti. "65 Years since Brown v. Board of Ed, School Segregation Persists." NBC News. May 17, 2019. https://www.nbcnews.com/news/nbcblk/65-years-brown-v-board-ed-school-segregation-persists-n1006356.

Richardson, Heather Cox. *How the South Won the Civil War: Oligarchy, Democracy, and the Continuing Fight for the Soul of America*. New York: Oxford University Press, 2020.

Ritterhouse, Jennifer. *Growing Up Jim Crow: How Black and White Southern Children Learned Race*. Chapel Hill: University of North Carolina Press, 2006.

Roche, Jeff. *Restructured Resistance: The Sibley Commission and the Politics of Desegregation in Georgia*. Athens: University of Georgia Press, 1998.

Rosenberg, Gerald N. *The Hollow Hope: Can Courts Bring About Social Change?* 2nd ed. Chicago: University of Chicago Press, 2008.

Rosette, Jacob. "A School Board for the People: Baltimore Freedom Fall." *Race, Poverty, and the Environment* 14, no. 2 (Fall 2007): 23–24.

Rothstein, Richard. *The Color of Law: A Forgotten History of How Our Government Segregated America*. New York: Liveright, 2017.

Ruane, Janet M. *Introducing Social Research Methods: Essentials for Getting the Edge*. Hoboken, N.J.: Wiley-Blackwell, 2016.

Rustin, Bayard. *The Bayard Rustin Papers*. Compiled by Nanette Dobrosky. Frederick, Md.: University Publications of America, 1988.

Shabazz, Amilcar. *Advancing Democracy: African Americans and the Struggle for Access and Equity in Higher Education in Texas*. Chapel Hill: University of North Carolina Press, 2004.

Smith, John David. *An Old Creed for the New South: Proslavery Ideology and Historiography, 1865–1918*. Athens: University of Georgia Press, 1991.

Smith, Robert Collins. *They Closed Their Schools: Prince Edward County, Virginia, 1951–1964*. Chapel Hill: University of North Carolina Press, 1965.

Sokol, Jason. *There Goes My Everything: White Southerners in the Age of Civil Rights, 1945–1975*. New York: Alfred A. Knopf, 2006.

Sommer, Barbara W. *The Oral History Manual*. Walnut Creek, Calif.: AltaMira, 2009.

Span, Christopher, and Ishwanzya D. Rivers. "Reassessing the Achievement Gap: An Intergenerational Comparison of African American Student Achievement before and after Compensatory Education and the Elementary and Secondary Education Act." *Teachers College Record* 114, no. 6 (2012): 1–17.

Stoper, Emily. *The Student Nonviolent Coordinating Committee: The Growth of Radicalism in a Civil Rights Organization*. Brooklyn, N.Y.: Carlson, 1989.

Synnott, Marcia. "Desegregation in South Carolina, 1950–1963: Sometime between 'Now' and 'Never.'" In *Looking South: Chapters in the Story of an American Region*, edited by Winfred B. Moore Jr. and Joseph F. Tripp, 51–64. Westport, Conn.: Greenwood, 1989.

Tamura, Eileen H., ed. *The History of Discrimination in U.S. Education: Marginality, Agency, and Power*. New York: Palgrave Macmillan, 2015.

Thuesen, Sarah Caroline. *Greater than Equal: African American Struggles for Schools and Citizenship in North Carolina, 1919–1965*. Chapel Hill: University of North Carolina Press, 2013.

Tillman, Kayla L. "Tifton: From Indian Trails to I-75." *Tifton Magazine*, December 1990.

Titus, Jill Ogline. *Brown's Battleground: Students, Segregationists, and the Strug-*

gle for Justice in Prince Edward County, Virginia. Chapel Hill: University of North Carolina Press, 2011.

Todd-Breland, Elizabeth. *A Political Education: Black Politics and Education Reform in Chicago since the 1960s*. Chapel Hill: University of North Carolina Press, 2018.

Trounstine, Jessica. *Segregation by Design: Local Politics and Inequality in American Cities*. New York: Cambridge University Press, 2018.

Troy, Gil. *Leading from the Center: Why Moderates Make the Best Presidents*. New York: Basic Books, 2008.

Tuck, Stephen G. N. *Beyond Atlanta: The Struggle for Racial Equality in Georgia, 1940–1980*. Athens: University of Georgia Press, 2003.

Tushnet, Mark V. *The NAACP's Legal Strategy against Segregated Education, 1925–1950*. Chapel Hill: University of North Carolina Press, 2004.

Tyack, David B. *The One Best System: A History of American Urban Education*. Cambridge, Mass.: Harvard University Press, 1974.

Tyack, David B., and Larry Cuban. *Tinkering toward Utopia: A Century of Public School Reform*. Cambridge, Mass.: Harvard University Press, 1995.

Urban, Wayne J., and Jennings L. Wagoner Jr. *American Education: A History*. 5th ed. New York: Routledge, 2013.

Walker, Vanessa Siddle. *Hello Professor: A Black Principal and Professional Leadership in the Segregated South*. Chapel Hill: University of North Carolina Press, 2009.

———. *The Lost Education of Horace Tate: Uncovering the Hidden Heroes Who Fought for Justice in Schools*. New York: New Press, 2018.

———. "Second-Class Integration: A Historical Perspective for a Contemporary Agenda." *Harvard Educational Review* 79, no. 2 (Summer 2009): 269–84.

———. *Their Highest Potential: An African American School Community in the Segregated South*. Chapel Hill: University of North Carolina Press, 1996.

Ward, Jason Morgan. *Defending White Democracy: The Making of a Segregationist Movement and the Remaking of Racial Politics, 1936–1965*. Chapel Hill: University of North Carolina Press, 2011.

Watkins, William H. *The White Architects of Black Education: Ideology and Power in America, 1865–1954*. New York: Teachers College Press, 2001.

Webb, Clive. *Massive Resistance: Southern Opposition to the Second Reconstruction*. New York: Oxford University Press, 2005.

Wells, Amy Stuart. *Both Sides Now: The Story of School Desegregation's Graduates*. Berkeley: University of California Press, 2009.

Welsh, Richard O., and Shafiqua Little. "The School Discipline Dilemma: A Comprehensive Review of Disparities and Alternative Approaches." *Review of Educational Research* 88, no. 5 (October 2018): 752–94. https://doi.org/10.3102/0034654318791582.

Westbrooks-Griffin, Lulu. *Freedom Is Not Free: 45 Days in Leesburg Stockade; A Civil Rights Story*. Hamlin, N.Y.: Heirloom, [1998?].

Whitfield, Stephen J. *A Death in the Delta: The Story of Emmett Till*. Baltimore: Johns Hopkins University Press, 1991.

Williams, Heather Andrea. *Self-Taught: African American Education in Slavery and Freedom*. Chapel Hill: University of North Carolina Press, 2005.

Williams, Juan. *Thurgood Marshall: American Revolutionary*. New York: Times Books, 1998.

Williamson-Lott, Joy Ann, Linda Darling-Hammond, and Maria E. Hyler. "Education and the Quest for African American Citizenship: An Overview." In Gates et al., *Oxford Handbook*, 581–90.

Williford, William B. *Americus through the Years: The Story of a Georgia Town and Its People, 1872–1975*. Atlanta: Cherokee, 1975.

Willis, Vincent. "'Let Me in, I Have the Right to Be Here': Black Youth Struggle for Equal Education and Full Citizenship after the Brown Decision, 1954–1969." *Citizenship Teaching and Learning* 9, no. 1 (December 2013): 53–70. https://doi.org/10.1386/ctl.9.1.53_1.

Woodson, Carter G. "Fifty Years of Negro Citizenship as Qualified by the United States Supreme Court." *Journal of Negro History* 6, no. 1 (January 1921): 1–53. https://doi.org/10.2307/2713827.

Woodward, C. Vann. *The Strange Career of Jim Crow*. Commemorative edition. New York: Oxford University Press, 2002.

Yow, Ruth Carbonette. *Students of the Dream: Resegregation in a Southern City*. Cambridge, Mass.: Harvard University Press, 2017.

Yow, Valerie Raleigh. *Recording Oral History: A Guide for the Humanities and Social Sciences*. Walnut Creek, Calif.: AltaMira, 2005.

Zieger, Robert H. *For Jobs and Freedom: Race and Labor in America since 1865*. Lexington: University Press of Kentucky, 2007.

INDEX

Albany Movement, 43–44, 117, 121, 123
Allen Temple A.M.E. Church, 63, 174
Americus, Ga., racial history, 76–78
Appeal for Human Rights, 21, 40, 43
Arkansas, 21, 24, 26, 39, 57; Little Rock
    Nine, 27
arrest and incarceration of black youth, 86,
    102, 131; student activism, 39, 41
A. S. Staley High School, 81, 92–93, 96–98,
    102
Atlanta Committee for Cooperative Action,
    39
Atlanta University (AU), 1–2

Baltimore, 24–28, 155, 163
Beals, Melba, 27, 156
Bell, Mary Kate, 103
Bennett, Marion D., 41. *See also* Appeal for
    Human Rights
black bodies, 28, 40, 45–46, 105, 145
black businesses (economic), 50, 81, 84
black education: Albany State University,
    15; Atlanta University (AU; now Clark
    Atlanta University), 1–2; climate, 12, 20,
    55, 94; Howard University, 42, 139
black freedom struggle, 41, 142. *See also*
    educational equality
black schools: advocacy, 109, 121; best prac-
    tices, 42; cultivated, 53–54, 107, 147,
    149; out-of-classroom activities, 47;
    overcrowding, 81, 91, 102, 169, 175;
    resources, 37–40, 55, 57–59 (*see also* tax

dollars); without, 27, 122, 131, 157, 160,
    168
black youth: agency, 65, 98; better educa-
    tion, 12, 74, 148; burden-bearers, 28, 80,
    101; definition of equality, 16; desire, 42,
    45–46, 139, 144, 153 (*see also* educational
    equality); Fourteenth Amendment, 7, 44;
    humanity, 77, 79, 93; ideas, 23–24, 157,
    159, 176; law, 142; literacy, 53, 90; mar-
    ginalized, 138–39, 144, 153, 156–57; per-
    sonal connection, 96, 148, 154; practi-
    cal issues, 126; treatment, 77; voting, 14;
    youth movement, 50, 73–74, 173–74
Bridges, Ruby, 26, 101
Brown, Linda, 22, 156
Brown, Minnijean, 26, 32
Brown v. Board of Education (*Brown*):
    avoidance of attention, 38, 118; celebra-
    tion, 29–31, 107, 109; climate, 19–20;
    desegregation, 28 (*see also* black youth);
    doubt, 21, 24, 29, 36, 45; enforcement,
    148; hope, 24–25, 29, 31, 34; Hunt, Net-
    tie, 21; Hunt, Nickie, 21; segregation (Jim
    Crow), 6, 14, 24, 46–49, 69
Brown v. Board of Education II (deliberate
    speed), 23, 36, 161–62, 165, 168, 172
brutality, 86, 88, 97
business and Jim Crow, 28, 49–50

Campbell, Mamie, 103
Central High School (Little Rock, Ark.), 27
Charlie A. Gray Elementary School, 109

Civil Rights Commission, 152–53
civil rights movement: activities, 60–61,
    64–65; historiography, 38, 43, 85, 110
Clarke, Don, 41. *See also* Appeal for Human
    Rights
Collins, Addie Mae, 60
Colquitt County, Ga., racial traditions, 119–
    23, 156
Colquitt County Training School, 107, 109
compromise, 141, 144
contrasting ideas, 16. *See also* black youth;
    white citizens; white officials
Crawford, Lectured, 2
*Cumming v. Richmond County Board of
    Education*, 47, 112, 138

democracy, 3, 28–29, 33, 35, 88
desegregation. See black youth; *Brown v.
    Board of Education*
direct action, 50, 61, 70, 87, 104, 162
dissatisfaction, 87, 124, 131, 152. *See also*
    black youth
Dixiecrat, 12
Du Bois, W. E. B., 137, 157
Dykes, Walter, 54, 93, 148, 156, 174

economic independence, 85, 87. *See also*
    black businesses
economic opportunities: mobility, 51, 80, 87,
    112, 146; restraint, 111
educational equality, 22–24, 57, 101, 161
educational farrago: contentiousness, 9, 13;
    contradictions, 9, 12–14, 18, 20, 67, 142;
    defined, 9–10; post-Brown complications,
    20–21, 106, 153; regression, 45; theoreti-
    cal framework, 9–10, 13. *See also* educa-
    tional equality; inequities
Eisenhower, Dwight, 140
events: federal decisions, 5, 8–10, 13, 137–
    38; freedom of choice, 76, 102, 145;
    Youth March for Integrated Schools, 21,
    31–36, 78, 144, 167–68. *See also specific
    legal decisions*

Fair Employment Practices Committee, 110
Felder, James, 41. *See also* Appeal for
    Human Rights
first class, 43, 53, 55, 79, 90, 175. *See also*
    black schools; black youth

functionality, 84, 143. *See also* educational
    farrago

Georgia, 39, 141
Georgia Teacher and Education Associa-
    tion, 134
Glenn Bill, 39, 52, 55
Gordon, John, 1
gradualism, 61, 69, 143, 147
Green, J. W., Jr., 118–19, 125, 129

hand-me-down (secondhand goods), 37, 55,
    115–16, 148
harassment, 39, 114
Historical African American Pedagogical
    Network, 42
Holton, Jimmy, 116, 118, 122–23, 156
Hoover, Herbert, 11–12
Hopkins, Charles Lee, 103
Houston, Charles Hamilton, 6. *See also*
    National Association for the Advance-
    ment of Colored People: Legal Defense
    Fund

implementation of law, 1–2, 15–16, 20
inequality, 67, 77, 91, 109. *See also* hand-
    me-down
inequities, 23, 29, 41, 49, 55, 140
inhumane treatment, 96–97
intergenerationalism, 61. *See also* black
    schools

Johnson, Lyndon B., 139
Jordan, Joanne, 157–58

Kennedy, John F., 140
King, Martin Luther, Jr., 33–35, 62, 65–66,
    69, 78, 104
Kitchen, Fran, 51, 145
Kitchen, Herman, 122, 127–28
Koinonia Farm, 82–84, 176
Ku Klux Klan, 83–84, 95

Lamar, Eddie Lee, 103
learning institutions, 148
Leesburg Stockade, 95, 98, 103, 105–6, 159
Little Rock Nine, 27

Mahone, Sam, 79, 85–86, 89, 156

Mansfield, Sandra, 79, 89, 91, 106
Marshall, Thurgood, 19, 28, 161, 165
Mason, Ruth, 111
Mays, Willie, 41. *See also* Appeal for Human
  Rights
McBurrows, Johnny, 44, 112
McCay Hill School, 80–81
McLaurin v. Oklahoma State Regents, 5
McNair, Carol Denise, 60
Melton, Daughtry, Sr. (Doc), 50
Melton, Ella (Dee), 50
Morrison, Toni, 154
Mott-Litman Gymnasium, 46–47, 67–68
Moultrie, Ga., race relations, 111. *See also*
  black businesses
Moultrie High School for Negro Youth,
  107, 111

National Association for the Advancement
  of Colored People (NAACP): Legal
  Defense Fund, 19, 81, 137; Youth Coun-
  cil, 167; Youth Program, 31
National Council of Negro Women, 155
Nixon, Solomon, 61, 73, 173

Obama, Barack, 108
occupation: domestic, 51, 110–13; economic
  stagnation, 141, 146; tenant farmer, 17,
  111
opposition to change, 52; in Georgia, 39,
  141. *See also* Arkansas; Baltimore; Tennessee; white citizens

Parry, James, 122, 124, 133–34
Pertilla, Alton, 54, 93, 148, 156
Plessy v. Ferguson, 5–8, 12, 18–19, 22, 37,
  45, 47, 79, 112, 118, 162
Pope, Roslyn, 41. *See also* Appeal for
  Human Rights
power, 19, 29, 40, 97–98, 107. *See also*
  black youth; National Association for the
  Advancement of Colored People; white
  officials
progress, 37, 45, 119, 146. *See also* educational equality; educational farrago
progression, 82, 100, 153
public schools: academic institutions, 52,
  57, 152; history, 20, 22–23, 141–42, 154–
  55; indictment, 146–47; integration, 116,

152; intrasegregation, 158; laboratories,
  151; legal decisions, 19, 138, 143–46, 160;
  mistreatment, 95–96, 101–2, 125, 158;
  overdisciplining, 147; partnership, 14,
  22, 140, 152, 158; purpose, 11, 13, 133,
  166–67; race, 48–49, 97, 110–11, 158–60,
  176; relationships, 51, 53, 68, 108–9, 112,
  171; segregated schools, 47, 148; special needs, 147; standards, 25, 42, 64, 154;
  tension, 61, 104, 142, 147

racial harmony, 30, 60, 82–83
racial hierarchy, 48, 155, 170
Ram Round-Up, 107–8
Randolph, A. Phillip, 144
Ricks, Willie (Mukasa Dada), 89, 133
Robertson, Carole, 60
Roberts v. City of Boston, 4
Roosevelt, Franklin D., 80
Roosevelt, Theodore, 10
Rustin, Bayard, 31, 165, 167

Sabbs, Lorena, 79, 139, 156
second class, 96, 98, 119, 163
sedition trial, 85–86, 89
self-determination (self-help), 13, 41, 143
Sherrod, Charles, 43, 156, 170
Shield, Robert, 132
Simpkins, Isaac, 122, 127–29
1619 Project, 159
16th Street Baptist Church, 60, 173
Smith, Hoke, 163
Smith, Mary Ann, 41. *See also* Appeal for
  Human Rights
Southern Association of Colleges and Secondary Schools (SACS), 126
Southern Christian Leadership Conference
  (SCLC), 61–63, 99, 143, 149
Southwest Georgia: disenfranchisement, 12,
  15, 44, 140–41; public schooling, 21–22,
  47, 153, 160, 164; white opposition, 27,
  41, 43, 45. *See also* Albany Movement;
  civil rights movement
State of Missouri ex rel. Gaines v. Canada, 5
states' rights, 24. See also *Brown v. Board of
  Education*
student activism, 39, 41
Student Nonviolent Coordinating Committee (SNCC), 15, 44, 85, 90

Sumter County, Ga., racialized pedagogy, 76–77, 84, 156
Supreme Court, 2, 4. *See also* white comfort; white officials
Sweatt v. Painter, 5–7

Taft, William Howard, 11
Talmadge, Herman, 141
Tate, Horace, 134, 146, 169
tax dollars, 2, 64–65, 70, 81–82
Tennessee, 21, 26, 29
Terrell, Johnny, 51, 93, 148, 156
terrorism, 60
Thompson, Annie Ruth, 111
Thurmond, Strom, 12
Tift County, Ga., racial stagnation, 46–47, 50–52, 55
Tift County Improvement Club, 50. *See also* black businesses
Tift County Industrial Elementary and High School, 47
Tifton, Ga., racial tensions, 44, 46–76, 78, 80–81
Tifton Youth Chapter of the Southern Christian Leadership Conference (TYCSCLC), 62–63. *See also* Southern Christian Leadership Conference
Truman, Harry S., 12
Turner, Lena, 103

Virginia, 21, 24, 26–27, 39, 57, 74, 101
voter suppression, 146
Voting Rights Act, 145

Walker, Ann Whea, 91
Washington, D.C., 21, 24, 26, 32–33
weaponization, 144. *See also* opposition to change

Wesley, Cynthia, 60
Whatley, Aultman, 103
Wheeler, Ann, 20, 26, 44, 112
white citizens: resistance, 43; way of life, 22, 140
white comfort: backlash, 44, 49, 78, 88, 138; white flight, 158, 162, 164, 174, 176; white fragility, 56, 172, 174; white guilt, 56; white racial frame, 56, 172, 175
white officials: acknowledgment of inequality, 72, 119; adversarialism, 81, 111, 147; apathy, 56, 120; deficiency, 42, 53, 77; dismissiveness, 134; loyalty, 49, 101, 120, 138, 142, 159; minimalist framework, 117; neglect, 72; negligence, 118, 134; obstructionism, 7, 9, 78; ordinances, 66–67, 70; police, 25, 86, 88, 131–33, 158; public office, 103; school board, 70; separate but equal, 56, 128 (see also *Plessy v. Ferguson*); Sibley Commission, 39, 52; superintendents, 71–72, 129–34; violence, 25–26, 50–51 (*see also* white citizens); voter registration, 90–91, 101, 103, 122
William Bryant High School, 107, 114, 155
Williams, Dale, 118, 156
Wilson, Anthony, 2
Wilson, Johnny, 53, 171
Wilson, Juanita, 79, 101, 145, 156
Wilson Elementary and High School, 47
Wise, Gloria, 103
Wright, Major (J. K. Obatala), 60, 62, 64–65, 74, 148–49

Youth March for Integrated Schools, 21, 31–36, 78, 144, 167–68

CPSIA information can be obtained
at www.ICGtesting.com
Printed in the USA
LVHW052358120721
692490LV00007B/318